A Slight Case of Libel

A Slight Case of Libel

Meacher v Trelford and Others

Alan Watkins

Duckworth

First published in 1990 by
Gerald Duckworth & Co. Ltd.
The Old Piano Factory
43 Gloucester Crescent
London NW1

ISBN 0 7156 2334 6

British Library Cataloguing in Publication Data

Watkins, Alan *1933–*
    A slight case of libel : Meacher v. Trelford and others.
    1. England. Libel. Laws
    I. Title
    344.20634

    ISBN 0–7156–2334–6

The author and publisher are grateful to the following for supplying and giving permission to reproduce illustrations (sources in italics): Alan Watkins: *Express Newspapers*; Donald Trelford: *Observer*; Stephen Nathan: *Sue Adler*; Richard Hartley: *Topham Picture Source*; Sir John Hazan: *Universal Pictorial Press*; Paul Fox: *Photographia*; David O'Callaghan: *Photographia*; John Knight: *Syndication International*; Robert Taylor: *Observer*; Lewis Chester: *Times Newspapers*; Anthony Howard: *Observer*; William Millinship: *Observer*; St Margaret's Farm: *Mail Newspapers*; House in Berkhamsted: *South Bedfordshire News Agency*; Canon Wilkinson: *Canon Wilkinson*; Eric Moonman: *Monitor Syndication*; Kenneth Clarke: *Monitor Syndication*; Michael Meacher, 3 October 1988: *Independent*; Michael Meacher and Lucianne Sawyer: *Mail Newspapers*; Michael Meacher, 10 June 1988: *Independent*.

Photoset in North Wales by
Derek Doyle & Associates, Mold, Clwyd
Printed in Great Britain by
Redwood Press Ltd, Melksham

Contents

Contents

Part Four. The End of the Case

Plates between pages 86 and 87

Acknowledgments

My principal debts are to Barbara Rieck, who typed the ms. speedily and impeccably, and to Anthony Howard, who read it, corrected several errors and made numerous suggestions for improvement, most of which I accepted. Sydney Reynolds of Berkhamsted supplied me with valuable information about the town and the school, particularly about Michael Meacher's days at the latter. Julia Braybrook of the *Observer* obtained the transcript of Mr Meacher's observations about the case on BBC television during the 1988 Labour Conference.

Geoffrey Wheatcroft put the idea of the book into my mind. At the end of *Meacher* v *Trelford and Others* he said to me that there ought to be a '60,000-word instant paperback' in the case. What follows has turned out to be rather longer.

Giles Gordon of Anthony Sheil Associates was, as always, helpful and encouraging. Deborah Blake of Duckworth tidied up the ms. admirably and saw it through the press meticulously. I am grateful to them both.

I have relied chiefly on the notes I took during the trial, on the solicitor's notes taken on behalf of Turner Kenneth Brown which were kindly supplied to me by David O'Callaghan of that firm, on the correspondence between the firm and me and – above all – on the transcript of the trial.

It may be worth saying something about transcripts. During a trial of the kind described in the following pages, speeches and evidence are recorded by means of a large, old-fashioned tape-recorder concealed from general view but just visible to a witness. The tapes are then put in the charge of the Mechanical Recording Department of the Royal Courts of Justice.

Transcription of the tapes is, however, in the hands of a private enterprise, C.H. Blackwell and Partners of Dulwich. Transcripts ordered from Blackwells have first to be authorised by the Mechanical Recording Department. They are charged for at a hefty rate: the transcripts for this medium-length trial cost over a thousand pounds. As a party, a co-defendant, I was entitled to a cut rate, but not such as to avoid hitting the pocket hard.

Now, I see no reason why a court official should be empowered to authorise the issue of a transcript to a citizen: *a fortiori* if the person concerned is, as I was, a party to the case. There might be an argument for requiring the person requesting the transcript to show an interest, however widely or narrowly defined. But if, for example, a complainant to the Press Council is not compelled to possess an interest as lawyers understand the word – if recourse to that body is open to any well-meaning or even officious member of the public – then it is difficult to see why merely asking for a court transcript should be subject to a more exigent test. What that test is I am still not sure.

I ought to explain that transcripts are commonly not ordered *en bloc*, though of course they can be. The barrister, solicitor or author will usually order those sections which he or she wants. Blackwells are exact in their transcriptions, both courteous and efficient in dispatch.

I see no reason, however, why C.H. Blackwell and Partners should hold an Elizabethan monopoly, even if it is today sustained by the Royal Courts of Justice. In these days of electronic technology, it should be possible to supply any citizen with the part of the transcript required at a reasonable cost.

Christmas Eve 1989   Alan Watkins to the memory of my parents

DAVID JOHN WATKINS
1894-1980

and

VIOLET MARIA HARRIS
1893-1986

Introduction

> While I have a profound belief in the good sense of English law and regard
> those who spend their lives in applying it and making it work as engaged in
> a noble calling, I do not much care to revive the memory of ancient
> encounters in court, which may have created a sensation at the time, but
> have now passed into an oblivion which to some concerned may be welcome.
>
> John Simon, *Retrospect*

Comedy is always implicit in melodrama, and throughout the case of
Meacher v *Trelford and Others*, in which I was one of the others, I kept
being reminded of passages from Charles Dickens, W.S. Gilbert, A.P.
Herbert and, above all, J.B. Morton ('Beachcomber'), whose creation Mr
Justice Cocklecarrot introduces several of the chapters that follow. This
was one reason for writing an account of the case: it was not only a good
story but a funny one as well.

When I got into the witness box I determined to do my bit. I may well
have overdone it. Here also there were historical parallels, some of them
dangerous. While the journalists present at the trial, or most of them,
thought I was putting on a reasonably amusing performance, the lawyers
thought I was damaging our case by making jokes which only the
journalists could properly understand.

I must, however, pay tribute to the late Mr Justice Hazan, who
presided over the trial. He often seemed quite amused himself; the more
so as he was trying to conceal his merriment. It is always encouraging to
have an appreciative audience. And, if the jury looked blank, as they
often did, the judge was always fully in command of the proceedings. This
did not mean that he was at all dictatorial or heavy-handed. On the
contrary: he allowed Michael Meacher to reply to counsel at what I
thought was often excessive length, and me to bandy words with Mr
Meacher's counsel on several occasions during my own evidence.

In what follows there is, I hope, no element of gloating or of what the
late Philip Toynbee used to call 'putting on dog'. During the trial I felt
angry wih Mr Meacher for causing me much worry and inconvenience
over what I considered a trivial matter. I was even more incensed
with his counsel, Gordon Bishop, for his, as I thought, crass and
impertinent comments on the business of writing a political column.
Friends pointed out that such an emotion was unworthy of me personally

1

and reflected ill on my legal knowledge. Mr Bishop, they said, was simply doing his job. I can only report what I felt at the time.[1] Luckily I managed to keep my temper and tried to be funny instead. (Why is it, Malcolm Muggeridge once asked, that it is only in England that 'trying to be funny' is considered an offensive activity?) I have already remarked the conflict between the lawyers and the journalists about the merits or otherwise of this approach. Nonetheless I was worried when my friend Frank Johnson reported to me the muttered observations of a regular court-watcher as he left his place during my evidence: 'Every joke he makes adds £500 to the damages.'

In the end there were no damages but defeat for Mr Bishop and substantial costs for Mr Meacher. As soon as the case was over my feelings for Mr Bishop became wholly benign. I continue to make inquiries of my friends and acquaintances at the Bar about his progress in that profession. For Mr Meacher I felt sorry, whereas during the trial my feelings for him had been the same as my feelings for Mr Bishop; I wanted him destroyed, humiliated. I said as much to Colin Welch of the *Daily Mail*, one early evening in the Press Gallery bar of the House of Commons while the trial was going on. Mr Welch replied that he was disappointed in me – he had never thought of me as a vindictive person – but that he was sure I should feel differently when the case was over. He was right; though whether he would still have been so if Mr Meacher had won is another matter.

Lord Chesterfield says in one of his letters to his son that people much prefer to be entertained than informed, because the imparting of information implies a deficiency on their part. One purpose I had in writing this story was to inform. I thought it would be useful to provide an account of a libel case, from the background of the words complained of, through the preliminary skirmishes, to the trial itself, the verdict and its consequences. Though there have been accounts of single libel actions in the past (that of the Laski action against the *Newark Advertiser* and the *Daily Express*, published by the latter, comes to mind), the various 'famous trials' series understandably rely chiefly on the criminal law for their subject-matter.

This account would still, I think, have been informative even if we had lost. In June 1988 the number of libel cases which had gone successively against the defendants was just over 40. A year later the total had risen to 50, and *Meacher v Trelford and Others* was still the sole exception. It is not, I hope, vanity which leads me to believe that the rarity of the case adds to its interest.

Throughout the pages that follow I have tried, as far as possible, to steer clear of lawyers' language. However, there are some places where it

---

[1] Cf. Peregrine Worsthorne, 'A Verbal Mugging in the Courts of Justice,' *Daily Telegraph*, 31 January 1990, where Mr Worsthorne describes his feelings of shock caused by the hostile cross-examination of Richard Rampton, QC, counsel for Andrew Neil in *Neil v Worsthorne*.

cannot be avoided and there are some – only a few – where it is positively desirable in the interests of clarity. Moreover, if a jury hauled in from duty at the Old Bailey could be required to absorb the outline of the law of libel from Mr Justice Hazan and two barristers, readers of this book can reasonably be expected to make a similar effort.

One part may prove useful to lawyers and students. This is the section that concerns the admission of Mr Meacher's proof of evidence – what he told his solicitor, which then formed the basis of his examination-in-chief by his counsel. Owing to a mistake by his counsel, Mr Meacher was recalled to the witness box and cross-examined for a second time by our counsel. The episodes concerned (the mistake, the legal argument and the recall) are dealt with in Chapters 8 and 18. These events, which may or may not have been crucial to the outcome of the case but were certainly important, lead me to my first modest proposal for reform.

Some modest proposals

Proofs of evidence should be exchanged before the trial, becoming disclosed documents. This already happens in some civil actions. I was about to add: 'and I see no reason why the practice should not be extended for trials for defamation'. But there is a reason, which is that, of all civil actions, libel trials perhaps most closely resemble criminal trials and, in the latter, proofs of evidence are guarded like gold bars.

In libel trials there is almost always a jury. The damages tend to be punitive in fact even when they are not supposed to be so in law. Counsel for the plaintiff behaves as counsel for the prosecution used to do in the days before it became considered bad legal form to press for a conviction at all costs. The defendant, as I can testify, feels himself to be on trial. The difference is that there is a greater chance of an acquittal in a criminal trial than there is of a verdict for the defendant in a libel case.

However, if various reforms are carried out (always a risky assumption to make), libel trials will become less like criminal trials than they are at present. Besides, even under the existing practices and procedures, there is a case on balance for exchanging proofs. If this had been done in *Meacher* v *Trelford*, the apparent conflict between 'I have always described myself as the son of a farm worker' (in Mr Meacher's proof) and 'I have never described myself as the son of a farm worker' (in his evidence at the trial) could have been resolved – or the attempt could have been made to resolve it – early in Mr Meacher's evidence, instead of on the last day of the case for the defendants.

The exchange of proofs would not, I may add, have benefited me. In my own document I had omitted to mention two matters which I considered important. In 1987 I had re-examined the press cuttings relating to Mr Meacher's campaign for the Labour deputy leadership in 1983, and concluded that he must indeed have claimed to be the son of a farm worker. In 1984, following the publication of the offending column, not a single MP, or indeed anyone else, had commented on it as far as the references to Mr Meacher were concerned. Naturally, Mr Hartley did not ask me about these matters in his examination-in-chief. I managed to work them into my answers to Mr Bishop's cross-examination. If my proof of evidence had been made available to him, he might well have objected: 'Why are you telling us all this at this late stage? Why is it not in your proof ?' And I might have replied: 'Idleness, Sir, pure idleness.'

After Mr Meacher's first day of evidence, Mr Hartley said to us that he would be kept in the box for the whole of the next day as well – as, indeed, turned out to be the case. The implication was that he would slowly be exhausted by his experience. We did not know then that Mr Meacher would be subjected to the additional ordeal of being further cross-examined on his proof of evidence. I was not in the box for as long as Mr Meacher, though I gave evidence for three part-days. Mr Meacher's counsel, Mr Bishop, kept asking me to repeat evidence which I had previously given: not, I may say, to our counsel, Mr Hartley (whose examination-in-chief of me had proved to be comparatively brief) but to him in his cross-examination. Several times he asked me to explain how I went about writing my weekly column.

As it happens, I do not believe that this was an attempt by Mr Bishop to exhaust me, or not predominantly so: I think he had forgotten what I had previously said, and was incidentally engaged in what the lawyers call a 'fishing expedition': a line of questioning which is not leading – is not intended to lead – anywhere but is being pursued in the hope that something useful may be turned up. I protested perfunctorily but Mr Justice Hazan did not intervene, except to advise Mr Bishop, at the end of a particularly repetitive afternoon of cross-examination, to take stock of the situation. Mr Howard had a similar experience, and was constrained to tell Mr Bishop that they had been, as he put it, around those bushes earlier in the day.

The remedy lies in time-limits, greater judicial activity or a combination of both. I have no faith in the ability of judges unguided to control irrelevance and repetitiousness by counsel, partly because they have been brought up to believe that a good judge is he whose yoke is easiest, and partly because most of them earned their livings as learned counsel themselves. It is no use complaining about the length of the trial, as Mr Justice Hazan did after the verdict, if you yourself have presided over the trial, as he had. I see no reason why judge and counsel should not agree among themselves on the length of a witness's evidence. The length of both the examination-in-chief and the re-examination by the party's own counsel should be easy enough to fix. The difficulty would be caused by trying to estimate the length of the cross-examination by the opposing party's counsel. Nevertheless the attempt should be made. When the whistle goes, the barrister should be required to justify extra time by satisfying the judge that he has certain specific questions still to ask, or matters still to clarify.

In the account of the case, I have, as far as is consistent with accuracy, tried to steer clear of 'the pleadings'. These are the written statements (and, in this instance, re-statements) of the case, prepared by the barristers, and expressed in lawyers' language. I have followed this course because, though 'the said Howard', 'the defendant Watkins', 'did falsely state' and all the rest of it have a certain comic value at first reading, they grow tedious by repetition.

They are nonetheless important. Thus, after the verdict, such usually accurate reporters as the *Financial Times* and the BBC Television News said that I had called Mr Meacher 'a louse'. Other organs stated during and after the case that I had accused him of 'despicable conduct'. I had, of course, done neither. They were relying on the agency reports of the first day's proceedings, particularly of Mr Bishop's opening speech for the plaintiff, which had been based – entirely properly – on the pleaded meanings of the words complained of. My actual words were, as the reader will see, somewhat different.

The pleadings were also called in aid by Mr Bishop during his cross-examination of both Mr Howard and me. I got off comparatively lightly. Mr Bishop asked me why it had taken us so long to amend our defence to the effect that Mr Meacher had indeed told various journalists that he was the son of a farm worker. I simply replied that I was not responsible for what our legal advisers may or may not have done. Mr Howard made a similar response, but Mr Bishop harassed him for rather longer: partly because he had discovered that Mr Howard had been called to the Bar (which he had not discovered about me) and partly because the defence on which Mr Howard was giving evidence – that Mr Meacher had agreed to my initial apology, called technically 'accord and satisfaction' – was more susceptible to this kind of attack.

The judge grew perceptibly impatient with Mr Bishop but made no attempt to protect Mr Howard. We had both of us, Mr Howard and I, devoted a good deal of time to studying 'the bundles', as they are called, in the two days that had been available to us before the trial. But the pleadings were not included in the ring-binders which Messrs Turner Kenneth Brown had dispatched to us. We had seen the pleadings, admittedly, some months previously. But the excellent David O'Callaghan of that firm had not told us that it would be necessary to master them. Nor had Mr Hartley or his junior in the case, Stephen Nathan, who had in fact drafted them. I assumed that pleadings were wholly a matter for legal argument between counsel and judge. I am sure Mr Howard assumed the same.

If two legally qualified witnesses could be made to feel uncomfortable through being cross-examined on the pleadings, at what a disadvantage could lay witnesses be placed? Accordingly my fourth modest proposal is that witnesses should not be liable to examination, cross-examination or re-examination on the pleadings in libel (or any other) cases, on which they are, after all, unqualified to speak.

The law, the press and the public

While I was writing this book, in 1988-9, the subject of the law, the press and the public was much discussed. There were three sub-heads: the creation of a right of privacy; the creation of a right to reply to factual inaccuracies or, in some versions of this proposed new right, to other mis-statements; and the reform of the law of defamation, particularly as to trial by jury and, a connected matter, the measure of damages. In this period, privacy and the right of reply were the subject of Private Members' Bills in the House of Commons. John Browne, a Conservative MP, tried to inaugurate a right of privacy. Tony Worthington, a Labour MP (and, before him, a member of the same party, Ann Clwyd), attempted to establish a right of reply.

Members proved sympathetic to both proposals, but the government detected a can of worms. Accordingly Mr Browne's and Mr Worthington's Bills were voted out on the instructions of the party Whips. The Minister in charge, Tim Renton, promised an inquiry into the press. The precise status of the investigation was left somewhat vague at the time: understandably so, as the Prime Minister, Margaret Thatcher, had long set herself against Royal Commissions and Departmental Committees, regarding them – with some justification, it must be said – as indications of unclear vision and infirm purpose. Nor was it wholly clear that the proposed committee under David Calcutt, QC, would investigate defamation. The then Leader of the House, John Wakeham, said that it would almost immediately after the award of £600,000 damages against *Private Eye* to Sonia Sutcliffe.[2] It then turned out that Lord Mackay, the Lord Chancellor, would be conducting a separate inquiry.

The other development of note in this period was the publication of a draft House of Lords Defamation Bill by Mr Justice Hoffmann: a Chancery rather than a Queen's Bench judge, but a highly regarded academic lawyer before his return to practice and his elevation to the judiciary. This measure provided for a simplification and acceleration of procedure but left substantive law untouched. It provided an opportunity for summary decisions in libel cases similar to those available in most other types of claim.

Plaintiffs could obtain swift corrections, with damages up to a

---

[2] *Private Eye* appealed, and succeeded on damages. The Court of Appeal was about to reassess them when the parties agreed a settlement of £60,000. This was an opportunity that was lost to inject some rationality into the law. In November 1989 the jury's award of £1½ million against Nikolai Tolstoy and Nigel Watts in the Aldington case convinced most people that damages ought to be taken out of the jury's hands. In February 1990 Lord Mackay announced his intention to change the law to enable the Court of Appeal to vary a jury's award irrespective of the parties' wishes. The jury's function, however, remained unchanged.

maximum of £5,000. Defendants, for their part, could apply to dispose speedily of trivial or gold-digging claims. This would happen only if the judge thought the matter fit for the summary procedure, but there would be a right of appeal. Some cases, however, would still merit the present extended treatment because of a good, arguable defence of justification (that is, truth) or because the article contained such layers of alleged innuendo that the meaning itself would have to be decided at the trial.[3]

The Report of the Faulks Committee on Defamation[4] fell on barren soil: Mr Justice Hoffmann's measure appears at the time of writing to be the most promising development since Harold Lever's Defamation Act of 1952. It is worth noting, however, that even under the unreformed law of defamation it was always possible to have the action tried by a judge alone, if both parties agreed. Plaintiffs almost always insisted on a jury because they considered – with every reason – that with a jury they were more likely to win not only the case but also enormous damages. I now come to my own further proposals for reform.

A right to privacy

There is a case for establishing a right to privacy by means of the creation of a separate tort entitled invasion of privacy, comparable to trespass, assault or whatever. The case would have been substantial even without the excesses of the popular press over the past decade. Indeed, it is surprising that the judges have not created this tort on their own, through the common law. When you consider the – in my opinion – monstrous and oppressive edifice which they have made out of breach of confidence, unheard of 40 years ago, it may be fortunate that they stayed their hand.

For a law of privacy is not nearly so simple and straightforward as some people imagine. Though, as will appear, I tried to protect the privacy of Mr Meacher's family – and though, as will also appear, I found myself in trouble on that account – it is still possible that what I wrote would have fallen foul of Mr Browne's Bill. If there is to be a law of privacy, there should be a defence of 'public interest' comparable to the defence in defamation of fair comment, which is, after all, only public interest dressed up in a different suit of clothes.

Lord Deedes once told me that, when he was in charge of the *Daily Telegraph*, he experienced great difficulty over whether to 'follow up' the story about Major Ronald Ferguson's visits to massage-parlours. There seems to me to be a legitimate public interest in the private activities of some people but not of others. As Mary Kenny put it, after the manager of the England football team had been betrayed in a Sunday paper by a lady

[3] See David Eady, QC, 'A Bad Defence of a Good Name', *Independent*, 14 April 1989.
[4] Cmnd 5909 (1975).

with whom he had been having an affair: 'It is obvious that a football manager is not in the same position of public trust as a government minister or a servant of the Crown.'[5]

Just so. The politicians, as Anthony Howard speculated in an article immediately after the Meacher case,[6] would be unlikely, however, to pass a law which allowed open season for them – even if journalists were to be added as a makeweight, as perhaps they ought to be anyway. The solution is to allow public interest to be settled by judicial interpretation, much as fair comment has been established. It is the absence of a law of privacy that has been the principal cause of the number of libel cases in the past decade, of the jury's disposition to find for the plaintiff and of the exorbitant sums awarded in damages. A law of privacy should, however, be kept separate from the law of defamation. This separation was urged by the Younger Committee on Privacy,[7] and the Faulks Committee agreed.[8]

The jury retained

The jury should be retained, though I hope Mr Justice Hoffmann's more expeditious procedure is introduced also. The Faulks Committee recommended that the jury should decide either where both parties wanted it or where the court considered it proper in the circumstances. The committee also recommended a right of appeal over the latter to the Court of Appeal, without leave. The earlier Porter Committee on Defamation had recommended that the jury should be retained.[9] Faulks took the view that it was unfair that one party, usually though not necessarily the plaintiff, should be able to impose his or her will on the other.

I disagree. Defamation *is* different from other civil wrongs. It involves the freedom of speech. Historically – most notably in the late eighteenth century – the jury was the citizen's safeguard against the government. Today juries tend to see themselves as protecting the citizen from the press. That is largely the fault of the newspapers.

Damages, however, should be taken completely out of the jury's hands and given to the judge. I see little merit in the 'banding' proposal which some commentators have put forward, whereby judge instructs jury to award a sum within a given range if they find for the plaintiff. Nor is there much merit in Lord Donaldson's ruling in the Sutcliffe case – if it is a ruling, rather than a *dictum* – that in future judges should instruct juries on the income derivable from various capital sums.

[5] *Daily Mail*, 12 June 1989.
[6] *Observer*, 12 June 1988.
[7] Cmnd 5012 (1972), para. 71.
[8] para. 67.
[9] Cmd 7536 (1948).

A test of literacy

After the Sutcliffe case, P.F. Carter-Ruck, a solicitor who specialises in libel and is the author of a standard work on the subject, wrote to the Attorney-General suggesting special juries for fraud and libel. I am not sure that the two are comparable (though in the past special juries sat for all kinds of disparate cases). A jury trying a fraud case has to be able to follow a series of usually complicated transactions involving companies, property and money. A jury trying a libel case has to understand words and their meaning. Jurors must be literate rather than intelligent, even though the two qualities often go together. Libel jurors should be required to pass a simple literacy test.[10]

It would, however, be oppressive if, having been forced to disrupt their lives, jurors were to be subjected to the further hardship of being compelled to sit an examination, however elementary it might be. I would accordingly introduce an element of self-selection for libel juries: only volunteers would risk failing the test. The risk would be that such a self-selected group would contain a high proportion of those opinionated busybodies who are forever writing to newspapers and complaining to the Press Council and are unrepresentative of the population at large. To be so representative is the function of the jury. But it is also the function of a jury in a libel case to read and to understand. Voluntary or not, it seems to me that a literacy test is necessary.

A new definition

The Faulks Committee suggested a statutory definition of libel, as part of a new Defamation Act: 'Defamation for the purpose of civil proceedings shall consist of the publication to a third party of matter which, in all the circumstances, would be likely to affect a person adversely in the estimation of reasonable people generally.' This is a softer test – a test more favourable to the plaintiff – than that laid down by Lord Atkin: 'Would the words tend to lower the plaintiff in the estimation of right-thinking members of society generally?'[11] This seems to be the most popular criterion still. Certainly it was the one used in *Meacher* v *Trelford*, though 'right-thinking' was not always appended to 'members of society generally'. 'Hatred, ridicule or contempt' – a harder test for a plaintiff to satisfy – has gone quite out of fashion.

Damage should be proved

I should be prepared to accept the Faulks test, however. With the addition of an alternative test concerned with 'substantial and material

---

[10] In Jeffrey Archer's case, July 1987, one juror could not read the oath and admitted to being illiterate: Adam Raphael, *My Learned Friends* (1989), 20.
[11] *Sim* v *Stretch* (1936) 52 T L R 669 at 671.

inaccuracies', it would largely satisfy the proponents of a 'right of reply'. There would, however, be no question of damages, unless damage could be proved. Damage still has to be proved in actions for slander (subject to certain exceptions). Faulks wanted to subsume slander under libel. I, on the contrary, should like to see libel made virtually identical with slander, as far as damages are concerned.

Let me take the case whose course is charted in this book as an illustration. Mr Meacher feels aggrieved. He is entitled to go to the court to seek redress, either with a jury or under Mr Justice Hoffmann's new, expedited procedure. If he succeeds, he is entitled to: a declaration by the court, with a statutory obligation on the *Observer* to print it in its next issue; his costs; and a modest sum to compensate him for time, trouble and hurt feelings. Whether under the Hoffmann procedure or with a jury, this sum would be fixed by the judge.

But the idea of someone's reputation as a great, amorphous yet delicate mass would be jettisoned. Damages would have to be proved. Mr Meacher would have found it difficult to prove damage. The 'words complained of' made little impression at the time, either on him or on anyone else. Nor did they have any greater impact in the longer term. For Mr Meacher was re-elected to both the Shadow Cabinet and the National Executive Committee of the Labour Party in the three years (1985-7) between the publication of the alleged libel and the trial of the action. Mr Meacher lost his seat on the Executive in 1988, after his action had failed, though in that same autumn he was re-elected to the Shadow Cabinet.

The pages that follow tell most of this sorry yet comic story.

Dramatis Personae

The Judge:
  Hon. Sir John Hazan
The Plaintiff:
  Michael Meacher, MP
The Defendants:
  Donald Trelford, The Observer Ltd and Alan Watkins
Counsel for the Plaintiff:
  Gordon Bishop and Michael Lazarus
Counsel for the Defendants:
  Richard Hartley, QC, and Stephen Nathan
Witnesses for the Plaintiff:
  Michael Meacher, MP, Sarah Burton, Ann Rouse and
  Canon Wilfred Wilkinson.
Witnesses for the Defendants:
  Alan Watkins, Anthony Howard, Rt Hon.Kenneth Clarke, QC, MP,
  Robert Taylor, Lewis Chester and John Knight
Solicitors for the Plaintiff:
  Larry Grant and Sarah Burton of Seifert Sedley Williams
Solicitors for the Defendants:
  David O'Callaghan and Paul Fox of Turner Kenneth Brown
The Usher:
  Elizabeth Gadd

11

Part One
The Background

1

Politicians as Plaintiffs

In the end most things in life – perhaps all things – turn out to be appropriate.

Anthony Powell, *Casanova's Chinese Restaurant*

In the first week of May 1988 William Millinship, the then managing editor of the *Observer*, took me aside – it was on the pinky-grey editorial floor of the paper's new building over Chelsea Bridge – and spoke to me with unaccustomed force, even severity. Did I realise, he asked, that I was about to be sued for libel in the Queen's Bench Division of the High Court and that the action was set down to begin on Monday, 16 May? Did I further understand that the proceedings might last a week or even longer (the estimate given to me later, as a matter of fact, was 10 days), that they would prove gruelling and that I would be compelled to give evidence subject to cross-examination? He appreciated, he went on, that my 'style' was, as he put it, 'laid back': but there was a limit beyond which casualness was transformed into irresponsibility. Mr Millinship did not actually utter the last words. But the implication, what libel lawyers call the innuendo, was there; and it was more or less justified.

Would I therefore, he concluded, be kind enough to telephone David O'Callaghan, of Turner Kenneth Brown, the *Observer*'s solicitors? Mr O'Callaghan was anxious to take down my 'proof of evidence', which is the witness's statement to his solicitor of what he intends to say in court, and forms the basis of the barrister's examination-in-chief. (In Michael Meacher's action against Donald Trelford, The Observer Ltd and me, Mr Meacher's proof assumed a possibly crucial importance.) I accordingly telephoned Mr O'Callaghan and arranged to call on him at his firm's spacious offices in Fetter Lane, all potted plants and haughty girls carrying files, and more reminiscent of an American television series than of Jarndyce and Jarndyce.

Mr O'Callaghan and his team

I had met Mr O'Callaghan before, though I had not been to his offices until 10 May. We had attended several conferences in 1987-8 at the chambers of Richard Hartley, QC, at 1 Brick Court, Temple, in the company of Stephen Nathan, Mr Hartley's junior, and of Anthony Howard, , the *Observer*'s then deputy editor. We had corresponded frequently over 'this bloody Meacher business', as I tended to call it, or 'this wretched affair', as Mr Howard preferred to describe it. Mr O'Callaghan was the son of an Army NCO and had been educated at Farnham Grammar School. His father had been a champion bantam-weight boxer and Mr O'Callaghan himself – sandy, square, with a large nose and a slight puffiness around the upper cheeks and the eyes – had something of the pugilist about his demeanour. The eyes themselves were particularly menacing, of an intense blue. I caught them once when giving evidence and always tried to look elsewhere afterwards, even though his personal friendliness and helpfulness were overwhelming. As the case progressed my admiration for the intelligence, resource and, above all, resilience of Mr O'Callaghan grew. I was similarly impressed by his young articled clerk, Paul Fox, by Monique Bonville-Ginn and by Marion Tudholpe. Indeed, if it had not been for the intensely hard work done by the four of them on Mr Meacher's family background (work whose thoroughness put most journalists to shame), the case could not have been fought as effectively as it was. The work was not completed until 11 o'clock on Friday 13 May, two days before the case was due to start. Most of it was done on that day and on the days immediately preceding. Mr O'Callaghan told me afterwards that he had never worked so hard in his life.

The implication was that he had not really expected the case to come on at all. I certainly did not expect it. When I took my place in Court No.14 on the first day I thought I was having a dream or sitting in the front row of the stalls for a performance of *One Way Pendulum*. Mr Howard experienced similar feelings of dissociation from reality. We had both thought that the bloody business or wretched affair would be settled somehow. Mr Millinship perhaps saw more clearly than either of us that Mr Meacher, his solicitors or both were determined to have a fight.

Reading for libel

In 1985 the *Observer* had no 'in-house' lawyer. Perhaps this was odd, though it did not strike me so at the time. But in my days on the *Sunday Express*, 1959-64, Express Newspapers had a legal manager with an office and secretarial staff. When I wrote a political column for the *Sunday Mirror* in 1968-9 there was a legal manager employed by the group. Indeed, at a meeting chaired by Sir Edward Pickering and attended by various other grave gentlemen in suits, this particular legal person had insisted that I apologise to Reginald Maudling for some animadversions of mine concerning Maudling's connection with Jerome

Hoffman and the Real Estate Fund of America.[1] He had said firmly that, without wishing to be offensive, if a London jury had to choose between Maudling and me, they would unfailingly prefer the Conservative politician.

In 1985, when the letter from Mr Meacher's solicitors arrived, Mr Millinship was the *Observer*'s legal manager. The paper was then 'read for libel' on Friday and Saturday by several young barristers who came in under a rota system. There was also a senior libel barrister. When I started on the *Observer* in 1976 this was Alec Grant, an old acquaintance of mine from university Labour politics, and an old friend of Mr Howard. Mr Grant left to become a High Court Master. Oddly enough I enjoyed an easier relationship with Mr Grant's effective successor, Mr Nathan, who was of a younger generation. He had been at New College with my friend Geoffrey Wheatcroft and was dark, somewhat Italian in appearance, with quick, brown eyes. Occasionally he would proffer advice, I would decline it, he would insist and I would go off to the editor, Mr Trelford, who would almost always support me. Mr Nathan would look petulant and flounce a little (Nigel Lawson often wore a similar expression when thwarted) but he bore no ill-will. These infrequent disagreements tended to arise over charges by me of dishonesty or untruthfulness in a politician. Mr Trelford had a more robust approach: 'not defamatory', 'fair comment' or, more frequently, 'he (or she) wouldn't dare to sue'. One of his favourite maxims was that only trivial or possible libels were argued about strenuously in newspaper offices – that the really serious ones slipped through. This was certainly so in the case of *Meacher* v *Trelford and Others*. No one raised any alarm.

Mr Nathan was a skilled newspaper lawyer, besides being an accomplished barrister. Indeed, it is arguable that, if anyone won the case for us, it was Mr Nathan. It was he who spotted the action of Gordon Bishop, counsel for the plaintiff, when he put Mr Meacher's 'proof of evidence' before the court. This led to the recall and extended cross-examination of Mr Meacher. This episode will be dealt with later, in its proper place. We are now at the pre-trial stage, with Mr Nathan in his role of the *Observer*'s principal weekend lawyer.

Political journalists' privilege

Political journalists, I should explain, enjoy an unofficially privileged position in relation to the law of libel. They enjoy it irrespective of whether they are political columnists, lobby correspondents or parliamentary sketch-writers – since the arrival of the incomparable Frank Johnson and, later, Edward Pearce, the most derisive group of the three. They occupy this protected place because of custom and practice.

---

[1] See Michael Gillard, *A Little Pot of Money* (1974), 150.

The practice varies from politician to politician and, indeed, from administration to administration. Harold Wilson was not averse to securing the dispatch of a minatory letter from Lord Goodman, the greatest solicitor since Cicero. But Edward Heath prohibited members of his administration from having recourse to the law at all in matters of defamation. Nevertheless the prudent political journalist will avoid those words which remain legally incandescent, such as 'fraud', 'cheat', 'liar' and 'coward'.

'Hack', was established as being similarly perilous when in October 1956 Randolph Churchill successfully sued the *People* for so describing him and was awarded £5,000 as a consequence. But the word has since been devalued for purposes of litigation by its constant use in *Private Eye*.

Where politicians lose most heavily, however, is in their vulnerability to suggestions that they are bad at their jobs. An imputation of incompetence in one's trade or profession is regarded as highly defamatory. Journalists are particularly prone to rush off to their solicitors if someone says they are past it or were never up to it. However, critical journalists, of the theatre, the cinema, television or whatever, enjoy some latitude. They do so partly because of the available defence of fair comment on a matter of public interest (provided the defence is not destroyed by malice) and partly also because of custom and practice. In reality the courts recognise that the work of a critic cannot be carried on properly, or at all, unless he or she is free to write that a performer is no good. The case of Charlotte Cornwell's shape and Nina Myskow's comments on it in the *News of the World* diverted many onlookers.

The contrast between the treatment of actors and performers on the one hand, and businessmen and financiers on the other, could hardly be greater. The most respected financial journalists in the most reputable newspapers can easily find themselves, or their papers, liable for £50,000 or so owing to an incorrect forecast, a misplaced zero or merely an unhappy choice of phrase. Politicians are regarded – indeed, regard themselves – as being closer to actors and performers than to businessmen and financiers. In some respects, in fact, they are treated worse than actors.

In 1966-7, for example, there was a cry that Douglas Jay was a 'bad' President of the Board of Trade. Mr (later Lord) Jay was uninspiring, an embodiment of the privations of the 1940s under the Attlee government. But he was both intelligent and industrious. One of his principal political beliefs was that Britain should not join the Common Market. The bulk of the press thought we should join, especially the *Mirror* papers, which were also the most persistent in their questioning of Mr Jay's competence as a Minister. As the Wilson government's policy towards Europe had changed in 1966, it is arguable that Mr Jay should have been moved from the Board of Trade instead of being dismissed in the following year. Yet he did not, as far as I know, contemplate any legal action to impede this campaign of denigration. It was regarded by everyone as part of the rough-and-tumble of political life.

Some case studies

Sometimes, however, politicians do sue. In 1946 Harold Laski sued the *Newark Advertiser* for stating that he advocated revolution by violence. Though a scholar, he was also active in Labour politics, being chairman of the National Executive Committee in 1945, and one of the first of numerous Labour bogeymen that have made comet-like appearances in our newspapers, from Laski, John Strachey and Aneurin Bevan to, more recently, Tony Benn, Arthur Scargill, Ken Livingstone and Bernie Grant. The *Daily Express* was pursuing Laski with special zeal and, though the first defendant was the local paper, the other – real – defendant was the *Express*, which had picked up the offending words and featured them prominently. They were extracted from Laski (though their precise form was always in dispute) in an altercation with James Wentworth Day. Day was a Conservative journalist who cultivated a jaunty and picturesque appearance and wrote chiefly on farming matters. At the meeting in Newark market square, however, he was present as an 'adviser' to Conservative candidates in the region. On this occasion he seems to have behaved more as an *agent provocateur*.

In the cross-examination of Laski by Sir Patrick Hastings, the question at issue became not what he had actually said at the meeting but what he had written on the subject. Understandably, he had written a great deal. Did saying that revolution was inevitable also mean that one was advocating it? Laski's replies were, equally understandably, honest but involved. The jury found for the defendants. Laski had a bill of costs of around £13,000.

The Labour Party inaugurated a fund, using the slogan: 'Save Laski's Library'. Some £2,000 over the sum required was collected, with which a Laski Memorial Fund was established. Laski composed a somewhat self-pitying though well-written article entitled 'On Being a Plaintiff', which was discovered among his papers after his death.[2] Oddly, Laski did not object to the judge, Lord Goddard, the Lord Chief Justice, who had arguably allowed Sir Patrick too great a latitude in cross-examination and, at the same time, unduly restricted the plaintiff in his replies. Lord Cudlipp, in *Walking on the Water* (1976), describes his cross-examination by Gilbert Beyfus, QC, when he appeared as a witness in the case of Liberace against the *Daily Mirror* and 'Cassandra' (William Connor). Cudlipp accused judge and counsel of being in a conspiracy to cow witnesses, and claims he was unfairly restrained by Mr Justice (later

[2] Reprinted in Kingsley Martin, *Harold Laski* (1953, paperback edn. 1969), 263; the case is dealt with at 159ff. See also Joseph Dean, *Hatred, Ridicule or Contempt* (1953, paperback edn. 1955), 212; *Laski Libel Case*, Daily Express, 1946.

Lord) Salmon from replying to Beyfus in kind. Laski did not object greatly to the cross-examination itself. What he complained about was the publicity, especially the photographers.[3]

Laski was not being 'bankrolled'. He had no rich, generous or (as is sometimes, sadly, the case) vindictive patron urging him on, willing to pay the bill if necessary. Another group of Labour politicians, Aneurin Bevan, Richard Crossman and Morgan Phillips, had the support of a Socialist millionaire, Howard Samuel. Their case concerned a Socialist congress in Venice and a resulting article in the *Spectator* of 1 March 1957 by Jenny Nicholson. The words complained of were these:

> And there was the occasional appearance of Messrs Bevan, Morgan Phillips and Richard Crossman who puzzled the Italians by their capacity to fill themselves like tanks with whisky and coffee, while they (because of their livers and also because they are abstemious by nature) were keeping going on mineral water and an occasional coffee. Although the Italians were never sure if the British delegation were sober, they always attributed to them an immense political acumen.

The case of *Bevan and Others* v *The Spectator Ltd* was tried before Lord Goddard and a jury on 21 November 1957 and lasted two days. Miss Nicholson had not written specifically that the plaintiffs were drunk all the time. Indeed, it might have been argued that, according to her account, the Italians were surprised by the Labour politicians' ability to remain sober in view of the amount they had taken on board. But this – possibly fanciful – approach was not tried. Lord Goddard took a dislike to the paper's proprietor, Ian Gilmour, and much of the case concerned the content and conditions of any apologies offered, if offered they had been. The plaintiffs were awarded £2,500 each.

Crossman was relieved at Lord Goddard's instruction that, if damages were awarded, the plaintiffs should each receive the same amount. He thought that Gilbert Beyfus disliked him but liked Bevan, and that he was elevating Bevan and Phillips into major political figures, while treating him as a 'mere journalist'.[4] However, Phillips presented difficulties for the plaintiffs' case. Crossman wrote:

> We had to endure the cross-examination of Morgan Phillips. At lunch Goodman [Arnold (later Lord) Goodman, solicitor to the plaintiffs] had said that whether a witness is good or bad depends on his self-confidence and quickness of wit. That is why a man like Fearnley-Whittingstall [W.A. Fearnley-Whittingstall, QC, leading counsel for the defendants] is so surprised when he is confronted with Nye or me, because the usual witness can be hectored or bullied and made to take the attorney's line, whereas we gave a good deal better than we got. But, directly Morgan got into the box, it was clear he was a sub-normal witness – shifty, fearful, sweating with panic (legitimately, for he'd been dead drunk for most of the conference) – and

---

[3] Laski is more bitter about the judge, the jury and the law in 'My Day in Court' in M. Rubinstein (ed.), *Wicked, Wicked Libels* (1972), 168, reprinted from *Atlantic Monthly*, 1952.

[4] Janet Morgan (ed.), *The Backbench Diaries of Richard Crossman* (1981), 632.

within ten minutes the cross-examiner was exploiting his inferiority complex and forcing him to admit things he'd never thought of admitting an hour before.[5]

Phillips, the most powerful general secretary of the Labour Party since 1945, was a more formidable person than Crossman allowed. He was, however, famous for drunkenness. His favourite watering-hole was the Marquis of Granby, conveniently situated just across the road from Transport House in Smith Square. Bevan was a substantial consumer of wine and spirits. He would become more voluble, go red in the face and sweat perceptibly, but was rarely seen drunk (though he was reckless about driving his car after he had had too much to drink). Crossman was less of a *bon vivant* than Bevan but imbibed generous quantities of gin and wine, though not whisky or brandy.[6] In the time I knew him, roughly the last decade of his life (he died in 1974), I did not once see him drunk or, indeed, the worse for drink.

Nevertheless, at a *Private Eye* lunch in the early 1970s I heard him admit that the three of them had been drunk 'all the time' in Venice. Others present at the lunch included Richard Ingrams, Patrick Marnham, Auberon Waugh and Geoffrey Wheatcroft. On being asked what they had drunk, he replied 'Valpolicella', adding that no one but a fool would drink whisky in Venice. This connects with Michael Foot's apologia in his life of Bevan:

> To return to the libel, and the incident (rudely referred to sometimes by his friends as 'the Venetian blind') it was, among other oddities, highly improbable that he would be drinking whisky when so well-situated to call upon the immobile delights of Soave and Valpolicella.[7]

Mr Waugh wrote in a profile of Lord Goodman in the *Spectator*:[8]

> Fifteen years later, Dick Crossman was happy to boast to a party of journalists in my hearing that he and Bevan had both been as pissed as newts.

Mr Waugh's phrase 'pissed as newts' has led some observers to conclude that Crossman never said it, because the phrase was not part of his normal discourse. Nor was it; nor did Crossman use it on the occasion in question. As the lack of quotation marks indicates, Mr Waugh was putting what Crossman had indeed said into his own more demotic language. Others who claimed that the plaintiffs had committed perjury were Iain Adamson, reporting Beyfus's opinion, in his biography of the advocate[9] and Sir David Llewellyn, writing under the pseudonym of 'The Junior Member for Treorchy' in the *Western Mail*.[10] Sir David

---

[5] ibid., 631.
[6] See Alan Watkins, 'Richard Crossman' in *Brief Lives* (1982), 41.
[7] Michael Foot, *Aneurin Bevan*, II (1973), 537-8.
[8] 15 April 1978.
[9] *The Old Fox* (1963), 236ff.
[10] 9 July 1963.

was Conservative Member for Cardiff North, 1950-9 and, with Ian Gow, MP, one of that group of Conservatives who were fascinated by Bevan. Mr Foot doubts the claims of Mr Adamson and Sir David.[11]

One of Crossman's principal characteristics was his desire to shock. My view is that he wanted to shock us journalists by claiming to have perjured himself. In any case, what is perjury in these circumstances? Drunkenness is not an absolute condition, like having scarlet fever: it is more like influenza, coming in many degrees and manifold forms. In his diaries, admittedly, Crossman wrote: 'I still think the risk we took was appalling.' But the sentence that immediately followed made it clear that he was referring to the danger of receiving small damages: 'If it hadn't been the Lord Chief Justice but a more moderate judge, the damages might have been quite small.'[12] The *Spectator* had in fact offered each plaintiff £1,000 and paid 500 guineas apiece into court.[13]

Crossman was not one of those politicians who have a taste for litigation. Indeed, one of the strongest impressions which he derived from his father, a Chancery judge, was Crossman senior's horror at the prospect of anybody's becoming mixed up with the law.[14] A few politicians acquire a taste for the courts. John Lewis[15] was a notable litigant, possessing as he did a vindictive disposition. His neighbour in Lancashire, Barbara Castle,[16] was more admirable personally but equally persistent legally.

However, one of Mrs Castle's first expeditions to the courts was as an unsuccessful defendant. In July 1948 she apologised through counsel to the *Daily Express* for suggesting on a BBC broadcast in which she had participated that the *Express* 'Hustings' meetings were rigged. These were a combination of public meeting and opinion poll, subsequently reported in the paper. Counsel for the *Express* stated that the purpose of the meetings was to ascertain the state of political opinion. The people attending them were invited to record by secret ballot their answer to the question: 'Does the country need a change of government?' The ballots were conducted by independent persons. Mrs Castle was constrained to agree with this account – though it should be remembered that, throughout the period of the Attlee government, the *Express* was campaigning for its removal.

She was more successful as a plaintiff. In May 1960 she and the late John Stonehouse, in separate but simultaneous actions, successfully sued Associated Newspapers for an accurate report in the *Daily Mail* of some observations by the Mayor of Lusaka. Mrs Castle had an arrangement to

[11] See above, n.9.
[12] op.cit., 632.
[13] For the offer of payment into court, see pp. 61-2.
[14] Richard Crossman, 'My Father', *Sunday Telegraph*, 16 December 1962.
[15] 1912-1969; Labour MP for Bolton, 1945-50, and Bolton West, 1950-1.
[16] 1911-; Labour MP for Blackburn, 1945-50 and 1955-79, and Blackburn East, 1950-5.

report Harold Macmillan's African visit for the *Sunday Pictorial*. Mr Stonehouse, who had lately been declared a prohibited immigrant by Rhodesia, to much publicity, was also in the journalistic market, on a more loosely freelance basis. As host at a lunch for the British Prime Minister, the Mayor, who had been a settler for 35 years, attacked the two Labour MPs:

> They come here to make money, to create trouble, to write sensational articles without regard to truth. The more sensational the articles were, the more they slammed the white man in Africa, the larger the size of the type in the headlines and, no doubt, the size of the fee.

Mrs Castle and Mr Stonehouse won apologies, 'sums of money by way of compensation' and costs.

In February 1964 she took similar action against the *Yorkshire Post*. On this occasion also her co-plaintiff was a Labour MP, George Wigg: but the action was unitary, *Castle and Another* v *Yorkshire Conservative Newspaper Co. Ltd*. The offender was not a mayor but an irate letter-writer, for whose words the paper was legally responsible. The letter was published in October 1963, after the Profumo Affair, in which Mr Wigg and Mrs Castle had played an important part. Indeed, it is now often forgotten that she had asked embarrassing questions on the first night the matter was raised in the Commons. After various uncomplimentary references to the Labour Party, the writer of the letter proceeded to assert that the only weapon which the party had in Parliament was 'a muckrake wielded by Wigg, Castle and Co.'. I should have thought the defence of fair comment could have been mounted, as it could not have been – anyway it would have presented greater difficulties – in the Mayor of Lusaka's case, owing to his charge of having no regard to truth. But the *Yorkshire Post* action was settled, to the satisfaction of the two plaintiffs.

July 1979 saw the case of *Castle* v *English and Others*. The first defendant was David English, editor of the *Daily Mail*; the Others were Associated Newspapers Ltd and Anthony Bevins, then one of the paper's political correspondents.[17] In an article entitled 'Parliament Heads Blacklist of Britain's Non-attenders', Mr Bevins had accused Mrs Castle, among others, of neglecting her parliamentary duties. This is a distinct form of political article in which 'Crossbencher' of the *Sunday Express* used to specialise. Originally, it was based on a scrutiny of division lists. More recently, attendances of Members at parliamentary committees have been examined. It can often be unfair to the Member concerned, because 'pairing' arrangements are not taken into account – and because an MP's work on behalf of his or her constituents is not measurable. At all events, the action was settled to Mrs Castle's satisfaction.

[17] Later a political correspondent of *The Times* and political editor of the *Independent*.

Mrs Castle's best-known litigation concerned the behaviour of British troops in Cyprus during the revolt against this country's occupation of the island (the 'emergency' of the 1950s). On 3 September 1958 she told Geoffrey Johnson Smith on the 'Tonight' television programme:

> I don't think life in Cyprus is anything but extremely difficult for our troops. The position is critical there simply because of the government's policy ... If the government adopts a tough political policy, it is not surprising that the troops use toughness in carrying out that policy and that brings about a tough attitude in the villagers.

These views did not cause much excitement. The outcry against Mrs Castle came nearly three weeks later, following some remarks of hers in Nicosia on 21 September 1958:

> I believe the men are being permitted and even encouraged by the authorities to use unnecessarily tough measures in searching villages in areas where a shooting incident has taken place on the grounds that the men are engaged in hot pursuit.

The words produced two legal actions, one of them famous, the other more obscure. The little-known case arose after Major Michael Pope, retired, of Porthcawl had written a letter to the *Glamorgan Gazette* in June 1959, alleging that Mrs Castle had described British troops in Cyprus as 'murderers'. Subsequent events were more curious. Mrs Castle sued the Major and the paper. On 9 May 1961 Mr Justice Havers entered judgment for £1,350 in her favour. On the following day he set the order aside when Major Pope protested that he had been unaware of the hearing. On 13 July 1961 the action was settled. The Major protested a second time, saying he would have no part of it. Mrs Castle said:

> I brought this action because he refused to withdraw his allegation in the *Glamorgan Gazette* that I had described our troops in Cyprus as murderers. That this allegation was unjustified was made clear both by the apology in open court on behalf of the newspaper and by the evidence in my action against Mr Chataway. My purpose was never to make money out of him but to get him to admit that he was wrong.

The action against Mr Chataway to which Mrs Castle referred was far better known. On 2 October 1959 Christopher Chataway, then MP for Lewisham North, said in a party political broadcast:

> Yes, Barbara Castle particularly, and a number of others, have continually made very serious allegations about British troops, sometimes implying that they have tortured Cypriots and others. Is this true?

Mrs Castle sued Mr Chataway and the BBC and lost, probably undeservedly. As the quotations given earlier have shown, she was always careful not only to use the word 'tough' or 'toughness' of the troops' behaviour but also to attribute this behaviour to the then government's 'tough' political policy. Some observers attributed her failure to her loyal employment of a fellow-Labour MP, William Wells, as her leading counsel. Though a QC, an experienced lawyer and the author of an introductory students' textbook, *How English Law Works*,[18] he was not a leader of the libel bar. Mrs Castle took her defeat well, saying: 'I have lost a lawsuit, but my consolation is that I helped to win a peace.' The costs were estimated at £10,000, and a Labour Party appeal was got up.

Mr Howard

The *New Statesman* was particularly active in furthering the appeal, both in its editorial pages and at the paper's offices. Mrs Castle was, after all, one of the paper's most distinguished alumni. She had numerous friends and acquaintances at or around the *NS*. Mr Howard, then the paper's newly appointed political correspondent, asked me, then on the editorial staff of the *Sunday Express*, whether I proposed to contribute. I said no: anyone going into a libel action in the High Court as plaintiff should be presumed to understand the risks involved. Others took a different view, and the appeal raised the money that was required.

In 1970-6 Mr Howard and I were colleagues on the *New Statesman*. In 1976 I left to become political columnist of the *Observer*; from 1981 to 1988 he was deputy editor of the same paper. By 1981 he and I had already gone through several crises together and were to go through some more. Of these, the Meacher case was, in the professional sense, perhaps the gravest yet. But neither of us really thought it would happen.

[18] 1st edn 1947.

2

A Farm Worker's Son

Lady Bracknell: Who was your father? He was evidently a man of some wealth. Was he born in what the Radical papers call the purple of commerce, or did he rise from the ranks of the aristocracy?

Oscar Wilde, *The Importance of Being Earnest*

In 1970 Mr Meacher began his parliamentary career auspiciously by winning back Oldham West from the Conservatives. They had won the seat from Leslie Hale – one of the most independent, influential and amusing backbenchers of modern times – on his retirement in 1968. Mr Meacher was 30, perhaps the best age at which to start in the House of Commons. He gave his occupation as 'university lecturer', and his places of education as Berkhamsted School, New College, Oxford (where, it was known, he had obtained a first in Greats) and the London School of Economics. It was known further that he had contested Colchester at the 1966 general election, that he was a member of the Fabian Society and that he was chairman of the Hull branch of Clive Jenkins's union, ASTMS. He had been a lecturer in Social Administration at the University of York and, on his election to Parliament, lectured in the same subject at the LSE. In 1969 the Fabian Society had published his pamphlet *The Care of Old People*.

The result of the 1970 election had come as a shock to Harold Wilson and his entourage and to most of the Conservative Party. The Labour Party, or the party's activists, at any rate, were less surprised. There was a feeling among them that the Wilson administrations of 1964-70 had 'betrayed' the Movement; just as there was an identical feeling after 1979 about the Wilson-Callaghan administrations. In this earlier period after 1970 Mr Meacher 'placed' himself on the left of the party, but there was nothing specially extreme about his opinions. During the party conferences of the early 1970s he made, in 1973, a speech on public investment and the National Enterprise Board (a favourite *restoratif* of the time among virtually all sections of the party) and, in 1971, a speech on welfare services which was applauded enthusiastically.[1]

[1] Labour Party Conference Report, 1971, 203; 1973, 182.

A genuine radical

He secured an early reputation in Parliament also as a tenacious questioner of Ministers on matters concerning the social services. There had long been Labour specialists on poverty, from Eleanor Rathbone to Jim Griffiths. In the 1950s the subject was transformed into an academic discipline or meta-discipline. The pioneer was Richard Titmuss of the London School of Economics. His principal followers were Professor Peter Townsend and Professor Brian Abel-Smith. Indeed, it was angry essays by these two in the symposium *Conviction* of 1958 which was probably, more than anything, responsible for the taking-up of poverty by Labour's intellectuals. Richard Crossman was swift to show interest, even though his chief concern was the establishment of a state pension scheme. When, in 1973, Dr Townsend joined the Board of the *New Statesman*, Corinna Adam nicknamed him the Professor of Poverty.

By this time Crossman had departed the editorial chair. In 1970, when he had just assumed it, and throughout his comparatively brief period of editorship, he was assailed by unsolicited articles from Mr Meacher. 'Another article by Meacher,' Crossman would announce in desolate tones. 'Quite unusable, I'm afraid, but you might see what you could do with it, Tony,' thrusting a ms. in the direction of Mr Howard, then his assistant editor. One week the groans were louder – maybe more theatrical – than usual. 'Good God,' Crossman said, 'there are two of them. There are two Meachers. There's somebody called Molly Meacher,' thrusting another ms. in the direction of Mr Howard, with two names on it. Molly was Mr Meacher's then wife, herself an expert on social policy and administration.

It was at this time that Mr Howard first met Mr Meacher – he thinks it was at a party conference – and they became acquaintances. I did not know him, then or subsequently. As far as I was concerned, this was one of the odder features of the case. I had been a political journalist for the entire period, from 1970 onwards, during which Mr Meacher had been an active politician; and yet we had not once met. Why was this? The answer, I suspect, was that I knew – without the need to think about it too much – that we should not get on with each other. There was something of the disciplinarian school prefect about Mr Meacher: that stiff walk, that narrow mouth, those cold eyes, the spectacles! He must be clever – his academic record demonstrated this – but he had no sense of style, as his proffered articles showed only too clearly. He was industrious but he was also something of a prig.

By February 1974, when Labour, unexpectedly again, won a general election, Mr Meacher had consolidated his parliamentary reputation as a harrier of Ministers. He was also an early admirer of Tony Benn. He became Parliamentary Under-Secretary at Mr Benn's Department of Industry. Harold Wilson shifted Mr Benn in June 1975. Barbara Castle records in her diaries:

> Tony Benn was sitting at his desk, a figure of tragedy, surrounded by a
> cortege of political advisers: Michael Meacher, Joe Ashton and other figures
> I could barely make out, because the curtains were drawn against the
> brilliant sun. The heat was stifling. 'Have you heard anything?' I asked.
> 'Yes,' he replied, 'I am to be moved to Energy.'[2].

Next day Harold Wilson told her that he was going to give her the
junior Minister for whom she had first asked as Minister at the DHSS, Mr
Meacher. 'Oh, he'd be first class,' she responded.[3] Alas, Mr Meacher's
transfer was part of yet another of Harold Wilson's plots: 'Glad as I am to
have him at DHSS, his transfer is just part of Harold's determination to
denude the Department of Industry of all its former devotees.'[4] He was an
assiduous junior Minister, sending back those letters which had been
placed before him for signature 'not so much for redrafting as for
reconsideration of policy'.[5] He and Mrs Castle worked harmoniously
together until James Callaghan became Prime Minister and she was
dismissed, despite the unavailing protests of Michael Foot. Moreover:

> Michael Meacher was outraged ... The most moving letter of them all was
> from young Michael Meacher. He is no time-server. He is extremely able
> and a genuine radical. It was a matter of pride to me that he should write
> about my 'patent burning sense of socialist purpose and drive', and my
> 'capacity to inspire'.[6]

Mr Benn's high tide

Mr Meacher stayed in James Callaghan's government but was moved to
another department, Trade, where he was Parliamentary Under-
Secretary of State until Labour lost the election in 1979. His reputation
was that of an administratively competent but politically partisan junior
Minister. He had been an admirer of Mr Benn both in the pre-1974 period
of opposition and in his first spell of junior office at the Department of
Industry. The next two years saw the high tide of Mr Benn's influence. It
secured the mandatory reselection of Labour MPs by their general
committees. It led also to a change in the method of choosing the leader
and deputy leader of the party. Mr Benn and his followers failed in their
attempt to make the election manifesto subject to the control of the party
conference. Besides, reselection turned out to be a less fearsome weapon
in the hands of the constituency activists than had once been expected.

[2] *The Castle Diaries 1974-76* (1980), 410, 9 June 1975.
[3] ibid., 413, 10 June 1975.
[4] ibid., 416, 11 June 1975.
[5] ibid., 425, 20 June 1975.
[6] ibid., 727, 732, 8 and 12 April 1976.

But the change in the method of electing the leader and the deputy leader was a fundamental one. For the first time, the trade unions and the constituency representatives were given a formal role in the choice of leader and deputy. (The unions had always enjoyed an unofficial say in the election of leader, at least, though its precise strength was a matter of dispute. But it is generally allowed that the approval of the big unions sealed the choice of Hugh Gaitskell over Aneurin Bevan and Herbert Morrison.) The Labour MPs lost 70 per cent of what had previously been their exclusive power; and, such was their condition of fear and demoralisation, to which James Callaghan and Michael Foot had both largely contributed, they made no effective attempt, indeed no attempt of any description, to retain that which had formerly been theirs alone. At the special Wembley conference of 24 January 1981 the party hurriedly chose a system whereby the leader and deputy leader should be re-elected each year by the conference with 40 per cent of the vote allocated to the trade unions, 30 per cent to the parliamentary party and 30 per cent to the constituency parties. This was called the electoral college, though it was known in some quarters as the electoral comprehensive.

The system was first used in autumn 1981, when Denis Healey narrowly defeated Tony Benn and the late John Silkin for the deputy leadership. In the second, final ballot Mr Healey obtained 50.4 per cent of the vote to Mr Benn's 49.6 per cent. Mr Meacher was one of Mr Benn's principal supporters at this time. Several colleagues in the party, and observers of the passing scene outside it, expressed surprise not so much at his support for Mr Benn personally as at his commitment to the policies and, above all, the jargon of the 'hard Left' generally. 'Accountability' – one of the hurrah-words of Mr Benn's faction – was much on his lips in these months.

And yet, colleagues and observers agreed, Mr Meacher did not naturally belong to this section of the party. True, he was and always had been of the Left. But it was what might best be described as the old *New Statesman* Left: rational (or apparently so), with a Victorian respect for Blue Books and statistics; paternalistic, knowing what was good for the workers better than they knew themselves; puritanical, with an equal distaste for the extravagances of the rich and the pleasures of the people; unaesthetic; somewhat humourless.

This was a tradition which, though it was formed in the Edwardian era, probably reached its apogee in political power from 1939 to 1951, during the war years and those immediately following, under the Attlee government. It was a tradition which took a battering from the Wilson governments' misfortunes after 1964; it may be significant that the *New Statesman*'s circulation began to decline fairly steadily after 1966, the year of the 'July measures'. Nevertheless it was to this tradition that Mr Meacher belonged.

At the general election of 1983 Mr Benn lost his seat at Bristol East and did not return to the Commons until the following year, when he won a by-election at Chesterfield. Mr Foot went into honourable retirement from the leadership. Helped and encouraged by his wife Jill, his favour fell upon Neil Kinnock. The trade union leaders David Basnett and Clive Jenkins agreed, announcing their intention to 'skip a generation'. The 'dream ticket' of Mr Kinnock as leader, with Roy Hattersley as his deputy, was born, a nice combination of acceptable Left with moderate Right. But Mr Hattersley (it is now often forgotten) contested the leadership as well, as did Eric Heffer and Peter Shore. The deputy leadership was contested by Roy Hattersley, Michael Meacher, Denzil Davies and Gwyneth Dunwoody. Mr Heffer allowed himself to be used by the Left: 'What we want from you, Eric, at this stage of the war, is a pointless sacrifice.'

The Left wanted – or, for the time being, were prepared to put up with – Mr Kinnock in preference to Mr Heffer, as the ballot of the constituency parties was to demonstrate, 27 per cent of their 30 per cent share going to Mr Kinnock, and only 2 per cent to Mr Heffer. But the Left wanted Mr Meacher to defeat Mr Hattersley for the deputy leadership, and thought they had a chance of bringing this about. Robert Taylor, then the labour editor of the *Observer*, was one of the first journalists to take Mr Meacher's campaign seriously.

> Many of Labour's left wing [he wrote in a news story] want to prevent the establishment of the so-called 'dream ticket', with Mr Kinnock and Mr Hattersley interchangeable as leader and deputy leader. They are running Mr Michael Meacher as a serious challenger for the deputy leadership. He can expect to pick up considerable constituency party support as the bearer of Mr Benn's brand of socialism, and the Left is also hopeful of considerable support in unions such as the Transport and General Workers.[7]

In fact Mr Meacher had detached himself slightly from Mr Benn since that time, almost two years previously, when Mr Hattersley had complained on the BBC:

> If you look at the leaflets that are being given out by Michael Meacher's friends outside this [1981] conference ... I think the far Left have acted in a typically intimidatory way ... I include the organisation of which he is a prominent member, the LCC (Labour Co-ordinating Committee).[8]

With Mr Benn *hors de combat*, a regrouping was in process. But Mr Taylor was in good company. Mr Kinnock, as will be seen,[9] shared his view of Mr Meacher as Mr Benn's surrogate.

---

[7] *Observer*, 19 June 1983.
[8] David and Maurice Kogan, *The Battle for the Labour Party* (1982), 117.
[9] See p.36 below.

A farm worker's son

The next week Mr Taylor interviewed Mr Meacher and wrote a story which was, if anything, even more favourable to his chances and included the following passage:

> At first sight, Mr Meacher looks an unlikely man to win through, but appearances are deceptive. The son of a farm worker, he is a public school classicist who won a first class Greats degree at New College, Oxford. His first ambition had been to enter the Church, but he went to work at Nelson Hall in Southwark after graduating and discovered grinding poverty. 'I am very conscious of my privileged background,' he says. 'My strongest motivation in politics is guilt.'[10]

Mr Meacher's admission to feelings of guilt about his background was to recur, becoming a feature of the case. But why should a farm worker's son who had won his way to Berkhamsted and New College, Oxford, feel guilty about anything? On the one hand, perhaps Mr Meacher thought that privilege remained privilege, however hard won it had been. He may have considered it even more objectionable on that very count – because it separated him from family and friends. Works of fiction and autobiography by (predominantly) sons of working-class parents born roughly 1930-40 and published in the late 1950s make the same point.[11] On the other hand, he may have been aware of coming from a fairly prosperous background in the first place.

The seriousness with which Mr Taylor took Mr Meacher's prospects seemed excessive to Mr Howard. He was sceptical not because he was a friend of Mr Hattersley but because his political nose told him that Mr Hattersley would win. Mr Howard also thought that Mr Taylor was being unduly influenced by Mr Meacher's campaign managers, in particular by Alan Meale.[12] Mr Taylor, however (whose own political leanings were some way to the social-democratic side of both Mr Meacher and Mr Howard), stuck to his prediction, despite the deputy editor's doubts. He wrote in a news story:

> Mr Meacher is increasingly confident that he can win the deputy leadership. 'If I was elected with Neil Kinnock as leader it would be a united ticket.' he said yesterday. 'Hattersley's election would produce a conflict ticket.'[13]

A week later, he wrote that the decision of the National Union of Public Employees to support Mr Kinnock as leader and Mr Meacher as his

---

[10] *Observer*, 26 June 1983.
[11] Cf. Dennis Potter, *The Glittering Coffin* (1960).
[12] Then 'parliamentary and political adviser' to Mr Meacher. Labour MP for Mansfield since 1987.
[13] *Observer*, 24 July 1983.

deputy was 'a setback for the cause of Mr Roy Hattersley'.[14] Mr Taylor was certainly the first journalist to take Mr Meacher's prospects seriously – even though he had established his credentials, up to a point, by unsuccessfully contesting the Party Treasurership in the previous year. But altogether he enjoyed a remarkably favourable press. In an interview-cum-article in the *Morning Star*, Mick Costello wrote:

> The general secretary of Britain's agricultural workers' union ... is tonight chairing a conference fringe meeting in Douglas [Isle of Man, where the union were holding their conference] at which one of the speakers will be Michael Meacher, MP. This is a suitable association as Mr Meacher is the son of a farm worker who will need the support of all sections of the Labour Party, especially the trade unions, to win the deputy leadership of the party against the right wing.[15]

The Times's experienced parliamentary reporter, John Winder, was equally friendly. In a 'Man in the News' feature entitled 'The Toiler with a Social Conscience', he wrote that Mr Meacher was:

> Born in Hertfordshire 43 years ago, the son of a farm worker. He won a scholarship which gave him a public school education at Berkhamsted, and another which took him to New College, Oxford.

Mr Winder added something on his subject's by now famous feeling of guilt. Contrary to popular belief, it was not his childhood and education that gave him the feeling which led him into the Labour Party but, rather, 'what he saw after university in inner London's slums'.[16]

In that week John Knight, the columnist of the *Sunday Mirror*, also thought it worth having a look at the candidate for the deputy leadership: 'His eyes blink earnestly behind rimless spectacles, and Oscar, the family poodle, darts around our feet as we stand in the long garden of his house in London's prosperous Highgate.' He went on to describe Mr Meacher as 'very much his own man' rather than Mr Benn's, as 'coolly intellectual' and as 'a brilliant statistician ... He has four delightful children aged from 11 to 20, and his wife, Molly, is the Director of Information to the National Association of Citzens Advice Bureaux.' Moreover:

> Meacher has an immaculate background which appeals to Socialist romantics. His father was a farm worker (outside lavatory and bath in kitchen), and his brainy son won a scholarship to a public school and went on to get a First at Oxford.[17]

There is an old Fleet Street story – though its origins lie in the BBC

[14] *Observer*, 31 July 1983.
[15] *Morning Star*, 4 July 1983.
[16] *The Times*, 2 August 1983.
[17] *Sunday Mirror*, 7 August 1983.

rather than with the press – about a correspondent who regularly claimed expenses for lunches with a certain Colonel Obolensky of the Russian Embassy. His superior, who countersigned his claim, became suspicious and checked with the Embassy. He was told that there was no Obolensky on the staff and never had been. He confronted his correspondent with this intelligence, who replied: 'I, too, have always had my doubts about the *bona fides* of the Colonel.' It was at this stage that I began to have doubts about the *bona fides* of Mr Meacher. I had two reasons, or sets of reasons.

First, he did not look like the son of a farm worker. Mr Howard, with whom I discussed the matter perfunctorily several times, had the same doubts. He mentioned them in his evidence[18] five years later. Even though he prefaced his observations by saying that this was a delicate area, he briefly lost the sympathy of Mr Justice Hazan. I did not bring the matter up because I was not asked and saw no reason – anyway, had no opportunity – to do so. In my experience you can generally tell roughly what sort of background people have. I should have guessed that Mr Meacher was the son of a bank official or a local government officer. But I should not have been surprised to be told that he was the son of a schoolmaster, a Nonconformist minister or an Anglican clergyman – though a complete absence of raffishness in his character, indeed a certain Goody Two-Shoes quality about him, militated against the likelihood of an upbringing in vicarage or manse. The truth turned out to be stranger and sadder.

Second, and as far as I was concerned more persuasive, my knowledge of the English educational system told me that it was unlikely that the son of a farm worker would win a scholarship to a public school at the age of ten. This was not because such children were inferior: they might well go on, later, to win scholarships to Oxford or Cambridge. But a scholarship at ten, I considered, made it highly probable that the boy would already be enmeshed in the fee-paying system, at a preparatory school. However, the scholarship which he won (and which would have been open to boys from county primary schools also) was awarded under Hertfordshire's assisted-places scheme. The *Observer*'s profile, anonymous but in fact written by Christopher Price,[19] got the scholarship right but repeated the error about his origins.

> He won a scholarship from humble agricultural worker origins to Berkhamsted, a minor public school [which, however, nurtured Mark Boxer, Sir Hugh Greene, Graham Greene and Peter Quennell.] (Years after the Second World War, Hertfordshire was continuing to offer scholarships to a range of public schools, including Eton.)[20]

[18] See below, p. 144.
[19] Journalist, author and director of Leeds Polytechnic. Labour MP for Birmingham, Perry Barr, 1966-70; Lewisham West, 1974-83.
[20] *Observer*, 4 September 1983.

This parenthesis about the assisted places scheme might have dispelled or, at any rate, diminished my doubts. Mr Price had explained the scheme for the first and, it often seemed at the trial, the only time: counsel for the plaintiff and the defendants, and also Mr Meacher himself, persisted in referring to it as a 'State scholarship', which it was not. But I cannot recollect the passage's making any impression on me at the time. If it had, I might – wrongly, as it was to turn out – have said to myself: 'Ah, Meacher senior could have been a farm worker after all.' The story of the State scholarship was repeated in Lewis Chester's profile in the *Sunday Times* of the same day:

> Born in 1939, the only child of an elderly farm worker near Berkhamsted, Hertfordshire, Meacher cannot recall much in the way of political education in the house other than his father saying of the Attlee government: 'If Labour goes on this way, they'll bankrupt us all.' They were poor, but loyal Tories. The family home had an outside lavatory, a bath in the kitchen and facilities for him to study in the front room with a hot water bottle over his knees in winter. He won a State scholarship to the neighbouring public school and bent himself to the fulfilment of his mother's hopes – to become an Anglican priest.[21]

Lunch at the Gay Hussar

Some days before these profiles appeared, Mr Meacher had recommended a referendum on the retention of Polaris if Labour won the election.[22] This was a new element in the argument about the party's defence policy, certainly not an element whose introduction commended itself to Mr Meacher's natural supporters.[23]

As it happened, it was something of a week's wonder. It was, however, one of the considerations in Mr Howard's mind when he invited Mr Meacher to lunch at the Gay Hussar restaurant in Greek Street, Soho, on Wednesday 7 September 1983. In any case, Mr Howard wished to talk to him about the course of the deputy leadership generally.

The Gay Hussar had long been the Left's favourite – perhaps its only – restaurant in London. The then owner, Victor Sassie, looked after his regular customers but, like any competent restaurateur, was not averse to recommending those dishes which were not 'going' that day. ('You'll be having the carp, Michael, lovely piece of fish.') Mr Sassie kept his prices down by mixing cheap dishes, such as minced pork and lentils, with more expensive ones, such as pheasant. Lord Longford used to treat the place

---

[21] *Sunday Times*, 4 September 1983.

[22] *The Times* and *Daily Mail*, 30 August 1983.

[23] Though it may be remembered that in the early 1970s Mr Benn had successfully urged a referendum on the Common Market as a means of keeping us out of Europe. This change in party policy brought about the resignation of Roy Jenkins from the deputy leadership in 1972. Its implementation cemented us in Europe in 1975.

as a kind of cocktail party laid on for his benefit, walking up and down the restaurant after he had finished his lunch – it was organised on the banquette principle, with a corridor down the middle – and joining those tables whose occupants took his fancy. Lord Bradwell (Tom Driberg) died as he would have wished, after collapsing at dinner there.

Mr Howard and Mr Meacher had an agreeable lunch. After some conversation, Mr Howard asked his guest to tell him something of his background. What was all this he had been reading about his being the son of a farm worker? Mr Meacher smiled in his diffident way and said that he was a little embarrassed about it. He would tell his interlocutor what it had really been like. His father had been much older than most fathers – 56 – when he was born. He had gone to London to try to become an accountant but he possessed a nervous disposition, suffered a breakdown, returned to live with his father (Mr Meacher's grandfather) and worked on the family farm. Mr Meacher also told of his father's fear of thunderstorms.

In those pre-Battersea days I went to the *Observer*'s offices in Blackfriars, EC4, three or four times a week, on Tuesday, Wednesday and Thursday mornings and on Friday afternoons. It was my habit to drop into Mr Howard's room for a chat which lasted a quarter of an hour or so, or to have a drink with him at the new El Vino's in Bridge Street, which lasted longer. On this occasion, the day after the lunch, we talked in his room. He was quite excited about his discovery. At last, he said, he had found out the truth about Michael Meacher. He was not really a farm worker's son at all. Having tried to become an accountant, his father had merely pottered about the family farm. I also understood from Mr Howard's story that young Michael had lived in an *ex gratia* cottage adjoining the main farmhouse: accordingly the information about a bath in the kitchen and an outside lavatory made sense.

In this case, incidentally, all the parties, together with the press, were guilty of a lack of both social and historical sense over outside lavatories. Their presence was assumed to be a sign of deprivation or poverty. But educated, ambitious and relatively prosperous families continued to have an outside lavatory solely until well into the last half of this century. Margaret Thatcher, as a girl in Grantham, the daughter of a prosperous shopkeeper, had an outside lavatory.[24] My aunts, the Misses Harris of Gorslas, Carmarthenshire, schoolteachers both, continued to have an outside lavatory at their detached house until their deaths in the 1970s. Moreover, the word 'loo' was used anachronistically throughout the trial: originally upper-class slang, it did not come into popular usage until the late 1960s.

About the only other episode of note before the election was an interview by Jilly Cooper with Neil Kinnock in the *Mail on Sunday*.

[24] See Peter Jenkins, *Mrs Thatcher's Revolution* (1987), 84.

There was more controversy over whether Mr Kinnock had been speaking on or off the record than over the content of the interview itself. In the course of it he had said:

> People over-emphasise the 'Militant' danger. They're terrified of Meacher. They regard him as Benn's vicar on earth, and use his name to frighten their children. In reality, he's kind, scholarly, innocuous – and as weak as hell.[25]

The phrase 'Benn's vicar on earth' was not wholly original, though it was ever afterwards attributed to Mr Kinnock. In his interview in the *Sunday Times* three weeks previously,[26] Mr Chester had quoted an unnamed Scottish MP referring to 'Mr Benn's representative on earth.'

The Pendennis article

On the Friday afternoon before the Labour elections on Sunday 2 October 1983, Peter Hillmore, the author of the widely-read 'Pendennis' column, paid his weekly visit to Mr Howard, who would go over his copy with him. On this occasion Mr Howard complained that the column contained not a single reference to the forthcoming contest at Brighton. Mr Hillmore replied that he could not think of anything to say. Mr Howard said he would try to come up with something. Being self-reproachful about the *Observer* profile, which had preceded the lunch and perpetuated the error, he provided Mr Hillmore with the information on which the following item was based:

> I do hope that Michael Meacher and his supporters are not going to start any more 'working-class stock' nonsense as a last-ditch attempt to win support. It's nonsense. Mr Meacher's father was not a 'farm worker' or agricultural labourer, as is often claimed. It is true that he worked on a farm – but he trained as an accountant, and went to work on a farm owned by his brother. Which is not quite the same thing.[27]

Libel lawyers employ a Procrustean principle when referring to parts of a newspaper. Everything becomes an 'article': leading articles, feature articles, political columns, beauty hints, recipes, interviews, profiles, news stories and, as here, gossip column items. 'The Pendennis article', as it was called, was perhaps the most crucial in the case, because it anticipated my own alleged libel by over a year, and in more forthright terms. I read it at the time but did not pay much attention. (For instance, I did not notice that Mr Hillmore referred to a 'farm owned by his brother', which had been Mr Howard's erroneous impression after his

[25] *Mail on Sunday*, 25 September 1983.
[26] See above, p.34.
[27] *Observer*, 2 October 1983.

lunch with Mr Meacher. I had simply assumed – correctly, but this was luck – that the farm was owned by his father, that is, by Michael Meacher's grandfather.) Mr Meacher did not read the item at all. It created no stir of any kind. It almost certainly played no part in the result of the election for the deputy leadership, which was declared on that Sunday night, and was:

	TUs	CLPs	MPs	Total
R. Hattersley	35.2	15.3	16.7	67.3
M. Meacher	4.7	14.4	8.8	27.9
D. Davies	0.0	0.2	3.3	3.5
G. Dunwoody	0.0	0.1	1.2	1.3

In the election for the leadership, Mr Meacher voted not for Mr Heffer but for Mr Kinnock.

3

A Shabby Episode

When a man is determined by his own inclination either to act or not to act in a particular manner, he invariably sets about devising an argument by which he may justify himself to himself for the line he is about to pursue.

Lord Melbourne in his Notebook, quoted in
David Cecil, *The Young Melbourne*

The trial was fought on two sets of allegations by me, which were known as 'the father allegations', often varied to 'the background allegations', and 'the Moonman allegations'. In the last chapter I tried to outline the political and journalistic framework of the father or background allegations, which was set mainly in 1983, the year of the contest for the deputy leadership. In this chapter I try to do the same for the Moonman allegations, which derive mainly from 1984, the year of Mr Meacher's questionnaire to Labour members of health authorities, of Eric Moonman's resignation from the Labour Party and of the column which – so unexpectedly to everyone at the *Observer* – led eventually to Court No. 14 at the Royal Courts of Justice.

The Moonman allegations received comparatively little attention in the press reports of the trial. This was understandable enough. I make no complaint whatever about the omission. The background or father allegations – their connection with class, with deception (if deception there had been) and with playing the game of Lowlier Than Thou – were more attractive material to any newspaper. They were, moreover, fairly easy to follow. The Moonman allegations were not. They were difficult to explain; even to someone with a rough working knowledge of Labour politics and British public administration.

Indeed, it is possible to argue plausibly that they should never have been allowed to come before a British jury at all, or a British judge for that matter. Not only in security matters, but in a whole range of cases also, the courts are prone to say: this is a case for the Minister, or for Parliament, to put right, or (if it is a case of parliamentary privilege or contempt) for Parliament to regulate according to its own procedures, with which the courts will not interfere. There has, it is true, been an increase in the courts' readiness to over-rule or modify Ministers' decisions with the development of the doctrine of judicial review over the last quarter-century. The high point of judicial restraint vis-à-vis government occurred in the middle decades of this century, roughly 1940-60. Nevertheless, the courts are still liable to say, in many different circumstances: This is not a matter for us. Your remedy lies elsewhere.

The Moonman allegations did not involve a government or minister but a political party. In fact they were pretty typical of the rows which periodically convulse the People's Party, to the general increase in the public stock of harmless pleasure. Mr Meacher used – or was allowed to use – the law of defamation to try to remedy a party grievance.

The first questionnaire

On 13 August Mr Meacher wrote from the House of Commons to all Labour members of health authorities. He began 'Dear Colleague' and went on to refer to the 'blatant political bias within the membership of some District Health Authorities and Regional Health Authorities which, to say the least, does nothing to challenge the Tory ideology which is destroying the cornerstone of our Welfare State'. He asked the recipient to 'liaise with the other Labour supporters on your health authority' to produce the following: a list of all members of the authority, with their occupations and political affiliations, to reach the House of Commons by 24 September 1984; an analysis of how 'cuts' had affected the health service in the area concerned; politically useful case histories; and the name, address and telephone number of one Labour member of the authority with whom he could 'liaise regularly'. He signed himself 'Yours sincerely'.

At the same time Mr Meacher circulated a paper of some 1,600 words entitled 'Guidance for Labour Members of Health Authorities'. It complained about 'officer prepared agendas' which reflected 'the priorities of Tory policy' and 'the lobby of medical professionals'. It urged Labour members to 'take the lead in developing socialist priorities for health care'. To this end, they should 'monitor health inequalities in their districts by social class, ethnic origin, sex, geographical area'. They should also 'produce plans for lessening health inequalities' and 'make inequality in health a political issue of the highest concern to Labour CLPs (Constituency Labour Parties), District and County Parties'.

After much else along the same familiar lines, the paper went on to a section entitled 'Involving the Party'. Labour members of health bodies, it averred, had 'a special responsibility to the Party'. Accordingly they should 'take the lead in developing a local socialist perspective on health' and 'report back to the Party on the business of health bodies and their role on a regular basis. Members should *insist* [all italics in original] space be made available in CLPs, District and County Parties and Councils to receive regular reports.' Moreover, 'local authorities as *elected* bodies can play a key role in monitoring the affairs of *unelected* health authorities'. The most effective method of so doing, and of 'developing socialist policy', was for Labour groups which were in control of local councils to 'form health committees along the lines of those already working successfully in Greenwich, Sheffield and Oxford'.

No great stir was created by the dispatch of the letter or the circulation of the paper. As events developed, however, Mr Meacher was accused of wishing – or plotting – to introduce a 'caucus' system into health authorities. Some critics went further, alleging that he wanted the Labour members of these bodies not only to act as a group, concerting their votes and voices beforehand, but also to be required to take instructions from the local constituency parties. Certainly, Mr Meacher expected the Labour members to act together. And there is evidence in the paper, quoted above, that he wanted them to implement party policy as well. But it is clear also that his preliminary objective was to get the party to take an interest in the subject at all. It was not a case of the party instructing or mandating its representatives – the cause of some theorising in the public prints about the rule of party in totalitarian States. Rather it was a case of the representatives trying to interest the party in a matter which it was neglecting.

The second questionnaire

In any case, this point of political theory played the smaller part in the story. Mr Meacher found himself in trouble, instead, over his request of authority members to report on the voting habits and the political views or allegiances of their colleagues. At the beginning of November 1984 (the day was unspecified) he dispatched a letter, again from the House of Commons, to Labour members of health authorities. It started 'Dear Comrade', not 'Colleague' as the first one had done. It was subscribed 'With all good wishes'. According to Mr Meacher's assistant, Mr Meale, it was never intended to go to health authority chairmen (the post Mr Moonman occupied in Islington) but instead to Constituency Labour Parties for passing on to those members who were members of authorities.[1]

However this may have been – and it is difficult to see what difference it could have made – Mr Meacher wrote that he was 'very grateful' to those members who had taken the time to respond to his initial inquiries. A number of 'worrying trends' were appearing in the returns and he had therefore decided to write again, this time asking for 'specific information on areas of concern'. The questionnaire which was to cause so much trouble was attached for members of District Health Authorities, with a separate one for members of Regional Health Authorities.

The first question asked for the occupation, sex, age, voting habits and party political membership of each member of the authority. The second question asked how many Labour members had been dropped from the

[1] *Hampstead and Highgate Express*, 16 November 1984.

authority since it was set up. Did the recipient consider that they had not been reappointed because of their political affiliations? Of the new appointments, would the recipient say that the majority were Conservative or that there was an even political balance? The third question asked for the names of the Labour members who had been dropped. The fourth question asked for the number of 'ethnic minority members'. It went on to ask whether the authority covered areas which included a 'large ethnic community'. The fifth question asked whether meetings of the authority were attended by the public or advertised in the local press. Moreover, had the authority ever refused to provide information to any group or organisation campaigning on 'controversial issues, such as hospital closure?' There were three further questions which need not detain us, and a request to return the completed questionnaire to Mr Meacher by no later than Monday 19 November 1984.

Mr Moonman resigns

On 8 November Mr Moonman resigned from the Labour Party and Ivor Walker, a fellow-member of the Islington Health Authority, wrote a letter of complaint to Neil Kinnock about the questionnaire. Mr Walker said he did not think he had been appointed to the health authority

> in order to be a stool-pigeon to guess on people's sex, age or voting habits, and I very much object to being asked by a Member of Parliament, and particularly the Labour chief spokesman on Health and Social Security, to act in such a manner. I am ashamed that I can belong to a party where such letters are written and I look to you to ensure that this sort of activity does not continue.

Mr Walker received no reply from Mr Kinnock's office. Mr Moonman had somewhat better luck. When he first heard of the investigation in September 1984, he got in touch with the leader's office, to find that the staff there were unaware of the range of information which was being sought. They assured him, after inquiries, that no further questionnaires would be dispatched. 'Unfortunately, such is the power of the left wing today, the leader was unable to prevent a further distribution of questionnaires.'[2] Mr Kinnock gave a wide berth to Mr Meacher's activities, at the time of the questionnaire, before the trial and during the trial. In an affidavit which was obtained by our solicitors a few days before the case came on, he deposed that he was not consulted and knew nothing about the questionnaire and its background, though he added that Mr Meacher had been acting 'within his remit'. But he did not give evidence on Mr Meacher's behalf at the trial. Nor did any other Labour MP, frontbencher or backbencher. Indeed, Mr Meacher found himself a rather lonely figure.

[2] Letter, *Health and Social Services Journal*, 28 March 1985.

I had known Mr Walker, off and on, for some 15 years. We first met when he was a solicitor with the trade union firm of W.H. Thompson. Though we were friendly acquaintances, we did not consult each other either in 1984 or subsequently.

I first met Mr Moonman in the late 1950s when he took the chair at a lecture which I, then a research assistant at the London School of Economics, gave at Toynbee Hall. The subject was 'Britain and the United Nations'. He was later kind enough to send me a copy of a report he had written in a local newspaper. Reading it, I found I had not made as much sense as I had thought at the time. I later met him when he was a Labour MP[3] and I was political correspondent of the *New Statesman*.

Before Mr Moonman's resignation became public, Mr Meacher had quarrelled over the questionnaire with Kenneth Clarke, then Minister of State for Health, in the Debate on the Address to the Queen's Speech. Mr Meacher accused Mr Clarke of pursuing a campaign of 'political victimisation' against all those who supported the health service and opposed cuts. He intended to stop this 'Tory hit-listing' by providing the public with the details of what was happening. Mr Clarke replied that Mr Meacher probably suspected that so many of the recipients of his letters had been 'outraged' by their contents that many Conservative MPs had been shown copies of them. He was 'disgusted' and so were members of health authorities. If Mr Meacher would place a copy of one of his letters before the House, it would make clear that he had been seeking information on the political affiliations of members of health authorities and 'trying to introduce a whipping or caucus system involving pre-meetings with local Labour parties and Labour groups'. (This was presumably a reference to the document 'Guidance for Labour Members of Health Authorities'.)[4] It was 'sheer humbug' for him to complain about the introduction of politics into the health service and to criticise non-political appointments to authorities throughout the country. Mr Meacher responded that to accuse him of introducing politics into the health service was the 'most incredible hypocrisy' from Mr Clarke.[5]

Three days later, on 11 November 1984, Mr Moonman's resignation was revealed by that indispensable journalist Robert Taylor, who was having a brief spell as political correspondent of the *Sunday Times*, in between his longer periods of service to the *Observer*.[6] The story – what libel barristers choose to call the article – was headlined 'Labour Health Chairman Quits Over "Spy for the Party" Row'. The word 'spy' was repeated, though more in headlines than in the stories beneath them, throughout the following week: 'Labour's "Spy" Dossier Sparks Row', 'Moonman Quits Labour Over Left "Spying" ', 'Former MP Quits Party

[3] Billericay, 1966-70; Basildon, 1974-9.
[4] See above, p. 39.
[5] 67 H.C. Deb.6s.c.239, 8 November 1984.
[6] *Sunday Times*, 11 November 1984.

Over "Spying".'[7] 'Spy' was used several times by Mr Moonman himself in his quoted observations to journalists. He also accused Mr Meacher of 'Stalinism'. Mr Walker, for his part, appended 'KGB' to 'stool-pigeon'.[8]

Mr Moonman explains

By this stage Mr Moonman had become a public figure in a small way of business. As such, he was asked to contribute a leader-page (also called an opp.ed.-page) article to *The Times*. It was entitled 'Why Meacher was the Last Straw'. Mr Moonman wrote that it was easier to join a political party than to leave one. He complained about Mr Meacher's trying to mandate Labour members to vote in accordance with party dictates. Members of health authorities who were also Labour Party members were being asked details of the age, sex, political affiliations and voting habits of all the members of the authority. He did not know the politics of, for example, the nurses' or the general practitioners' representatives on the Islington Health Authority. Widening his field, Mr Moonman went on to attack the reselection of Labour parliamentary candidates. The party improperly wanted delegates rather than representatives. Altogether Mr Meacher was guilty of a 'gross intrusion into personal privacy'. Mr Moonman concluded:

> I joined Labour as a teenager, excited by the vision of a Socialist Britain. The party taught me tolerance and gave me comradeship. Now, it has become vituperative, even malicious, and brotherly love is out of fashion. Labour today is obsessed with control and the interests of tiny minorities. In the process it has lost touch with the aged, sick, and deprived who cry out for a caring government, indefinitely postponed by the alienating antics of the extreme Left. I used to think that Labour could be saved by Neil Kinnock and the sensible members of the parliamentary party and the National Executive. I now finally see they do not have the strength.[9]

In fact the doctrine of the mandate has a long and honourable history in the Labour movement. Burkean notions of representation have not, on the whole, found favour. Those members who attend the Labour Party conferences are called delegates, not representatives, as their Conservative equivalents are called. Sometimes these delegates are instructed by their general committees to vote in a particular way on a given topic, irrespective of the course which the debate may have followed. This process is called 'mandating' and is, or used to be, taken most seriously. The notion of a party member's subordinating his personal convictions to the will of the majority is as old as the party itself, anticipating by many decades the arrival of Mr Benn on the scene. A

---

[7] *Mail on Sunday*, 11 November 1984; *Daily Telegraph* and *The Times*, 12 November 1984.
[8] *Sunday Times*, 11 November 1984.
[9] *The Times*, 13 November 1984.

ward party sends a delegate or delegates to the general committee, which in turn sends delegates to the annual conference. These delegates are supposed to embody the views and aspirations of the majority of the body that sent them to the higher forum.

This way of looking at things has caused difficulties, notably over the relationship between a Labour government and the party conference, and between Labour MPs generally and the party in the country. *A fortiori*, it causes difficulties when party members are appointed by Ministers (often, as in this case, Conservative Ministers) to statutory bodies. Indeed, in September 1984 Mr Moonman wrote to Jim Mortimer, the general secretary of the party, making clear that he had the statutory duty as local health service chairman to work within the law.[10]

At this time, the Conservative government had a policy of privatisation within the health service. Mr Moonman implemented this policy, his degree of enthusiasm in so doing being a matter of dispute. Mr Meacher, replying to Mr Moonman's 'ridiculous allegations', wrote that this background had 'understandably' been left unstated. Labour members of the Islington authority had themselves asked him to resign the chairmanship. The Islington North and South constituency parties had both unanimously passed resolutions 'condemning his actions'. Having thus (Mr Meacher proceeded) rejected the principles on which Labour Party health policy was based, Mr Moonman had now used the questionnaire as an 'excuse' for a 'long-harboured intention' to leave the party, which he had now done 'with as much mud-slinging as possible'. In the 'ensuing furore', the purpose of the questionnaire had been 'totally ignored by Mr Moonman and the media'. There was 'abundant evidence' that political patronage had been abused in health authority appointments. And there was 'no implication whatsoever of spying on colleagues or of mandation of Labour members on health authorities.'[11]

Certainly, Mr Moonman thought there was something in Mr Meacher's point of view. When he received Mr Meacher's first letter, he suggested to Mr Kinnock's office that a better course would be to set up a 'working group' to investigate the whole question of health authority membership. This idea was not adopted. When he received the second, more detailed questionnaire, he decided to break his silence. However, his decision to leave the Labour Party had been prompted by an accumulation of factors which had caused him concern.[12] Despite his protests over the questionnaire, he favoured greater accountability and democracy in health authorities. He thought that the American system of direct elections might be the answer, though there were dangers in that approach. He believed in accountability to the public rather than to the party.[13]

[10] *Sunday Times*, 11 November 1984.
[11] Letter, *The Times*, 16 November 1984.
[12] *Hampstead and Highgate Express*, 16 November 1984.
[13] ibid.

The Times leader

The Times brought these developments together in a powerful though not always lucid leading article entitled 'Left in the Lurch'.[14] Mr Moonman was described as the 'authentic voice' of a Labour generation in its 'political dotage'. He had resigned; while others lapsed into 'political passivity', or into 'exhausting defence of their seats against the predators of the ultra-Left'. 'Vital organs' of the party were now controlled by those who said that Mr Moonman, Harold Wilson, James Callaghan and the other 'anti-heroes of the New Left' had 'betrayed the utopian dream'. Utopians were not new in the Labour Party. But in the 1940s they 'swam in the main stream'. Later, under Hugh Gaitskell and Harold Wilson, they were 'temporarily cowed'. In the 1970s, however, 'a new breed of militant utopians emerged, impatient with Parliament, strengthened by recruits from the new class of public functionaries created by Wilsonian socialism and Heathite corporatism and infused with a jumble of extremist ideas from the ideological ferment of the 1960s'. Since 1973 there had been no enemies and many openings on the Left.

This was a reference to the abolition of the 'proscribed list' at the party conference of that year. As it was unexplained, it must have puzzled those readers who were not well up on recent Labour history. There has been much misundersanding of this change, some of it brought about by ignorance of the Labour Party, but some, it must also be said, deliberate. The proscribed list contained the names of those organisations membership of which disqualified one from membership of the Labour Party. It did not include the Conservative Party, the Liberal Party, the Communist Party or – what is most to the point – any of those Trotskyist fringe parties from which Militant was to emerge. It did include various fellow-travelling bodies deriving largely from the 1940s and before, often with 'freedom', 'friendship', 'peace' and 'understanding' in their titles. The abolition of the list may have turned out to be a symbol of greater laxity, but it was undertaken because its existence implied that membership of equally sinister bodies which were *not* on the list was perfectly all right.

The *Times* leader continued: Mr Moonman's generation came to learn the limits of politics. Members of Parliament and local councillors were allowed 'space for judgment'. Respect was retained for 'a trade of civil administration outside the ambit of party politics'. Labour was now, however, beginning to function as a party in which members of the 'revolutionary parties' could find themselves at home. But Mr Moonman rejected 'a Leninist model of Labour Party organisation'. Mr Kinnock's task was 'not, yet, hopeless'. But he must realise that this was 'a sociological, a demographic quest', for Mr Moonman's generation had passed on, defeated. The Labour leader had somehow to appeal over the

[14] *The Times*, 15 November 1984.

heads of the extremists. Meanwhile the very least he could be seen to be doing was 'dressing down those members of his party – dupes or worse – who allow themselves to be the willing agents of Labour's Leninists for whom politics has no in-built limits of civility.'

I did not think this article was wholly wrong, though I did think it a little *exaggerated*, as the lady from Edinburgh said to her companion in the audience on first seeing a performance of *Swan Lake*. All I knew at this stage – it was a Thursday – was that I should probably be writing something that week about the poor old Labour Party. But neither Mr Meacher nor Mr Moonman was in the front of my mind.

4

The Words Complained Of

How matter presses on me! What stubborn things are facts.

William Hazlitt, *Table Talk*

For some years, it seemed to me when I sat down to write my weekly column for the *Observer*, the entire British press had been repeating the myth of the golden age of Labour decency and toleration, extending from 1945 and before to around 1970. I did not want to write the entire column on this subject, which I had touched on before, as I was to do later, often calling in aid the party's former National Agent, Sara Barker: 'a hint of heresy, a whiff of recalcitrance, and Sara's tanks would emerge at dead of night from the concrete garages deep under Transport House and move unstoppably towards the offending part of the country.'[1]

Down memory lane

I decided to utilise my experiences as a Labour councillor, 1959-62. Perhaps 'decided' is too strong a word. The first part of the column was to be about the mythical tolerant age. My local government experiences came to the top of the stew. So I began:

> There is an extraordinary notion going around that Labour was once the party of brotherly love. We can all write the script: 'Bevin ... honesty ... Attlee ... decency ... Gaitskell ... toleration ...' It is all great nonsense. I know. I was there. In the early 1960s (to take one more or less random example) I was a Labour member of the Fulham Borough Council. I represented the Hurlingham Ward, at the posher end of the borough, having been elected, I remain convinced, because my Conservative opponent was called Watson.
>
> I was not a specially active councillor, and tried to resign, quite properly, when the paper for which I was then working sent me to New York for six months. The local Labour agent was horrified by my conscientious offer, saying: 'We hate by-elections in Fulham.' So I went to America but stayed on the council. The local paper, I learnt later, ran a story getting my name

[1] *Observer*, 24 November 1985.

wrong, under the headline: 'Row over Ernie Watkins.'

The leader of the council was William Molloy, afterwards MP for Ealing North, now a Lord. Then, as later, Mr Molloy, who is from Swansea, talked a great deal. Indeed, it seemed that he never stopped talking. Having been brought up on lengthy renditions from that other *vox humana*, Jim Griffiths, I thought I could take Welsh oratory without its damaging the brain. Mr Molloy went on for longer than Jim and was considerably less entertaining. He went on chiefly at meetings of the Labour group. These lasted from mid-evening to three in the morning. At one in the morning I would stagger out, having had enough.

Meetings of the council, by contrast, lasted half-an-hour or so. No one spoke except one or other of the half-dozen miserable Conservatives and Mr Molloy, who would enjoy himself with elaborate displays of invective and scorn. There was no debate whatever. That had all taken place at the Labour group. Decisions went through on the nod. Nor were Conservatives made members of the important (or, as I remember, any) council committees. It was sheer Stalinism from start to finish. I am ashamed that I ever had any part in it.

After the column appeared, I was sorry I had used 'Stalinism', which was employed as an imprecise boo-word throughout the Moonman-Meacher affair. I was sorry also that I had offended or hurt several old party comrades from Fulham days. Lord Molloy, who considered me a friend, was distressed. People who had been with me in the local party or on the council – three of them – wrote to say that they had always quite liked me and thought I had enjoyed my time in their company. One former councillor, since gone over to the SDP, had a letter along these lines published in the *Observer*.[2] I felt guilty about having injured the feelings of some decent people. But what I had written nevertheless conveyed my honest emotions when I was a councillor, when I was composing the column and when I thought about it afterwards. There it was; it could not be helped.

Several other people, however, journalists and Labour MPs, expressed appreciation. The MPs said that it was high time the facts about Old Labour were known, the journalists that they never realised the party had been quite as I described it. This, roughly the first quarter, was the only part of the column to stimulate any comment whatever, as far as I was aware. I continued with the words complained of.

The louse and the flea

These recollections are prompted by, in particular, a leading article in *The Times* commenting on Mr Eric Moonman's resignation both from the chairmanship of the Islington health authority and from the Labour Party.

The resignation from the Islington Health Authority I simply got wrong. I assumed, from Mr Moonman's widely expressed dissatisfaction –

2 *Observer*, 25 November 1984.

from his general state of fed-upness – that he had resigned the chairmanship of the authority also. Not so: he had resigned only from the party. Mr Meacher's counsel played up this mistake like anything at the trial. I continued with what I thought was a statement of agreed and admitted fact, expressed in the most neutral terms:

> He resigned because Mr Michael Meacher asked him, in common with other Labour chairmen of health authorities, to report to Mr Meacher on the political predilections of his colleagues on the authority.

Nothing wrong with that, I thought. Indeed, the possibility of any libel trouble never crossed my mind. The next sentence caused me a good deal of worry. I cast and re-cast it in my mind, for several minutes. One of the more interesting things about Mr Meacher, I considered, was not that he dispatched questionnaires which tended to cause offence but that he misleadingly claimed to be the son of a farm worker or agricultural labourer. I drew no distinction in my mind between the two occupations, even though, as I realised on subsequent reflection, a cowman, say, was different from a general labourer. Certainly, Mr Meacher's own descriptions of his upbringing, at any rate as conveyed by journalists 13 or 14 months previously, suggested a background of rural privation. It seemed to me not only interesting but – what is somewhat different – a matter of public interest that Mr Meacher had made these false claims. On the other hand, it might be interesting that Mr Meacher's father had suffered a nervous breakdown but it was not a matter of public interest. That was a private, family matter. So I tried to tell the truth without mentioning the nervous breakdown:

> Mr Meacher likes to claim that he is the son of an agricultural labourer, though I understand that his father was an accountant who retired to work on the family farm because the life suited him better.

I specifically drew to Mr Howard's attention the sentence which I have just reproduced. After all, it was he who had provided me with the information, some 14 months previously. He was my sole source. I originally wrote that Mr Meacher senior retired to his father's (Michael Meacher's grandfather's) farm. Mr Howard said that by this time it was his brother's (Michael Meacher's uncle's) farm. We compromised amicably on 'the family farm'.

The next difficulty was more intractable. Mr Howard said that Mr Meacher senior had never really been an accountant. He had merely tried unsuccessfully to become one. I replied that a full explanation would entail the introduction of the nervous breakdown, which would, I considered, be tasteless. Mr Howard concurred. I recall his words, often used by him to express agreement: 'I think that's probably right.' But libel was far from his or my mind. We were concerned with accuracy. Over the claim to having been the son of an agricultural labourer, I did, however, rely on my memory of the 1983 articles about Mr Meacher. The column continued:

> But this by the way. It matters not, as the barristers say.

The barrister that I had in mind was Basil Wigoder in the unsuccessful prosecution of the *Sunday Telegraph* and Jonathan Aitken under the Official Secrets Act in 1971. Mr Wigoder was for the defence. I continued:

> Nor does the dispute between him and Mr Moonman matter greatly either, in itself. I should have thought Mr Moonman would have protested more effectively if he had advised Mr Meacher to jump off the Terrace into the Thames, and made this advice known to the press. What I am concerned about is the use to which the newspaper put this admittedly shabby episode.

Learned counsel for Mr Meacher chased me round the houses several times on the meaning of 'admittedly', of 'shabby' and of 'admittedly shabby'. When I wrote it down I thought I was using a phrase that was both accurate and mild. Defamation never entered my mind. I went on:

> It [*The Times*] said that Labour local authorities had become increasingly dictatorial, secretive and intolerant. Wrong: they have always been dictatorial, secretive and intolerant, as I have tried to demonstrate. The article also attempted to depict Mr Moonman as one of the last of the old Labour idealists – a follower of honest Bevin, decent Attlee, tolerant Gaitskell – driven out of the party by the likes of Mr Meacher.

Geoffrey Wheatcroft has suggested that a new typeface should be invented, called *Ironic*. The most intelligent and literate people often fail to spot irony. But there was no irony here. It was a perfectly straightforward sentence. Mr Meacher, however, persisted in interpreting it to mean that I was accusing him of having driven (or, as he often varied it, hounded) Mr Moonman out of the Labour Party. I continued:

> If it comes to a choice between Mr Meacher and Mr Moonman, I am tempted to recall the observation of Dr Johnson on the respective merits of the two poets: 'Sir, there is no settling the point of precedency between a louse and a flea.'

Here ended the words complained of. The last 15 of them, from the Doctor, caused as much trouble as any – perhaps more. Again, libel did not enter my mind as I wrote them down with the *Oxford Dictionary of Quotations* before me. I did think that I was perhaps being a little hard on both the comrades, but that the quotation was both apposite and quite funny. Certainly Mr Howard laughed when he read it that afternoon.

And, of course, Mr Meacher was not meant to be the louse: the entire point of the quotation is that the louse and the flea are interchangeable. I continued:

> As we are travelling down memory lane this week, I will tell you that I first met Mr Moonman in the late 1950s, when he invited me to come to Toynbee Hall to give a talk, which I did. He was not the warden but some kind of sub-warden.[3] Did I say to myself: 'This Moonman is anxious to do good to the poor of Aldgate and Bethnal Green'? No, I said: 'This boy is anxious to advance himself in the People's Party.' Advance he did. As an MP he appeared before our wondering eyes as a self-appointed expert on the Press and spokesman for the printing industry, though he had little if any practical experience of the business. He was a real busybody, more irritating even than Mr Meacher.

A mistake about Mr Moonman

I was harder on Mr Moonman than on Mr Meacher. Mr Moonman, however, had recourse to the letters column of the paper rather than to the courts. In particular he controverted me on his experience of the printing trade. After leaving school at 13, he wrote, he spent nine years as a printer on the shop floor, including a seven-year apprenticeship as a compositor. It was the print union that sent him to the university. Afterwards he was northern manager of the *Daily Mirror*, being involved in the launch of the paper into direct production in Manchester. He had represented the printing unions for 20 years as candidate and MP. I can only plead as Dr Johnson did, when asked why he had got various parts of a horse wrong in his *Dictionary*: 'Ignorance, ma'am, pure ignorance.'

Mr Meacher's counsel made a meal, rather, of my inaccuracies over Mr Moonman. He also made much of the word 'malice' in Mr Moonman's concluding sentence: 'Finally, after all that malice, it appears that Mr Watkins's conclusions about the state of the Labour Party are the same as mine!' These now followed:

> Let us leave Mr Moonman where he is, and return to the myth of Labour's golden age of honesty, decency and toleration.
> As with all myths, there is something in it. The error lies in making the contrast too stark, the white too snowy, the black too dusky, with no greys anywhere. The parliamentary leaders remain the embodiment of decency, even dullness. Mr Eric Heffer (who was undeservedly knocked off the Shadow Cabinet as a consequence of the campaign against Mr Tony Benn) now appears tolerant, though in fact he always was a bit of an old liberal underneath the neo-Marxist rhetoric.

Mr Meacher could certainly be numbered among the decent, even dull parliamentary leaders.

---

[3] See above, p. 42.

Mr Kinnock and the miners

But the party in the country, as we saw for ourselves in that horrible Blackpool conference, is much nastier than it used to be. It now contains some vicious characters. They are going to become quite rabid when the miners' strike collapses, as politicians of all parties now agree it will, either just before Christmas or just after. The activists will attack the Shadow Cabinet in general, Mr Neil Kinnock in particular.

The strike collapsed in February 1985. Mr Kinnock and his colleagues were duly attacked. Neither prediction needed much percipience on my part. I continued:

There is a view that Mr Kinnock was placed in a difficult position and could not have conducted himself any differently. The position was certainly difficult: but his conduct could equally certainly have been different. He could have been for a ballot and not only against violence (which, to be fair, he has been, though *sotto voce* a lot of the time) but against mass picketing as well. There is no constitutional right to picket in large numbers. With a ballot and picketing by small numbers, the strike would have been solid, and Mr Kinnock could have given it his full support.

Mrs Margaret Thatcher is not wholly correct when she says, as she did last week, that Mr Kinnock started off by calling for a ballot and then withdrew his demand. What he in fact said was that he understood the miners' union would shortly decide to hold a ballot, a decision he welcomed. When no such decision was made, he kept quiet.

Anyway, Mr Kinnock has contrived to have the worst of all words. He has at all events made himself more uncomfortable than he need have been. The activists are now pursuing him, though they will not dislodge him. My advice is that of the late Carwyn James, to get his retaliation in first.

The column was headlined: 'Neil should get his retaliation in first.' The reference puzzled many, including Mr Meacher, who said during the trial that he could not understand it. This was perhaps odd for a former rugby player, such as Mr Meacher also claimed to be. Carwyn James, of Llanelli and Wales, coached the British Isles team in their victorious tour of New Zealand in 1971. The New Zealanders were well-known for tactics of intimidation. Such play is often excused by the player to the referee with: 'I did it in retaliation, honestly.' James's advice was to hit them before they hit you. This was intended as a joke – but only partially. I was advising Mr Kinnock to attack Arthur Scargill and his friends before they attacked him. Mr Kinnock took my advice 11 months later, at the Bournemouth conference, after he had been subjected to numerous attacks.

I was quite pleased with this column. If I had been over-severe, it had been with Mr Moonman, my old colleagues on the Fulham Council and – possibly – Mr Kinnock rather than with Mr Meacher. I certainly did not accuse him of despicable conduct or call him a louse. Nor did I know that Mr Meacher had the same firm of solicitors as Arthur Scargill.

5

The Road to Court No. 14

'They've not been sleeping, I know that. Ah, they're very smart fellows –
very smart, indeed.'
   As the little man concluded, he took an emphatic pinch of snuff, as a
tribute to the smartness of Messrs Dodson and Fogg.
   'They are great scoundrels,' said Mr Pickwick.

Charles Dickens, *The Pickwick Papers*

The individual solicitor who, at this stage, was pursuing Mr Meacher's
interests – as she presumably saw them – was Sarah Burton. She was a
New York lady, small, dark, intense, of strong socialist convictions. She
had not been long qualified. I did not set eyes on her till the trial or deal
with her in any way: she was a name merely, which during 1985 I heard
Mr Howard and Mr Millinship pronounce with varying proportions of
irritation, resignation and despair.

The solicitors' letter

After the appearance of the column 'Neil should get his retaliation in
first', she was silent, as was Mr Meacher. No Member of Parliament
commented on what I had said about him. Christmas 1984 came and
went; the New Year came in. On 29 January 1985 a letter from Seifert
Sedley Williams arrived by hand at the *Observer*. It was written by Miss
Burton, addressed to the editor, with a copy to me. 'Dear Sir,' it started,
'We have been consulted by Michael Meacher, MP ...' and then followed
the publication details of the column, and the words complained of, from
'These recollections are prompted by ...' to ' " ... a louse and a flea." '
There were, the letter said, a number of untrue and highly defamatory
allegations made against their client. They included the following:
   First, Mr Meacher made false statements in relation to his family and
personal background. The implication was that he did so to appear 'more
politically credible to his constituents'. This allegation was 'completely
unfounded', a fact which, so Miss Burton asserted, I could have
ascertained for myself if I had possessed 'the courtesy to check these
statements with our client before publication'. Second, and arising from

53

the first allegation, there was a 'clear implication' that Mr Meacher was a 'dishonest and untruthful person'. Third, in carrying out his responsibilities as spokesman on Health and Social Security, he had been taking part in an 'operation designed for an ulterior purpose' referred to by me as an 'admittedly shabby episode'. And, fourth, Mr Meacher had thereby been responsible for the resignation of 'another member of his party' (that is, Mr Moonman) not only from that party but also from the chairmanship of a local health authority. 'Again, the true position could easily have been ascertained' by me. In the context of these allegations, the quotation from Dr Johnson was 'clearly designed to degrade our client further in the eyes of your readers'.

Messrs Seifert Sedley Williams had advised Mr Meacher that these 'serious and untrue allegations' were 'actionable by him against the newspaper in proceedings for libel'. Unless, within seven days of receipt of the letter, they had heard from us that we would meet their terms, proceedings would be 'commenced forthwith and without further notice'. The terms were: 'a clear and unequivocal undertaking' that the allegations would not be repeated; an apology, to be agreed before publication and 'printed with the same prominence in the newspaper as the original article'; payment of 'substantial damages' to Mr Meacher; and Mr Meacher's costs. A draft apology was enclosed. It was entitled 'Michael Meacher – an Apology' and continued:

> In the Political Diary of this newspaper on the 18th November 1984, we published an article written by Alan Watkins in which he referred to Mr Michael Meacher MP, a member of the Shadow Cabinet and Opposition Spokesman on Health and Social Security. In the course of that article it was alleged that Mr Meacher made false claims about his background and that conduct of his had led to the resignation of Mr Eric Moonman from the Labour Party and from the Islington Health Authority.
>
> We are entirely satisfied that those allegations are untrue and are pleased to take this opportunity to apologise to Mr Meacher for the distress which that article may have caused to him.

Accompanying both the draft apology and the letter setting out the terms there was a shorter letter. It said that Mr Meacher had 'no quarrel with the newspaper'. His 'attitude towards damages' would be influenced by the speed with which an acceptable apology was printed. Messrs Seifert Sedley Williams emphasised, however, that if they did not hear from us within seven days, 'proceedings will be issued'.

Mr Howard, Mr Millinship and I met shortly afterwards in Mr Howard's office. We were neither despondent nor alarmed but, simultaneously, amused and rather cross. Mr Howard was particularly exercised by Mr Meacher's behaviour. He was both puzzled and angry. This was understandable. Mr Meacher was, after all, a friend of his; had known him for 15 years or thereabouts. True, the friendship was not so much personal as political on Mr Meacher's side, journalistic on Mr Howard's: but nevertheless the two had a genuine regard, even liking for each other. Mr Howard had 'placed' occasional articles by Mr Meacher in the *New Statesman* between 1970 and 1974. Indeed, at the very time the minatory letter from Miss Burton arrived, he had in his drawer an article which Mr Meacher had just sent to him for possible inclusion in the *Observer*. Mr Howard could not get over it. Did we suppose Mr Meacher was quite right in the head? Had he temporarily taken leave of his senses? If he had not, what was he up to, what was he playing at, what was his game?

Mr Millinship and I could provide little enlightenment on Mr Meacher's motives or state of mind. The three of us, however, arrived at quick agreement under several heads. To begin with, the projected apology we consigned to the waste-paper basket. It was vague and simultaneously crawling. Above all, it was wrong about Mr Moonman. Mr Moonman had actually written, in *The Times*, that he had left the party on account of Mr Meacher's questionnaire. In the alternative, we were prepared to plead fair comment. I remember saying that whoever wrote the letter did not seem to know much about the law of fair comment. Over and above this, however, our inchoate view was that the Moonman allegations (though this is not what we called them at that stage) were non-justiciable.

The father allegations (as we came to call them) were, we recognised, somewhat different. Mr Millinship said I could well be right that the papers all reported in 1983 that Mr Meacher was a farm worker's son. That did not prove that Mr Meacher had said it. Of course he had said it, I replied; must have done, stands to reason, no other way it would have got into the papers. Mr Millinship remained properly sceptical: what would satisfy a journalist writing a column would not necessarily satisfy a court trying a libel action. We needed to see a direct claim by Mr Meacher: 'I am a farm worker's son … ' or 'speaking as the son of a farm worker … ' Even: 'Mr Meacher told me that, as the son of a farm worker, he … '

We agreed to divide the labour of checking. I would examine the files of *Tribune*, which had been active in propagating Mr Meacher's cause in 1983 and to which he had himself contributed a campaign column. At the same time Mr Millinship would ask the *Observer* library to search its own files for any claims to farm-working paternity by Mr Meacher. I duly went to the *Tribune* office in Gray's Inn Road, and came away slightly better informed about Mr Meacher's views on party accountability, but none the wiser about his father, a subject to which he did not advert. The *Observer* library reported to Mr Millinship: from what they could discover, Mr Meacher had made no such claims about his father. I do not blame the *Observer* library, for Mr Meacher had not indeed made any direct literal claim. But I do blame myself, for neglecting a second occasion for refreshing my memory of the flavour, the tone of the 1983 articles on Mr Meacher. The first occasion had been in November 1984; my omission had been less culpable then, for there was no idea at that stage that any legal trouble would ensue.

Mr Howard and Mr Millinship also agreed that Mr Howard would undertake negotiations with Mr Meacher on a personal, friendly basis. I said that, if I had made a mistake, I would willingly correct it. I added that if, despite our agreed views on the projected apology, the higher command at the *Observer* – Mr Trelford, or the managing director, or even 'Tiny' Rowland's representative, Terry Robinson – decided that it must be published, I would neither resign nor myself sue the *Observer*. I wished to have no part in it; that was all. We broke up amicably.

On 30 January 1985 I wrote a memorandum to Mr Millinship. Most of it I have already set down in these pages, at greater length. It ended:

> It might be a good idea to get a copy of Meacher's birth certificate. His *Who's Who* entry says his birth date was 4 November 1939 and he is son of George Herbert and Doris May Meacher. Tony [Howard] thinks that Seifert Sedley are trying it on and that Meacher's heart isn't in it.

The *Observer* had – still has – a system for getting hold of people's birth certificates. Perhaps 'system' is too grand a word: it is a matter merely of going through the correct procedures, which any citizen can do. Anyway Mr Meacher's birth certificate was produced within days. It showed that he had been born in the West Herts Hospital, Hemel Hempstead, on the date and to the parents named above. Under 'Rank or Profession of Father' was entered 'Farmer Retired' of 268 High Street, Berkhamsted. Mr Howard and I were chiefly interested in the rank or profession: at any rate Mr Meacher senior had never claimed to be a farm worker when he registered the birth of his son on 14 December 1939. We failed to spot the significance of the address in the High Street of Berkhamsted. For Mr Howard had assumed, following his lunch with Mr Meacher in September 1983, that he had been brought up on the family farm, living either in the farmhouse or, more likely – given the bathroom and lavatory arrangements adumbrated in the 1983 articles about Mr Meacher – in a farm worker's cottage tied to the farm. I assumed the same.

The second lunch

Mr Howard arranged to have a second lunch with Mr Meacher at the Gay Hussar on 7 February 1985. Though he is temperate in his habits, while Mr Meacher verges on the abstemious, this is really the tale of two lunches. Much of the misunderstanding of the way in which the case developed derived from a conflation of the two events. At the first one Mr Meacher told Mr Howard the story of his background, and Mr Howard repeated it accurately to Peter Hillmore and to me, Mr Hillmore using the information in October 1983, and I in November 1984. At the second one Mr Meacher spoke to Mr Howard in the following terms, which Mr

Howard related to me in the following fashion, almost immediately afterwards:

'I never said it, Tony.' This was a denial that he had ever claimed that his father was a farm or agricultural worker or labourer. Mr Howard, as he reported the conversation to me, replied: 'But it was in all the papers, Michael,' and went on to reproach him for not having corrected the error, as it was now accepted to be, at the time it was committed, in the late summer or early autumn of 1983. Mr Meacher admitted that he may have been dilatory or even negligent, but repeated that he had never made the claim. In that case, Mr Howard responded, an injustice had been done to him. It would be corrected as soon as possible; moreover, the *Observer* would pay his solicitors' costs to date. Mr Howard suggested to Mr Meacher that I should 'weave in' this correction: that is, incorporate it in the text of my next column, or one in the near future.

When Mr Howard reported this discourse to me, Mr Moonman played no part in it. As I have explained, Mr Millinship, Mr Howard and I were in accord that I could not possibly have committed any libel over Mr Moonman. Besides – a point that occurred to me subsequently – weaving Mr Moonman, Mr Meacher and their grievances into a column, in addition to Mr Meacher and his father's occupation, would present considerable technical difficulties. Mr Meacher and his father's occupation presented difficulties enough, as far as 'weaving in' was concerned.

I had and have no objections in principle to this practice. It involves inserting a sentence or sentences, often enclosed by brackets, into an article. It does not really involve much weaving. But the sentences of correction, parenthetical though they may be, must appear to arise naturally within the article. To begin with, the general subject must be appropriate: in Mr Meacher's case it would have to be some further thoughts of mine on the state of the Labour Party, or something of that nature. And, then, the words must be inserted at an appropriate place, often involving a playing with the words that precede and follow them. I explained this to Mr Howard, saying that my column, any column, had a pace and rhythm of its own. While I was perfectly willing to correct my mistake – that Mr Meacher had claimed to be the son of an agricultural labourer – I should greatly prefer to do so in a separate space at the end of my column. This would be technically easier and stylistically cleaner.

Mr Howard was not at all pleased at my attitude. He had, after all, persuaded Mr Meacher that 'weaving in' was the best course to take and had promised him that it would be followed. Furthermore, such a course would avert the indignity, as some newspaper executives see it, of inserting a formal, legal apology in the body of the paper. Indeed, my own suggestion of a personal correction at the bottom of the column came nearer to a formal apology than did 'weaving in'. I could see why Mr Howard was vexed with me (though we did not have a row). But I could not understand why Mr Meacher was so keen on 'weaving in'.

My apology or correction

Mr Howard agreed to follow the course I suggested. On 13 February he
wrote to Mr Meacher saying that, as I would be dealing with the Ponting
case this week, the incorporation of a correction would be difficult – as,
indeed, it would have been – but that I had agreed to insert the following
correction at the end of my column:

> In this column on 18 November last year I wrote that Mr Michael Meacher
> 'likes to claim that he is the son of an agricultural labourer, though I
> understand that his father was an accountant who retired to work on the
> family farm because the life suited him better'. Mr Meacher has asked me to
> make clear that his father was an articled clerk in an accountancy firm in
> the City who then worked at the family farm following an illness, and that
> he has never claimed he is the son of an agricultural labourer. I am happy to
> make this correction.

This expressed the truth as Mr Howard and I then understood it. I still
had a doubt at the back of my mind about whether Mr Meacher had made
the claim or not. But 16 months had now elapsed since the contest for the
deputy leadership and its accompanying articles. I was prepared to take
Mr Meacher's word or, at any rate, give him the benefit of that doubt
which I still retained. Friday 15 February 1985 – the last day on which he
could have expressed his views to Mr Howard on that Sunday's paper –
came and went, and there was still no communication from him. Mr
Howard did not hear from him for a whole week. In the afternoon of
Friday 22 February, bringing in my column to Mr Howard, I asked
whether the correction would be going in at last, and whether contact had
been established with Mr Meacher. Mr Howard raised his eyes to the
ceiling, as if to indicate the hopelessness of the task in hand, and
confessed to having difficulties.

I devoted my attention for the rest of that Friday to the week's column,
about Mrs Thatcher and related matters. On Saturdays I do not go into
the office. On Sunday 24 February I turned to my column to discover
whether the correction had been inserted at the end of it. A correction
there was. But it was not the one which Mr Howard and I had agreed and
which he had dispatched to Mr Meacher 11 days previously. It went:

> In my column on 18 November last I suggested that Mr Michael Meacher
> liked to claim that he was 'the son of an agricultural labourer'. I am now
> satisfied that Mr Meacher has never made any such claim – and I am happy
> to set the record straight.

It was now my turn to be vexed with Mr Howard. The dash and the
sentence that followed testified to his hand. 'Suggested' as opposed to
'wrote' or 'stated' betrayed a lawyer's hand: Mr Howard would have used
either of the more accurate words, as I should have done. My anger had,

however, abated by Tuesday. I confined myself to asking – rather crossly, it is true – what on earth had happened on the previous Friday. Mr Howard said he had had a dreadful time trying to make contact with Mr Meacher, who had wanted all references to his father's background deleted.

In fact Mr Howard had spoken to Mr Meacher twice, on one of the occasions with the latter in a call-box, about to catch a train from Euston Station. He had also spoken to Miss Burton. Mr Meacher certainly wanted the detailed references to his father removed. Even so, he remained dissatisfied. Miss Burton complained that the correction had not been incorporated in the text of the column and that Mr Moonman was unmentioned. Mr Howard said to Miss Burton that we did not accept that the Moonman allegations were defamatory and that, while he was personally sorry that the words did not satisfy Mr Meacher, they would appear that week.

The position could be summarised thus: Mr Meacher undoubtedly felt aggrieved – it was not put on – but did not at this stage want any money or indeed, to damage the *Observer* or Mr Howard in any way. His feelings towards me, whom he did not know, were less kindly. He was dissatisfied with the correction that had in fact appeared but neither he nor his solicitors proposed any alternative. While Mr Howard had made clear to him that the Moonman allegations were non-negotiable, he still felt that an injustice had been done to him – that, in a word which Miss Burton used to our then solicitors, Messrs Herbert Smith & Co., I had alleged that he had 'railroaded' Mr Moonman out of the Labour Party. I had written nothing of the kind. We did not see there was anything more that we could do.

On 4 April 1985 Miss Burton wrote to our solicitors formally 'commencing proceedings'. This was barely two months since we had first heard from her. In an accompanying letter she added that she was further instructed that, in an attempt to settle the matter before proceedings were served, her client was willing to accept £1,500 together with his costs to date, estimated at £500 plus VAT, 'in full and final settlement'. There was no mention of an apology, still less of any statement in open court. On 29 April the Writ was issued and duly served. On 11 June Seifert Sedley Williams served the Statement of Claim, drafted by the barrister Gordon Bishop. After quoting the words complained of (set out above in Chapter 4), it went on:

> The said words in their natural and ordinary meaning meant and were understood to mean (i) that the Plaintiff on numerous occasions had falsely claimed that his father was an agricultural labourer in order to ingratiate himself with his constituents and members of the Labour Party; (ii) that Mr Moonman had resigned from the Labour Party and from his chairmanship of the Islington Health Authority because of mean and despicable conduct on the part of the Plaintiff. By reason of the publication of the said words the Plaintiff has been seriously injured in his character, credit and reputation

and has been brought into public scandal, odium and contempt.

Mr Howard tries again

In July Mr Howard made another attempt to settle the case. He was presenting the BBC Radio 4 programme 'Talking Politics', which goes out when Parliament is in recess, replacing 'The Week in Westminster'. It usually takes the form of a personal (or more so than political) interview with a succession of politicians. Mr Meacher was one of these. The programme was broadcast on 10 August 1985. In his introductory remarks, Mr Howard said the Labour MP was:

> better known since he contested the deputy leadership of the Labour Party just two years ago. I discovered, though, another man, a man whose background was solidly Conservative, who enjoyed his time at an English public school and who very nearly became an Anglican priest.

Mr Meacher went on to say that he had met his first wife at a tennis school in Berkhamsted, after which there was the following interesting exchange:

> **Anthony Howard:** You were brought up in and around Berkhamsted, weren't you?
> **Michael Meacher:** Yes. I was born in Hemel Hempstead which is five miles away, and lived with … [dots in script.] I mean the family had always lived in Berkhamsted, and I lived there for 22 years.
> **Howard:** A lot of stuff saying that when you were young you had an outside lavatory and there was a bathroom in the kitchen and all that. Was it a fairly sort of severe and austere and, indeed, perhaps slightly humble background?
> **Meacher:** Well, that's perfectly true. The last thing I want to do is sort of flourish it and sort of display proletarian origins, which I suppose one's tempted to do in the Labour Party. That's not the case. I'm not working class. I wouldn't pretend to be, but my parents had pretty limited means. My mother was very ambitious, very thrifty, sort of full of the Protestant ethic, as I would now describe it, and, from fairly modest origins, sort of drove me forward. But it is true that we took in lodgers to eke out the money, so they took the only bathroom in the house, so we had a bath installed next to the kitchen sink. And there was this outside loo which one had to go down 15 steps to get to, and in the winter time, when there was snow on the ground, it was quite a dangerous and hazardous journey.[1]

Part of Mr Meacher's case at this stage was that he had never claimed to be the son of a farm worker. He made no such claim in this interview: quite the reverse. What rendered the interview more interesting still, however, was the light it shed on his early

---

[1] BBC Transcript.

circumstances. The bath in the kitchen and the outside lavatory – which, at the trial, were to assume almost the importance of the louse and the flea – were not, as we had supposed, the accompaniment of rural privation, with Mr Meacher senior, having failed to become an accountant, residing with his wife and son on the family farm. They were, rather, the consequence of taking in lodgers to supplement the family income. Mr Howard failed to spot the significance of the lodgers, for he was thinking of his next question; just as we had both allowed the address on Mr Meacher's birth certificate to pass us by.

It was an amicable occasion and a sunny day. Walking in the extensive garden of Mr Meacher's Highgate house, Mr Howard thought he had persuaded him to drop the action. The *Observer* would pay his costs and £500 to a charity of his choice and make an apology on terms to be agreed.

Almost immediately afterwards, on 26 July 1985, we served our Defence, drafted by the barrister Stephen Nathan. It denied that the words complained of bore the meanings attributed to them. It pleaded justification – truth – over the Moonman allegations and, alternatively, it pleaded 'fair comment upon a matter of public interest', namely the distribution of the questionnaire by Mr Meacher and the consequential controversy. Over the father allegations it pleaded 'accord and satisfaction' as embodied in my correction. It said that on 22 February, the Friday, neither Mr Meacher nor Miss Burton objected to the publication of the correction.

Over two months later, on 11 October 1985, our solicitors informed us that Miss Burton had telephoned them asking for £1,000 for Mr Meacher (rather than to charity), costs and an apology substantially on the lines of the one originally submitted to and rejected by us. On 15 October Mr Howard wrote to Mr Meacher complaining that his solicitors had not only varied but doubled the terms on which they had agreed to dispose of 'this wretched affair'. At this point Mr Meacher wanted to settle but was overruled by his legal advisers. Over a month later, on 19 November, in a letter drafted by those advisers, Mr Meacher replied, disputing Mr Howard's recollection. He had, he maintained, said that while 'financial recompense' was not his 'primary objective', a sum 'not exceeding £1,000 would be reasonable'. He repeated his 'main point that politicians simply cannot allow themselves to be treated like that'. He also wrote that he had 'never agreed that the libel regarding the Moonman episode did not merit an apology. On the contrary I have always said it did.'

Christmas 1985 came and went. On 10 January 1986 we paid £255 into court. Paying into court is, depending on the way you look at it, either a prudent insurance policy or a throw in that game of chance which is the law of libel. What it means is that, if the damages awarded (if any) are less than or the same as the payment, the plaintiff pays the costs incurred by the defendant after the date of the payment. The fact of the payment and its size are known to the plaintiff, but not to the judge or the jury. In this case Mr Meacher subsequently denied having been informed of the payment by his solicitors. We served our list of documents in February and Mr Meacher served his in April. In the same month the action was set down for trial. We were advised that it was likely to come on in the legal term beginning in October 1987.

Nothing very much happened in 1986. In 1988, immediately after the trial, friends and acquaintances would say: 'It must have been a terribly worrying three years for you.' In fact I gave Mr Meacher's action hardly a thought. The road to Court No. 14 was not nearly so pot-holed as this chapter suggests, owing partly to conflation, partly to retrospective knowledge. From time to time, every few months or so, I would address Mr Howard and Mr Millinship in jocular terms:

'How's Meacher this week, then?'

'Still going on, I'm afraid.'

An afternoon's research

In those days, Friday afternoons gave me a period of leisure. The column would have been written, typed, corrected, inspected by Mr Howard and sent down to the printers. After an hour-and-a-half or so it would come up in the form of a print-out (rather than a galley-proof, for we were then in the stage of intermediate technology). I would normally employ this time in what I called the administration of life, answering readers' letters, paying bills, writing postcards or doing my expenses, if I had not done them earlier in the week. Having finished these small tasks, I might read those weekly papers which I had not already looked at or, if it was a fine day, visit one of the neighbouring Wren churches, St Andrew-by-the-Wardrobe or, perhaps my favourite in the whole City, St Martin, Ludgate.

One Friday afternoon was wet. The administration of life had proved light. I decided to have a look at what had actually been written about Mr Meacher's background in 1983. I did so partly to satisfy my curiosity and to occupy a wet afternoon, but partly also to resolve the doubt that was still at the back of my mind. I had not looked at the press cuttings in November 1984, when I was writing the original column, but relied on my memory. I had not looked at them in February 1985, when Miss Burton's letter arrived, but relied on the *Observer* library's inspection. For the first time, I would inspect them systematically for myself. I did not reproach myself for my omission to do so in 1984 but in 1985. As I turned over the cuttings, which are summarised in Chapter 2, shame about my negligence was submerged under excitement about my discoveries.

In every single article, Mr Meacher was described as the son of a farm worker. Four of these articles were manifestly based on personal interviews with Mr Meacher by Lewis Chester, Mick Costello, John Knight and Robert Taylor (who, I erroneously assumed at that stage, had also written the *Observer* profile of Mr Meacher). Moreover, these were all experienced journalists, of high reputation, who would not have done what is known as a 'cuttings job'. They would not have gone to the library, copied down their predecessors' mis-statements, added a few of their own, and passed off the result as an interview or profile of their own composition. Mr Meacher must have told them himself that he was a farm worker's son: there was no other plausible explanation.

Though it was a Friday afternoon, and Mr Howard had other matters on his mind, I entered his room with unaccustomed briskness, told him what I had found out, and said that I was sick of all the lies. Mr Howard agreed that my short afternoon's work clearly put a different complexion on matters. Mr Millinship, whom I told next, remarked drily that it was a pity I had not chosen to undertake my researches in February 1985, when they would have made a difference. We had now apologised – admitted that Mr Meacher had never claimed to be the son of a farm worker. True, the apology was unsatisfactory to Mr Meacher, who was persisting in his action. Mr Millinship confessed he did not know enough about the law of libel to say whether we could now withdraw our apology or correction. Nor did I.

We plead justification

David O'Callaghan was more knowledgeable. In February 1987 the *Observer* changed its solicitors, for reasons unconnected wih the case. Mr O'Callaghan assumed responsibility for the Meacher action, which he examined with a fresh eye. He asked me why I had written that Mr Meacher liked to claim that he was the son of an agricultural labourer. In their correspondence his predecessor-solicitors had described this as 'an honest mistake' by me. How did it come about that I made such a mistake? I replied that I was now satisfied that there was no mistake at all and quoted the articles of 1983 by Mr Taylor and the others.

Mr O'Callaghan concluded that we could now plead justification for – in other words, the truth of – the father allegations. He suggested Richard Hartley, QC, as leading counsel, with Mr Nathan as his junior. It would be necessary also to take statements from the journalists who had interviewed and written about Mr Meacher in 1983 and to establish their willingness to give evidence on our behalf.

As we were becoming more confident, so Mr Meacher – or Miss Burton – was increasing his price. In Spring 1987 his solicitors re-stated their demand for £1,000 damages and costs but substituted a statement in open court for an apology in the newspaper. We were not having any of that – particularly as all four journalists confirmed in statements that Mr Meacher had indeed said that his father was a farm worker. Leave was given to amend our defence, which was served on 14 October 1987. The crucial addition was:

> The Plaintiff misinformed the said Howard. Unknown to the said Howard, the Plaintiff's said representation (that he had never claimed to be the son of a farm worker) was false and untrue. Particulars of the said falsity were set out ...

In December 1987 we made an offer to settle on the basis that Mr Meacher would pay a proportion of our costs. Larry Grant had by now assumed the supervision of Mr Meacher's case, but Miss Burton continued to act in tandem. On 5 January 1988 she wrote to Mr O'Callaghan saying she did not agree that the amended defence substantially altered Mr Meacher's case. What it would do, Miss Burton continued, would be to increase the costs of the action substantially. *'No doubt your clients are fully aware of recent trends in libel damages* [italics mine] since these negotiations broke down in May and that the level of damages discussed at that time (£1,000) was extremely reasonable.'

This was an attempt to frighten us with the record damages awarded in the case of Jeffrey Archer – and perhaps with other awards made against newspapers, whose unpopularity with libel juries was increasing perceptibly. But there was no reason for us to grant now what we had refused before.

Mr Meacher climbs down

Then a decidedly odd event occurred. All of a sudden Mr Meacher climbed down, or tried to. On 15 January 1988 Miss Burton wrote to Mr O'Callaghan saying that the problem – 'and I understand it', though 'and' may have been a mistyping of 'as' – was that we did not feel able to agree either to an apology in the paper or to a statement in open court. However, Mr Meacher, 'in the spirit of compromise', was 'willing to accept a letter of apology addressed to him, the wording of which can be agreed between us.'

It was not clear from this whether Mr Meacher had now relinquished also his demand for £1,000 and costs, or was merely modifying in a most curious way the form of apology which he was willing to accept. Nor was it clear from whom this letter of apology was to emanate, whether from me, Donald Trelford or the *Observer* as a body corporate. I informed Mr Millinship that, while I could not and would not choose to prevent anyone from writing to anyone else, I had no intention of sending a letter of apology to Mr Meacher. I had, I now considered, written nothing for which an apology was called. Mr Trelford took the same view about any letter signed by him. We repeated our suggestion that Mr Meacher should pay part of our costs and drop his action. He refused. The case was set down for hearing on 16 May. Twelve days before the trial was due to start I received a notice, signed by Mr Meacher's barrister (Gordon Bishop), that the plaintiff would be claiming I had been actuated by 'express malice'.

A plea of malice

'Malice' is a technical term whose meaning is not, however, vastly different from its ordinary meaning. A comment is malicious if the jury conclude that the writer did not honestly believe what he wrote. This can be so (though it is not always, in law, inevitable) if there is an *animus* on the part of the writer. Malice can also be implied if there is a history of attacks on the plaintiff either by the writer or by the newspaper. Nothing of the sort was involved here. I did not know – had not even met – Mr Meacher. He had, as he acknowledged, been always fairly, often favourably treated by the *Observer* over the years. In my own column he had made only the most infrequent and fleeting appearances. Nevertheless Mr Bishop, doing his best, had a go along these lines:

> The Plaintiff will rely upon the content and tone of the words complained of and in particular the inclusion therein of (a) the allegation that the Plaintiff had made false statements regarding his family background, (b) the suggestion that the Plaintiff should have been advised to jump into the Thames and (c) the comparison of the Plaintiff to a louse and/or flea. The Defendants wrote and/or published the said words and in particular the allegation that the Plaintiff had made false statements regarding his family background knowing them to be false and/or recklessly, indifferent to their truth or falsity and without any honest belief in their truth.

This missive occasioned much hilarity in the *Observer* office. But malice, if proved, is no laughing matter for the defendant. It destroys the defence of fair comment, which we were pleading to the Moonman allegations. The last-minute charge of malice could be regarded as a gamble worth taking – or, perhaps, as a gambler's somewhat desperate throw.

Mr Kinnock's affidavit

Mr O'Callaghan sprang a surprise of his own. He served a subpoena on the Leader of the Opposition – an action which would have perplexed Mr Justice Cocklecarrot as much as it would surely have delighted his creator. Unless Mr Kinnock had been prepared to disown Mr Meacher in court, which was unlikely, the summons served a tactical purpose only, that of showing that we were in earnest about defending ourselves. Mr Kinnock responded with an affidavit sworn under the auspices of Messrs Lewis Silkin.

His tone was injured, with some cause, I have to admit: 'I was not informed by the defendants of the matters regarding which my evidence was required, nor (as far as I am aware) was any approach made with a view to obtaining a statement from me.' He had 'no knowledge of any of the circumstances surrounding the issue of the questionnaire'. He 'would not have expected to be consulted about the decision to send out the questionnaire, nor was I, it being a departmental matter fully within the plaintiff's then areas of responsibility'. He did not recall being present at any meeting where the questionnaire had been raised. He would not have expected 'a matter of this nature' to come before the Shadow Cabinet, the National Executive or any other committee which he attended.

He possessed no relevant documents. 'If there were any in my office at the time, they would have been disposed of; as a matter of course, all documents no longer current are destroyed after 18 months have elapsed.' He had not himself received any complaints about the questionnaire, but he was informed by Patricia Hewitt (his press secretary in 1984) that Mr Moonman had spoken to her. He did not recall being told about this at the time. Had he been, he would have done nothing about it. He had been shown a copy (provided by our solicitors via his solicitors) of Ivor Walker's letter of 8 November 1984, but there was no record of it, of any reply to it or of any other correspondence, assuming there had been such correspondence, concerning the questionnaire.

Mr Kinnock's memory of the episode was, it appeared, a perfect and absolute blank. His reluctance to become involved in Mr Meacher's action may have been understandable, but the organisation of his office, as revealed in the affidavit, clearly left something to be desired.

Part Two

The Case for the Plaintiff

6

Mr Bishop's Opening Speech

Serjeant Buzfuz began by saying, that never, in the whole course of his professional experience – never, from the very first moment of his applying himself to the study and practice of the law – had he approached a case with feelings of such deep emotion, or with such a heavy sense of the responsibility imposed upon him – a responsibility, he would say, which he could never have supported, were he not buoyed up and sustained by a conviction so strong, that it amounted to positive certainty that the cause of truth and justice, or, in other words, the cause of his much-injured and most oppressed client, must prevail with the high-minded and intelligent dozen of men whom he now saw in that box before him.

Charles Dickens, *The Pickwick Papers*

Though I was not exactly looking forward to my appearance in the High Court, it was a bit like coming home. I had spent six years of my life in that part of London, at the *Sunday Express* and, before that, at the London School of Economics. My office at the school had been in a pre-1914 building, shining with linoleum, blazing with ancient gas fires, opposite St Clement Dane's Church. The offices accommodated also a Mr Peter Kroger, who proclaimed himself on his door as a dealer in rare and fine books. We LSE research assistants had a joke that from these dismal yet oddly romantic premises – recalling, if not Conan Doyle, then at any rate J.B. Priestley's *Angel Pavement* – Mr Kroger conducted a covert business in pornography. We did not imagine that he was a Russian spy, a member of the 'Portland spy ring'.

Some of the establishments I had continued to use: Louis Simmonds's excellent bookshop, and El Vino's, opposite the junction of Fleet Street with Fetter Lane ('El Vino's public house', as Lord Beaverbrook used to call it dismissively). Other places I had grown out of the habit of using, such as the Wig and Pen Club opposite the Law Courts, where neither wigs nor pens were greatly in evidence, rather, large men in public relations and red braces with trains from Waterloo to miss, and where, in the early days when I was not a member, I would sign myself in as 'Alastair Hetherington'. Other establishments had gone out of business or been pulled down, such as the Red Lion in Poppins Court by the *Express* building, known as Poppins and victim of the vandalism and greed of the new Express Newspapers. Also no more was a pleasant luncheon club, the Temple Bar Club, consisting of a high-ceilinged bar with early-nineteenth-century mouldings and a similar dining room, above a coffee shop, whose respectability was attested by the patronage of John Beavan (later Lord Ardwick) and Samuel Brittan.

The Law Courts were still where they used to be. They will still be where they are in the next century, as will Lincoln's Inn, Gray's Inn and the Temple. So will Harley Street, and Broadcasting House too. Doctors, lawyers, even broadcasters are treated – or treat themselves – with a measure of respect. It is only writing journalists who allow themselves to be pushed into inhospitable and often uninhabited regions of London by insensitive and grasping owners and managers. I had grown out of the habit of visiting the courts, even though I had, unlike Mr Howard, continued to be an amateur of legal matters, scanning the law reports in the papers, exchanging gossip with the criminal barristers who attended El Vino's of an evening and, from time to time, writing a column on grave constitutional matters. 'A Buzfuz piece this week, I'm afraid,' I would say apologetically to Mr Howard, who did not greatly care for this kind of thing, preferring me to keep to the broad highway of Westminster politics.

The judge and the jury

I first heard the name of the judge who would be trying the case on the Friday immediately before it started. Mr Justice Hazan, I was told, was 'very sensible'. As John Hazan he had been a well-known criminal barrister, chiefly a prosecutor, and subsequently an Old Bailey judge. In January 1988 he had, at the comparatively late age of 61, been promoted to the Queen's Bench Division. The Law Officers are keen to encourage such moves and to make the High Court Bench more open. Among my barrister friends he had the reputation of being scrupulously fair but a tough sentencer. 'He gave me 12 years for rape at the Bailey a few weeks ago,' one of them confided. 'Mind you,' he continued, 'it was a particularly nasty rape, and I deserved every bit of it.' His great love was opera.

In court he looked like a small, furry denizen of hedgerow or woodland, his features close together. There seemed to me to be an age-gap of more than six years between him and myself. He turned to the jury, on his left, and told them, in conversational but respectful tones, that they would no doubt be reading about the case in their newspapers. There was nothing wrong in their doing this, but they would be guided in their verdict only by what they saw and heard in the court. They would sit from 10.30 to 1.00, and from 2.00 to 4.15. They might think that these were easy hours, but when they came to listen to the case they would find it was hard work. (In fact Mr Justice Hazan sat from 10.30 to 12.45, and from 2.05 to 3.50. Two half-days and one whole day were also lost, in my opinion unnecessarily, the latter to facilitate Mr Meacher's marriage on the Whitsun bank holiday weekend. No doubt the trial was hard work for the judge as well as for the jury.) As he concluded his observations, Mr Millinship turned to me and said: 'He's trying to charm the jury.'

So were we all. Mr Howard, who was sitting in front of Mr Hartley and next to Mr O'Callaghan, was particularly assiduous in smiling and in opening and waving through doors. I thought it was probably all right for me to say 'Good morning' when one or two of them passed in the corridor or at the back of the court. On our side, we reposed particular faith in the two women: quite why I do not know, because they might equally well have been impressed by Mr Meacher's case. One of them – a tall woman with strong features – took notes later on, which we considered an encouraging sign. She sat next to a large, jolly-looking man with red hair. 'Time for a pint,' he said one day as they were leaving just before the lunch interval. In front of them the other woman sat, grey-haired, on the best of terms with the elderly man next to her, with whom she exchanged sweets and jokes.

In one of the middle seats of the front row was a juryman whom we designated 'the chap with the long hair'. For most of the time he looked bored; when he was paying attention he looked sceptical. He was about 25, I suppose. We regarded him as a wild card: someone who would support Mr Meacher either because he was sympathetic to the extreme Left or out of sheer perversity. Our prejudice was founded also on his refusal to wear a tie or to improve his dress in any other way. For the rest of the jurors smartened up as the trial progressed. On this first day they had been hauled in from the pool at the Central Criminal Court, looking dishevelled and disgruntled. Ties, suits, dresses, coats-and-skirts started to appear in greater profusion with every day that passed. Our friend with the long hair stuck to his tee-shirt and jeans. He was clearly unreliable.

Mr Bishop begins

No one on our side knew who Gordon Bishop was, apart from his being Mr Meacher's counsel. I looked him up in the Law List, to find that he was a BA from Cambridge, had been called to the bar by the Middle Temple in 1968 and occupied chambers at 10 South Square, Gray's Inn. (One of the changes which have occurred in the last decade or so is that barristers' chambers have been established, or re-established, in Gray's Inn.) These chambers, I also discovered, were headed by Andrew Bateson, followed by Charles Gray and Patrick Milmo, all leading QCs who did a good deal of libel work. Mr Bishop was the senior non-QC in a set of chambers housing 14 barristers altogether. It was accordingly reasonable to assume that he was a specialist in libel work. He had a pale pink complexion, curly red hair showing beneath the back of his wig, a large nose and even larger spectacles, transparent-rimmed, which seemed to fill up half his face. He had ginger hair on his hands and wrists. These were much on display, for he was a great shuffler of papers, snapper of files and tapper of pens, particularly at moments of strain or annoyance.

Mr Meacher, he told the jury, was 'no doubt well known to you'. The article of which the plaintiff complained made 'a number of general allegations' about the Labour Party. It also made 'two specific allegations' against him personally.

The first was that it accused him of 'mean and despicable behaviour' towards another member of the party, 'a Mr Moonman', who was chairman of the Islington District Health Authority, by sending him, together with others, a questionnaire asking him to report on the political views of other members of that health authority. My column asserted, according to Mr Bishop, that Mr Moonman resigned from the party because of Mr Meacher's 'shabby behaviour'. The second allegation was that Mr Meacher deliberately misled people by 'falsely claiming' that he was the son of an agricultural worker when his father was an accountant who had retired to work on the family farm because the life suited him better. 'Just to add insult to injury, the article also compared the plaintiff to a louse in respect of that behaviour.'

These allegations, Mr Bishop continued, were 'quite untrue'. The attack made on Mr Meacher was 'quite unwarranted'. However, apart from the 'half-hearted apology' which was published shortly after the original article and which now appeared to have been withdrawn, the *Observer* not only refused to apologise to the plaintiff for what they had said but persisted in claiming that the allegations were true.

Legally, this was complicated. We began by pleading 'accord and satisfaction' over the apology or correction: that is, Mr Meacher had accepted it in full and final settlement. We continued to plead this but added justification – truth – as an alternative plea. So we had not withdrawn the apology *in toto*. Mr Bishop did not make this wholly clear, but the jury were already looking bemused, as well they might.

Mr Bishop went on: Mr Meacher therefore came to the court to 'clear his name' of these 'unfounded allegations'. Mr Bishop would 'in due course' be asking the jury to find in Mr Meacher's favour and to make 'an appropriate award' of damages. He then read the whole column from start to finish, and afterwards took the sentence about being the son of an agricultural labourer. Mr Bishop proceeded to give us a fine piece of barristers' baroque, which might have ornamented a more spacious age at the bar:

Members of the jury, just look at that sentence for a moment. What does that mean, and why is it there? What relevance has it to the rest of the points made in this particular article? The answer of course follows in the next sentence: 'But this by the way. It matters not, as the barristers say.' Well, I am not sure that barristers do now say: 'It matters not.' Members of the jury, certainly it is by the way, is it not? It has got absolutely nothing to do with the article in question and it is put in there just as a nasty, unpleasant attack on Mr Meacher. And the attack consists of this: it suggests that Mr Meacher deliberately lied about his background, says he is the son of an agricultural labourer when his father was in fact an accountant, and obviously what is meant by that is that he is trying to gain support he would not otherwise be entitled to by making these false statements that his father was an agricultural labourer when in fact he was an accountant. A nasty, vicious attack on Mr Meacher.

Rounding off this splendid passage in appropriate style, Mr Bishop quoted the bit about jumping off the Terrace and said: 'That is the terrace of the Houses of Parliament, as I understand it.'

He turned to the Moonman allegations, the 'admittedly shabby episode'. What was being said by me here, according to learned counsel, was that Mr Meacher's asking Mr Moonman to report to him on the political predilections of his colleagues was 'a shabby act' by Mr Meacher, and that it was admittedly so. Admitted by whom? It was not entirely clear. It certainly had never been admitted by Mr Meacher. 'It may be that Mr Watkins was simply using the word "admittedly" there.' Perhaps the court would learn about that in due course. Learned counsel was suggesting here that I was using 'admittedly' as a makeweight word-phrase, familiar to most journalists, such as 'naturally', 'of course', 'perhaps', 'no doubt' or 'meanwhile'. But, perhaps inevitably, he did not make his meaning wholly clear.

As for the louse and the flea:

We can see who is referred to as the louse and who the flea by following the order of their mention earlier in that sentence. Mr Meacher is the louse and Mr Moonman is the flea. That again is another nasty attack upon Mr Meacher.

What was being said was that this was 'a shabby – that is, a mean, unpleasant, despicable – act on the part of Mr Meacher.' These synonyms, Mr Bishop did not tell us, were derived selectively from the *Oxford English Dictionary*.

The small house at Berkhamsted

Learned counsel then told the court something about Mr Meacher's background. It was the most interesting part of his opening speech, because it made public that which had previously been unknown, and which had become known to me only slowly. When Mr Meacher was born his father was 56. He had married Mr Meacher's mother, who was 20 years younger, in 1933. Mr Meacher was an only child. His paternal grandfather was the tenant of a farm just outside Berkhamsted. His father was the second of four children. In 1901, when he was 18, his father went to London as an articled clerk to a firm of accountants. They could have been solicitors but Mr Meacher thought they were probably accountants. After a short period – months or even weeks – his father suffered a 'nervous or neurotic breakdown' from which he continued to suffer for the rest of his life. As a result of that he returned to the farm of which his father was a tenant and worked there till his father, Mr Meacher's paternal grandfather, retired and gave up the farm shortly before his death in 1928.

On his retirement from the farm, Mr Meacher's grandfather acquired the lease of a house in Berkhamsted and lived there with his son and daughter, Mr Meacher's father and aunt. Mr Meacher's father continued to live there after the death of the grandfather. Mr Meacher's father did not work at all after the grandfather had given up the farm. On Mr Meacher's birth certificate, his father described himself as a farmer. Since, however, he never ran a farm but only worked on it, and never had any interest in it, 'it was not a strictly accurate description'.

Accordingly, my statement that Mr Meacher's father was an accountant who retired to work on the family farm because the life suited him better was 'simply not true'. He was never an accountant. Nor, Mr Bishop proceeded, did he retire because the life suited him better. 'He had to work on the farm because, as a result of his very unfortunate illness, he was not fit to do anything else.'

The charge of malice

Mr Bishop said that what I had written about Mr Moonman was fact rather than comment. In cross-examination later on I agreed with him about this. From the defendants' point of view, there was a good deal to be said for urging that the Moonman allegations were fact. We could and did plead justification of them as well as of the father allegations. We were also pleading fair comment about them, as we were not about the father allegations. It is only the defence of fair comment which is destroyed by a successful charge of malice. It was to this that counsel now turned.

> Malice in this respect has a different meaning in law from what it means in normal conversation. Normally, if we say someone is malicious we mean that he is spiteful or holds ill-will towards somebody. At law the word has a slightly wider meaning than that. What essentially it means is using the rights everyone has to comment for some improper purpose, i.e. to injure the plaintiff rather than simply using the right to comment. If it is shown – and it is for the plaintiff to show – that the predominant motive of the

person publishing the libel was to injure the plaintiff, then the defendant is held to be malicious and fair comment is no avail.

One way for a plaintiff to prove a defendant was malicious would be to show that the defendant knew that what he was saying was untrue or that he was 'reckless as to whether it was true or false'. In such cases, malice would be presumed, because it must be 'very rare', unless there was some other explanation, for someone to publish something which he knew to be untrue, or about the truth of which he was reckless, unless he intended simply to injure somebody.

Thus lawyers talk, and thus do they reason. It is mostly great nonsense. Most mistakes, in journalism as in life, come about through misunderstanding, through indolence or (what often amounts to the same vice) through the repetition of what someone else has said or written. Mr Bishop proceeded to say that, first, I knew that what I was saying about Mr Meacher was untrue or I was reckless as to whether it was true or false. Second, 'you can tell from the tone of the article itself that this was a malicious, nasty article aimed at injuring Mr Meacher'. Mr Bishop then pointed again to the (as he was trying to demonstrate) gratuitous nature of the reference to Mr Meacher's father.

In addition, you will see that Mr Watkins adds, in the next paragraph, that Mr Moonman would have protested more effectively if he had advised Mr Meacher to jump off the terrace and drown himself.

Mr Bishop quoted the bit about the louse and the flea again. He concluded this section of his address by saying that 'those allegations in there, those insults' showed that I was indeed malicious.

Well, members of the jury, you might well come to the conclusion at the end of the day that you agree with Mr Moonman on that point, that clearly was a very malicious and nasty article, where the facts were clearly got very much wrong, not only just in relation to Mr Meacher but it appears, according to Mr Moonman, in relation to him as well. Members of the jury, I have set out the main relevant facts in this case. I have done so fairly briefly, but I have taken up a fair amount of your time already, and the court's time, and no doubt what you would be interested to get on with is the evidence itself, and to hear from the participants in this trial, and, firstly, that will be Mr Meacher. So I will end my opening observations to you there and I will now call Mr Meacher to give evidence to you.

7

Mr Meacher's Evidence

We must stand on our heads, as men of intellect should.

R. Austen Freeman, *The Red Thumb Mark*

Numerous rival attractions presented themselves at the Law Courts while our case was beginning. Anne Diamond was in dispute with her former agent, Peter O'Toole with his former wife and Sam McCluskie with the present government. All these public figures were photographed daily, at one minute entering the courts, at another emerging from them, in various states of anger, resignation or relief. Mr Meacher could not hope to compete with these personages: but he was by no means neglected. I exchanged gossip before the days' proceedings began with old acquaintances of the camera from *Express* days. In this respect, again, it was quite like old times. I came to favour the back entrance in Carey Street, opposite the Seven Stars public house (which I had used during my LSE days, 30 years before). This entrance had the advantages of no baggage check – instead, a courteous wave through – and of being on the same first-floor level as Court No. 14.

Mr Meacher was wearing a blue-grey suit and a restrained tie. He had the voice of the home counties, which one hears over the public address system not only at Lord's cricket ground when Middlesex are playing but also at Highbury Stadium when Arsenal have a match. It is the voice of a whole group of South Eastern folk who exercise instructional or disciplinary functions in society, ranging from senior police officers to schoolmasters and Nonconformist ministers. It is often described as a 'classless' voice, but it is nothing of the kind. The accent is certainly regional, related to that of London itself.

Mr Bishop began by establishing or re-establishing Mr Meacher's identity to general satisfaction: for, as Lord Devlin has pointed out, under the English judicial system everything of any significance is said at least three times over.[1] Then followed an exchange of which J.B. Morton ('Beachcomber') would have been proud:

[1] Patrick Devlin, *Easing the Passing* (1985), 1.

76

Gordon Bishop: Can I ask you about your marital status at the moment?

Michael Meacher, MP: I am divorced.

Bishop: Are you about to remarry?

Meacher: I certainly hope so, in the next fortnight.

Bishop: My Lord, I raise this because there has been some publicity in the papers recently about Mr Meacher's forthcoming remarriage and some mis-statements about it, and I just wanted to clarify that at this stage.

Richard Hartley, QC: My Lord, I hope it is being made plain that it is not suggested that the *Observer* has been any part of this.

Mr Justice Hazan: It does not seem to me to have anything to do with the issues which the jury have got to try.

Bishop: My Lord, no, it will not have anything to do with those issues at all, but it has been put in the papers and I would just like to get it straight at this stage. Members of the jury, this has got nothing to do with the *Observer* at all, but you may have read matters about Mr Meacher in the paper recently; indeed, in the *Evening Standard* on Friday there was something published about this trial. So may I just ask you to say: you are about to remarry: is that right?

Meacher: Yes.

Bishop: I think it has been said in the newspapers that it is a South African lady who runs a private health clinic?

Meacher: All of those allegations are totally untrue.

Bishop: Is she South African?

Meacher: No.

Bishop: And does she run a private health clinic?

Meacher: No.

Hartley: If my learned friend is fighting another libel action, my Lord, it is quite improper for it to be done here, which might have some effect on the jury.

Judge: Members of the jury, you are not concerned, of course, with anything the *Evening Standard* or any other paper may have said. I think we had better pass from this and put it out of our minds altogether.

Bishop: I wanted to mention simply so that we could put it out of our minds.

Judge: Well, you have done so, yes.

The second Mrs Meacher, as she was soon to become, was much discussed before and during the trial. She was written about in the newspapers and talked about in Westminster and the clubs, for this was a case which really was talked about in Westminster and the clubs, even though not as avidly as was *Neil* v *Worsthorne* in 1990. This was another of its traditional English features. Indeed, it seemed to me, as a participant, that people could speak of little else. Though it was agreeable, to begin with, to become momentarily the centre of attention when I went down to the House of Commons in the late afternoon, the tasks of repetition and explanation soon became oppressive. Acquaintances were, however, chiefly interested in short answers to three questions: who is going to win, why is Meacher doing it and (a related question) who is paying for Meacher? It was generally assumed, erroneously, that the second Mrs Meacher was paying.

Mr Bishop took Mr Meacher through his academic and political career, and asked whether he knew anything about his father and his family.

> **Meacher**: Almost nothing, though I might say that the evidence that has been produced for this trial has certainly told me a few things that I didn't know before. My father, when I was nine, he was of retirement age, 65, and he talked extremely little. I never ever heard him talk about his mother, and indeed I didn't actually know her name until the last few days. But he talked a bit about his father, and I knew very well that his father was a tenant farmer at St Margaret's Farm.
>
> **Bishop**: A tenant farmer at St Margaret's Farm; where is that?
>
> **Meacher**: It is a little hamlet a few miles away from Nettledon, which again is a village a few miles away from Berkhamsted. I would think it is – I have never been there, I might say – I would think it is five, six, seven, eight miles away.

The revelation that Mr Meacher not only had been brought up away from the famous farm (which I realised fully only just before the trial) but also had never set eyes on the place: this entirely passed me by, I am afraid, while he was giving evidence. Mr Meacher then told Mr Bishop that his father had been educated at Berkhamsted too. This again I had learnt shortly before the trial: but it was the first time this information had become public. It went unreported in the newspapers. Mr Meacher added – what I did not know – that his father was very frightened of the then headmaster and sustained a nasty accident with a mangle, causing him to lose half a finger, which 'had some profound effect on his life'.

> **Bishop**: What about when he left school? Do you know what occurred then?
>
> **Meacher**: When he left school, to the best of my knowledge – and I have to say this is dependent on what my mother told me in a conversation which must now be about 30 years ago, and as far as I know that is the only source of information available – what I recollect she told me was that he went up to train to become, I think, an accountant, but I am not certain about that. He went up to

London; but that after a very short period of time, which I certainly understood to be a matter of weeks rather than months which you mentioned earlier, he had a severe mental or neurotic breakdown. I say neurotic rather than psychotic breakdown. He certainly wasn't a schizophrenic or like that at all, but he had a breakdown which actually crippled him for the rest of his life.

The court adjourned for lunch. Shortly after two o'clock, Mr Bishop began by asking Mr Meacher about the distinction between 'psychotic' and 'neurotic'.

Meacher: Well, I find both of those difficult. I am not a psychiatrist, first of all. By psychotic I understand, I suppose, typically schizophrenic illness, and it certainly was nothing of that kind. The second I find very difficult to answer because this happened around 1900, 1901, which is now 88 years ago. I was not even told about it until, I suppose, I was about 15, which would have been in the mid-1950s, which was 55, even 60 years afterwards. Therefore the exact nature of it I do not know. And nor indeed did my father ever once in his life talk about it. Nor indeed, I think, did my mother fully understand. But it manifested itself in his extreme nervousness, and he was very highly strung, and I have to say – which is perhaps rather difficult and rather painful – he was probably rather an inadequate man. For example, when he returned to St Margaret's Farm he was – when he went for a walk he would only be willing to walk in a circle round St Margaret's Farm so that he never lost sight of the farmstead buildings. He was also, which I do remember, on a number of occasions absolutely terrified of thunder. And whenever a storm blew up and it looked as though it would thunder, he would insist on my mother or me being present with him and holding his hand. But I suppose the most obvious manifestation of the condition was the fact that, until he was round about 45 to 50, he stayed with his parents and did not secure his economic independence. And I would have said the overwhelming characteristic of my father was that he was an excessively dependent man, first of all on his parents and then on his wife.

This was a terrible, sad story. Its happening so long ago only added to its pathos and power. If Berkhamsted had been in France, it could have been written by Balzac. Some of it I was aware of, from Mr Howard. I knew about the fear of thunderstorms, but I did not know that Mr Meacher senior would want his hand to be held by his wife or son. Nor did I know about his walking in a circle round the farm. I felt sorry for Michael Meacher: both for the sadnesses of his early life and for his having chosen to bring them out now, in 1988, in Court No. 14 of the

Royal Courts of Justice, before Mr Justice Hazan and a jury, together with numerous members of the public and representatives of the press. But I felt no guilt; nor do I feel any today. Mr Meacher, I was clear – am today equally clear – had chosen to take this course, even if encouraged by imprudent legal advice. But he was curiously unemotional about it all. He might have been talking (as he was indeed shortly to do) about the dreaded district health authorities. I am certain I should not have described my own father as 'inadequate', even if he had been, which he was not.

Mr Meacher added some more information. His grandfather left the farm in 1926, when he was 88. It was then being run by his father's brother, who had effectively run it for the previous 20 years or so. The tenancy was sold, and the new tenant farmer purchased the freehold. Accordingly the farm had been out of the Meacher family's hands for 12 years before Michael's birth. From this earlier date Michael's father had done no work of any kind but had resided, first with his own father and then with his wife, at the new home at 268 (renumbered 320) High Street, Berkhamsted. His father, however, enjoyed a long life, dying in 1969, as did his mother. Mr Bishop came to the crux of the father allegations.

> **Bishop**: So far as public statements about your background are concerned, have you been asked on occasions what your family background was and what your father did?
>
> **Meacher**: It is a subject that has come up exceedingly rarely. The only occasions that I can specifically remember being asked about my background was simply an opening shot in interviews when I was standing for the deputy leadership. I think it is possible that I may, for example, with people in my constituency, have talked briefly. But, as far as I can recall, they never specifically questioned me about it. And I must say I have always taken the view that who my father was was not a matter of material significance. It is what I am and what I do and what I say that matters politically.
>
> **Bishop**: When you have been asked about it, what have you said on the subject?
>
> **Meacher**: I have always, always said that my father, after he left school, went up to London in order to train, I thought, to be an accountant; that after a few weeks he had a severe breakdown which actually ruined his life; and he was therefore forced back to his father's farm, where he then worked helping his father on the farm for the next 25 to 30 years. That is always what I have said in answer to that question when it has, rather rarely, been asked.
>
> **Bishop**: Have you ever described your father as an agricultural labourer?
>
> **Meacher**: I am well aware that 'agricultural labourer' has associations, at least in my mind and probably in other people's minds, which certainly mean that it is not, in my view, an

appropriate description of my father. I have never said it.

Mr Meacher then dilated on regional and district health authorities. Tim Walker, who was covering the trial for the *Observer* – as a sketch-writer rather than a reporter – whispered to me: 'Our friend in the front pew with the long hair is completely zonked.'

As the trial progressed, it became evident that the judge possessed strong views about the political morality of the questionnaire, and that those views were not sympathetic to Mr Meacher. Indeed, they were more antipathetic to him than were mine – or Mr Howard's. Mr Howard thought that Mr Meacher had made a political mistake, a blunder. I thought so too but, additionally, that what he had done was wrong, however worthy his motives may have been. 'Shabby episode' expressed my opinion exactly.

Mr Bishop asked Mr Meacher whether he had framed the questionnaire himself. Mr Meacher replied that the work had been discussed by him with his front bench team, but that the work had actually been performed by his then researcher, Barbara Shepherd.

> **Judge**: Could you just tell me this as a matter of interest: if one of your supporters asked one of his colleagues on the health authority what his politics were and that lady or gentleman happened to reply: 'Mind your own business. It has got nothing whatever to do with the job that we are doing.' How would that have been? What happens? How is that recorded? Would you have counted that automatically as an opponent of yours, or what?
>
> **Meacher**: No, no, what happened, my Lord: We had 150 replies. One person objected.
>
> **Judge**: Only one?
>
> **Meacher**: Yes, only one. I never saw the letter, but I saw Barbara Shepherd's write-up of it. What she did, quite correctly, when she wrote up the survey was, she noted this fact and made public that there was one objection ... I have to say, in all honesty, that the columns 'sex', 'age' and 'voting habits': well, I don't know about the latter, but certainly the others were[2] added by Barbara Shepherd, I think in an excess of zeal. And it did actually reveal some interesting material about the maldistribution in terms of age and sex of the health authorities. But it wasn't actually asked for by me.

Mr Meacher told the court that he did not know Mr Moonman, had hardly met him. This was undoubtedly true, but it was even odder than

---

[2] The transcript says 'other was', but clearly Mr Meacher was referring to two columns headed 'sex' and 'age'.

my not knowing Mr Meacher. He proceeded to give his reasons for bringing the action. His counsel asked him when he first saw my column.

Meacher: I didn't see it actually on the Sunday, the day it was printed. I have to admit, which is a little embarrassing, that I am often rather behind in my reading of newspapers and, such is my anxiety not to miss things, that I will read newspapers several days later, not for the news but often for the articles or other material. I therefore read it, I think, some few days later.

Bishop: Could you look at it? ... What effect did it have upon you?

Meacher: Well, I was stunned, to be perfectly honest. I was casting my eye briefly over the article and suddenly saw reference to my name, read it, and was absolutely stunned. I read it again. I was angry. I felt that it was disgraceful that allegations like this, which were totally untrue, were clearly thrown into an article which is nothing really to do with me simply in order to do damage to me.

Bishop: Could you tell us which particular allegations it was in that article that ...?

Meacher: Well, first of all, clearly, as I have already made perfectly clear, my father of course was not an accountant, but the clear implication is that I was talking down my social origins in order to ingratiate myself with the Labour Party or with my constituency, a thing I have absolutely never done and never would, and have no reason to do so. It was then suggested that Mr Moonman – as I said, I have had no contact with him – but suddenly it is suggested that I have hounded him out of the party ...

That word 'hounded' again. Was Mr Meacher interpreting my column in this way because he thought he was thereby more likely to win his action? I do not think so. He had got an idea into his head and he refused to re-examine it. He is certainly not a natural actor; and what follows was delivered with genuine conviction, and a passion which was to be exceeded only once, during his recall.[3]

Meacher: ... because I sent him a questionnaire. I mean, it is just such a fantastic and absurd claim. I suppose my initial reaction might have been that the absurdity is something I could brush off as almost being comic, but the fact is it was put, when I re-read it several times, as a serious allegation and it is clearly extremely damaging. I am not the sort of person who has ever participated in chasing anyone out of the party, right or left, with whose views I might happen to disagree. I have always been someone who supported tolerance in politics. That has always been my style, and it certainly still is.

[3] See below, p. 189.

Already, on the first day of the trial, I was learning things I would not otherwise have known. Mr Meacher was exercised by my writing not only that he liked to claim he was the son of an agricultural labourer but also that his father was an accountant. Indeed, the latter allegation seemed to cause him the greater distress. He was equally exercised by his idea that I had written – even though I had not in fact written – that he had driven or hounded Mr Moonman out of the Labour Party. I was also learning about the past, at St Margaret's Farm, Herts, and at 268 High Street, Berkhamsted, where young Michael had spent the whole of his childhood and adolescence. I did not realise that Mr Meacher senior had been quite so odd; had been, in his son's own words – which, I confess, shocked me – so dependent and so inadequate. Nor did I fully appreciate the punitive, disciplinarian, prefectorial side to Mr Meacher, which emerged in part of his account of his second lunch with Mr Howard.

> **Meacher**: We then turned, or I think Mr Howard then turned, at the end of the meal, to the question of money, and I said immediately that, yes, I did want an apology on both counts and I did want reasonable and modest damages – I think that was my phrase as far as I can recall. He then said, and I remember this very distinctly: 'Are you gold-digging?' I had never heard the phrase ...

At this point the plump, jolly, ginger-haired juror looked amused and incredulous, and entered into a conversation with the woman juror on his left in the back row. I thought he was on our side. I thought she was too, because she had started to take notes.

> **Meacher**: ... and I turned to him and said: 'What do you mean?' He said words to the effect: 'Are you using this case in order to extract as much money as you can?' I said: 'No, absolutely not. I have made perfectly clear that is not my aim. I am not going for the *Observer* in a big way. I simply want redress which is sufficient to ensure that neither the *Observer* nor any other newspaper believes that they can make a scurrilous attack on me like this, simply print a few sentences some weeks or months later and then just walk away with impunity. I am absolutely clear that some modest damages must be paid to ensure that they respect that they cannot get away with it scot-free.'

A legal colleague who was sitting next to me, and who had been a contemporary of Mr Bishop at Cambridge, said that he tried to be aggressive but was not really so and was accordingly unsuited to the libel bar. Michael O'Flaherty of the *Daily Express*, who was one of the most assiduous observers of the case – and was certainly the most prolific writer about it – arrived at the same conclusion.[4]

Mr Hartley was a different matter. He was a leader of the libel bar. He was more colloquial in his expression and more easy in his manner than Mr Bishop. Off-duty – out of court but in his chambers – he would wear his Garrick Club tie. He loved making bets: 'Bet you £5 the next man who comes into the dining-room has a bald head.' His own head was small, snub, neat, white and curly – that was when he was not wearing a wig. With one on, he assumed an if anything even jollier, more Pickwickian aspect.

He could, however, arouse fear in opponents. He could also inspire hatred. He had been the successful counsel for a Mrs Marcie-Riviere in an action against the *Spectator* and its columnist 'Taki'; and the latter confessed to hating Mr Hartley as a consequence of cross-examination by him. However, this response was not universal among parties or witnesses who had confronted him. Christopher Silvester of *Private Eye* had been roughly treated by him during Robert Maxwell's successful action against that paper. Mr Silvester bore Mr Hartley no ill-will.

As these cases indicate, Mr Hartley was a plaintiff's man, as highly successful libel barristers tend to be. Similarly, successful barristers from outside the libel field who enter the area for special occasions tend to appear for the plaintiff. Mr Hartley was now appearing for the defendants. He began by taking Mr Meacher through all the articles (as, by this stage, we were all calling columns, features, leaders and stories) concerning Mr Moonman's resignation from the Labour Party.[5] Mr Hartley was trying to demonstrate that these articles had used such words or phrases as 'spying' and 'Stalinist tactics' but that I had confined myself to the neutral word 'report' and to the phrase 'admittedly shabby episode'. The following exchange gives the flavour:

> **Hartley:** The Labour members are spying on the other members to this extent: that the other members did not know that their details were going to be given by the Labour members of the authorities to you?
> **Meacher:** But, I mean –
> **Hartley:** Well, just answer me. Did they, would they know that?
> **Meacher:** Probably not.
> **Judge:** Have you ever heard of the expression 'Big Brother is watching you'?

A legal colleague turned to me and whispered: 'I think we've won.' I was not so sure. But I was cheered that the judge had said it, though I did not – still do not – think he should have done.

---

[4] *Daily Express*, 11 June 1988.
[5] See above, Chapter 3.

Meacher: I have indeed, my Lord

Judge: Did it ever occur to you that anyone might think, rightly or wrongly – I am not asking for your view on the matter: it might be right, it might be wrong – that anyone might think that that was the attitude of someone trying to do this to them?

Meacher: I would be extremely surprised, inasmuch as political balance is something that government takes very careful account of, for example, in appointments to the magistrates' bench. We know that for a fact. The Government also made clear, Mr Kenneth Clarke made clear, that they take account of political background in their appointments. Well, the Government has the capability of undertaking researches which is not given to under-provided-for members of the Opposition. The only way in which we can get that information, because we can't take soundings all over the country, is by sending out a questionnaire. I don't think what we were doing is any different at all from what the Government does.

On the next day, Tuesday 17 May 1988, Mr Hartley tried to clarify again the nature of the objection which Mr Meacher took to my references to him and Mr Moonman. Mr Hartley referred to Mr Moonman's article in *The Times* about Mr Meacher's being the last straw.

Hartley: I do not want to waste time. It has been read more than once. But would you agree with me that Mr Moonman in that article is making it plain that it was your conduct which was the last straw and made him decide to leave the Labour Party?

Meacher: That is what he is saying, yes. I strongly contest –

Judge: Yes, you are not being asked to agree with it. But that was his point?

Meacher: Yes.

Mr Hartley took Mr Meacher through my column. A substantial part of English legal procedure consists of reading aloud from documents which judge, jury, parties and solicitors for the parties already have before them. That the document in question has already been read aloud once, twice or even three times is no impediment. On the contrary, barristers seem to proceed on the principle that the old tunes are the best tunes. Used, re-used, picked at, pulled this way and that by the gentlemen in the wigs, my column was, I thought, holding together quite well.

Hartley: (*Quoting*) 'I represented the Hurlingham Ward, at the posher end of the borough, having been elected, I remain convinced, because my Conservative opponent was called Watson.' He is making a joke on his name being Alan Watkins.

Meacher: Even I picked that up.

Judge: Oh come, Mr Meacher, do not be so bashful. No one could accuse you of not having a sense of humour, if I may say so.

As Tim Walker wrote later in the *Observer*,[6] Mr Justice Hazan could be devilishly polite. Meanwhile Mr Meacher persisted in his view that he wanted – had always wanted – some monetary compensation.

Hartley: You wanted to punish the *Observer* and other newspapers?
Meacher: Well, you can put it like that, yes. I don't think that should have been written.
Hartley: That is what you are wanting. The money was to punish the *Observer*?
Meacher: A modest punishment, yes. That is right. Because unless people are punished they will do it again. That is one of the bases of psychology.

This occurred towards the end of the second day's hearing. Mr Meacher had already been in the witness box for well over a day. The next day's cross-examination produced three crucial pieces of evidence: on young Michael's scholarship to Berkhamsted (which was crucial because of what Mr Bishop later made of it); on his family circumstances, about which we came to know more; and on what he thought he had told Mr Howard at which lunch. It became clear to me that Mr Meacher had forgotten that, during the 1983 lunch, he had told Mr Howard the full story of his family background. He had also forgotten 'the Pendennis article' which had derived from that lunch. Though Mr Howard and I had forgotten it as well, we both remembered clearly that my reference to Mr Meacher's father in 1984 had derived from a conversation between Mr Howard and me in 1983, which had itself followed immediately on his lunch with Mr Meacher. Gordon Bishop never fully adjusted to this changed perspective.

Throughout the trial both Mr Meacher and his counsel had no success in persuading the judge that my article of 1984 was defamatory or maliciously libellous, whereas the 'Pendennis' article was neither. The other crucial piece of evidence emerged when Mr Hartley was asking Mr Meacher about Robert Taylor's interview with him. It concerned the scholarship to Berkhamsted. The point which Mr Hartley was trying to make was that, owing to family money in the background, the Meachers could have afforded to send Michael to the school, irrespective of whether he had won the scholarship or not, though doubtless it would have proved useful. Besides, Michael was already at the junior school – rather than at a State or preparatory school – while his father was himself an old boy of the senior school.

[6] 22 May 1988.

Alan Watkins

Donald Trelford

Stephen Nathan

Richard Hartley, QC

The Hon. Sir John Hazan

Paul Fox

David O'Callaghan

John Knight

Robert Taylor

Lewis Chester

Anthony Howard

William Millinship

St. Margaret's Farm, near Berkhamsted, Herts

The Rev. Canon Wilfred Badger Wilkinson

The Meacher house in High Street,
Berkhamsted

Eric Moonman   The Rt. Hon. Kenneth Clarke, QC, MP

Michael Meacher, MP, being consoled by Mrs Renée Short on 3 October 1988 when he lost his seat on the National Executive Committee of the Labour Party

Michael Meacher and Lucianne Sawyer on their wedding day, 27 May 1988

Michael Meacher surrounded by journalists on 10 June 1988

Hartley: If Mr Taylor gave evidence and said that he had got the clear impression that, but for your getting the scholarship, you would not, your parents would not, have been able to afford the fees, are you saying that that could not have been an impression that he got from your conversation?

Meacher: No, that is actually, I think that is probably correct. But I am saying to you that I would be very surprised. I don't actually remember this conversation. But I would be very surprised if the matter were raised. But, if it was, it is correct.

Hartley: That is your case: but for that scholarship, you could not have gone to that school?

Meacher: I think that is probably right.

Mr Hartley returned to this subject on the Wednesday afternoon, in the course of further question-and-answer on Mr Meacher senior's means. It was now clear that Mr Hartley had earlier misunderstood Mr Meacher. Mr Meacher had said merely that he would have been unlikely to discuss his removal from school with Mr Taylor.

Hartley: I think that this is important, Mr Meacher. Are you saying – and I did not think that you were – that you would have been taken away from public school if you had failed to get that scholarship?

Meacher: Yes, I did say that and I remember, I think – I am sure that I remember – my mother saying that to me and I perfectly well understand why.

Hartley: That is the first time – unless my recollection is going very badly wrong – that you have ever said that.

Meacher: Well, it may be.

It had been a hard afternoon, which had produced even more detail about the early circumstances of Mr Meacher. The significance of the lodgers was explained in relation to the bath in the kitchen and the outside lavatory.

Hartley: It was quite a substantial house, was it not?

Meacher: It was quite a large house, but half of it, of course, had been let off.

Hartley: But you did have a bathroom in the house and this was something that you say that the lodgers used?

Meacher: Yes, and it was theirs and it was not touchable by us.

Hartley: So the bath in the kitchen – so that we can get the whole picture – was not the only bath in the house but it was the bath that the family used. Is that right?

Meacher: Yes, the bath that was on the first storey was the one that was built for the house and the bath that was built in the kitchen was absolutely minuscule and clearly not intended to go there, but there was no other place to put it.

Both Mr Howard and I felt somewhat uneasy about the disclosure of the precise nature of the Meachers' domestic arrangements. But it was Mr Meacher who had brought the disclosure about, by telling the journalists in 1983 of the bath in the kitchen and the outside lavatory (leaving them with the clear impression that he had lived in a cottage or small farmhouse). He had brought it about also by bringing the action. Mr Howard became even more concerned about the effect on the jury which our production of the details of wills and inheritances could produce. They might, he thought, conclude that these were private matters which we were unjustified in pressing. But we had no choice if our case was to be fully and properly presented.

> Hartley: So 13 years before you were born, 1939, he lived in Berkhamsted?
> Meacher: That is right.
> Hartley: What did your father do in those days; do you know?
> Meacher: Frankly, I don't know. I think he lived on the income which he had inherited.

In 1912 the principal inhabitants of St Margaret's, Hertfordshire, were one Charles Lee, boot-maker and sexton, and George Meacher, farmer; by 1926 only Meacher and his family remained. On his marriage certificate of 20 November 1933 George Hubert Meacher, Mr Meacher's father, was described as 'gentleman' and his father, Mr Meacher's grandfather, as 'farmer'. Mr Meacher's grandmother, who died in 1926, left estate to the gross value of £6,308, net £6,192 – the equivalent, Mr Hartley pointed out, of £135,000 in 1988. In 1969 G.H. Meacher died leaving his wife £26,000 or £25,000 net. She died three months later and left Michael £19,000 net – the equivalent, so Mr Hartley claimed, though Mr Meacher disputed it, of £150,000 in 1988. (In total, Mr Meacher was left £40,000 in 1969.)

> Hartley: What I am really putting to you – and this is the purpose of those documents – Mr Meacher, is that it would be a quite wrong impression for anybody to have now that you were in any way the son of – that your father was an agricultural worker on hard times or anything like that?
> Meacher: First of all, I never say to people that I am the son of an agricultural worker. I never said, either, that he was a farm worker, as I have repeatedly said. As I have repeatedly said, I appreciate, for all the reasons that you have brought out, that my father's

background is complicated. First of all, he did seek to train as an accountant, for a very short period of time. He then went back to his father's farm after a serious breakdown and he worked there for 25 to 30 years, on a farm which he did not own and did not run. And, after his parents died, he inherited money on which he then lived, although he was extremely dependent, and that is the really most important factor, on, first of all, his parents – that is why he never broke away for 45 years – and, then, on his wife. His wife went out to work part-time (as a receptionist in a doctor's surgery) and he let off half his house to eke out his income. Those are the facts.

Hartley: What do you mean by 'eke'?

Meacher: Well, he lived on the income which he got from his investments. You have mentioned £26,000 in 1969, that is at the end of a fairly steady rise in the Stock Exchange throughout the 1950s and 1960s. I don't know what it was in, say, the early 1950s, but substantially less than that. He lived on it. I readily accept that. Now, how you describe a man with such a varied background in a single phrase, I simply do not know. I have always tried to be as fair and straight as I could by telling the truth. That is all I can say.

Mr Hartley asked about the school and the scholarship. Mr Meacher repeated that he would have been removed if he had not won the scholarship.

Hartley: ... I am suggesting that you have not disclosed – and deliberately not disclosed – the fact that your father was considerably better off than the press thought was the case.

Meacher: I have never been asked the relevant question. I have never had cause to give an answer ...

Mr Meacher was still in the box on Thursday 19 May. After some discussion of whether or not I had displayed malice, Mr Hartley summarised his case, as far as the father allegations were concerned, as follows:

Hartley: Mr Meacher, may I put it this way: if someone were asked: 'Do you own a motor car?' and the person answered: 'Yes, I have a battered old Ford Capri,' that answer, although literally correct, would give a completely false impression if the person also owned a Rolls-Royce, would it not?

Meacher: Yes.

Hartley: I suggest that that is what we have really got here whenever you are asked about your background.

Meacher: I disagree ... I don't think that I have ever said, in answer to the question: 'What was your father?' 'He was a farm worker.' I don't think that I have ever said that. I have given the fuller explanation that I have given now. ... I think it is wrong that politicians should be exposed to this sort of thing and, if you don't have damages, all that a newspaper has to do is a few weeks later put a couple of paragraphs saying 'We were sorry' and that allows them to get away scot free. I mean, that is a wonderful invitation to say absolutely anything you like about someone in public life and you just get away with it scot free. You don't have to pay for it. I think that people should be required to pay something in order to deter them from doing it again. That is what I am implying ... No one could say that I was claiming punitive damages. It was, if you like, a slap across the wrists ...

8

Mr Bishop's Mistake

Mr Tinklebury Snapdriver: I apply for a writ of *tu quoque*.
Mr Bastin Hermitage: And I for a writ of *sine mensis*
Mr Justice Cocklecarrot: Ah, that's better. That's more like the Law. I well remember in the case of the Pentagon Chemical Foodstuffs and Miss Widgeon *versus* Packbury's Weather Prophecies Ltd, Captain Goodspeed intervening, a colleague of mine laid down that – however, let us to the matter in hand.

J.B. Morton, *The Case of the Twelve Red-Bearded Dwarfs*

It was noticeable that Mr Hartley, as a 'silk' and a leader of the libel bar, was treated with more deference than Mr Bishop by the judge, who, though he was invariably polite to the witnesses, and consistently solicitous of the jury's comfort and well-being, could exhibit a certain tetchiness with Mr Meacher's counsel. When Mr Jusice Hazan's patience was being provoked, and he had decided not to say anything, he would purse his lips and blow air into his cheeks. With this expression, he looked like a baby about to throw a tantrum.

The purpose of re-examination by the witness's own counsel is to swing the case back in his favour – to undo any damage that may have been done in cross-examination and, incidentally, to clear up ambiguities or doubts. Mr Bishop asked Mr Meacher whether Estate Duty had been paid on the £26,000 which his father left: it had. He asked whether the house at Berkhamsted was included in this sum: it was. He asked how much Mr Meacher had paid for his house in Highgate: it was £20,000. He confirmed that Mr Meacher's father had not received any pension (apart, presumably, from an old age pension) but had lived on the interest from his investments.

He established that, in his *Observer* story of 1983, Robert Taylor had made a mistake in writing that Mr Meacher had spent a year in Italy working for the Danilo Dolci Trust: he had indeed spent that time working for the trust, but for 11 months in Britain, and for only one in Italy. He had Mr Meacher repeat what he had previously said, that his conversation with John Knight of the *Sunday Mirror* had not been a 'serious political interview' and had lasted 'under an hour'.

And then Mr Bishop committed his fatal error. For once the phrase, made famous 30 or 40 years before by Edgar Lustgarten in his short films on the exploits of Scotland Yard, was justified.

The fatal error

The fatal error came about in this fashion:

> **Gordon Bishop**: Could I here ask you a question about the scholarship you got? It was suggested in relation to the article by Robert Taylor that you left him with the impression that you would not have got to public school without this scholarship and then, yesterday afternoon, when cross-examined by my learned friend, you gave evidence that you remembered your mother saying that if you had not won the scholarship, they could not have afforded to –
>
> **Michael Meacher, MP**: I am sure that I do remember her once saying that, yes.
>
> **Bishop**: It was suggested to you by my learned friend that you had made that up at that moment.
>
> **Meacher**: Well –
>
> **Bishop**: It was the first time that you had mentioned it to anyone.
>
> **Meacher**: I certainly have not made it up. There is absolutely no question about that. One –
>
> **Bishop**: Well, can I just deal with it in this way. Do you recall, in fact, giving a statement to your solicitors – and I can prove it if necessary – but perhaps I can just read out one sentence from it: 'I do recall my mother saying that if I had not won a scholarship, they could not have afforded ...'?

I was sitting immediately behind Stephen Nathan, our junior, while Mr Nathan was sitting behind Mr Hartley. Mr Nathan turned round to me and whispered: 'He's put the whole statement in.' I did not immediately grasp what he meant, except that Mr Meacher's case had been done grievous legal harm. Mr Nathan then had a whispered consultation with Mr Hartley, in front of him, over the course of the next few questions and answers, during those intervals when Mr Hartley was not himself asking questions.

> **Richard Hartley, QC**: The usual way, if you are going to read from a statement, is to show me and I would, of course, accept if –
>
> **Mr Justice Hazan**: It is certainly permissible re-examination. If there is a suggestion that the least invention is made, you re-examine to show that that has been dealt with before.
>
> **Bishop**: If my learned friend thinks that I should have shown it to him previously then I apologise for not doing so.
>
> **Hartley**: My Lord agrees with me –

Meacher: I am sorry. I had not realised that we were talking about what I told you [presumably his solicitors]. I thought we were talking about whether I had mentioned it to other people [presumably the journalists who had interviewed him] in the course of the years before. But of course I have said – Yes.

Hartley: My Lord, as my learned junior points out, who is much more alert than I am on these things, in fact what my learned friend has now done is to put the whole of that statement in.

Judge: That is the danger.

Hartley: Well, he has done it.

Judge: If you adopt that course, yes.

Hartley: Well, I would like to see the statement.

Bishop: My Lord, I would ask, perhaps we can argue about that at a later stage.

Hartley: My Lord, I hope it is not being unfair, but my learned friend was making a point that I had accused Mr Meacher of lying. It is now being put forward to say that that is, in effect, something that I should not have done; had no justification for doing. He is now quoting from a statement and I do, therefore, ask to see the whole statement.

Judge: That is right. He is entitled to it.

Bishop: Well, my Lord, I will see if we can find a statement with no notes on it. It is really the statement which was originally given by Mr Meacher and that is what one is looking for, but we will try and provide one. My Lord, may I continue the re-examination for the moment? But I just wanted to be sure that what was being put was that Mr Meacher had in fact made it up [i.e. his being removed from Berkhamsted if he had not won the scholarship] on the spur of the moment. It appears that that was the case.

Judge: You mean you are putting in re-examination merely from your recollection of having seen some statement somewhere and you cannot lay your hands on it now. Is that it?

Bishop: My Lord, no, I am not. I read a passage from the statement that I have got.

Judge: Then why are you so vague about it? You have said that you will provide one in due course. Mr Hartley is asking for it. He is entitled to it.

Bishop: Well, my Lord, the copy that I have at the moment has my notes on it.

Judge: I see. You want a virgin –

Bishop: I want a virgin copy found.

Judge: Well, perhaps that can be arranged quickly, if it can be run off.

Bishop: My Lord, we are trying to find one.

Judge: Very well.

Throughout this crucial exchange my sympathies were with Mr Meacher. If anyone was blameless, it was he. The re-examination proceeded. It was comparatively brief, as these things go. William Keegan of the *Observer*, perhaps the most assiduous attender at the trial from among my friends, once departed for a cup of coffee with another friend and returned after three-quarters of an hour or so to find that learned counsel was asking the witness about the same point: he had missed nothing by his absence. At the end of the re-examination Mr Justice Hazan intervened to ask Mr Meacher whether he agreed that the questionnaire was bound to give rise to political controversy and possibly strong comment. Mr Meacher said he did agree. I thought this intervention was a good sign from our point of view, at any rate as far as the Moonman allegations were concerned.

Monday 22 May was set aside for legal argument, chiefly on the admissibility of Mr Meacher's statement to his solicitors or his proof of evidence. His evidence was followed by that of Sarah Burton, Ann Rouse and Canon Wilfred Wilkinson on his behalf. Late on the Friday morning I went into the box and remained there for the whole of Friday afternoon. My evidence was interrupted by the week-end, by legal argument and by the evidence of the Minister, Kenneth Clarke. All these witnesses will be dealt with in subsequent chapters. Here it is convenient to breach strict chronology and pursue the controversy over Mr Meacher's proof of evidence.

The legal argument

The court sat at ten on the Monday, half-an-hour before the usual time. Mr Bishop said the statement ranged over a number of matters and should not go before the jury. There were two questions: adoption and severability. Had Mr Meacher 'adopted' the statement – that is, waived its status as a privileged document? If he had not done so, the statement could not go in. If he had, the question of severability arose – that is, only those parts of the statement which were relevant to that particular line of questioning were admissible. Mr Bishop submitted that Mr Meacher had not adopted the statement: Mr Hartley had interrupted before he was in a position to do any adopting. The judge said, looking at the transcript, that he, as judge, had interrupted as well. The crucial answer was:

I am sorry. I had not realised that we were talking about what I told you. I thought we were talking about whether I had mentioned it to other people in the course of the years before. But of course I have said – Yes.

Mr Bishop said he did not know whom the 'Yes' related to: the judge said he did not know whom the 'you' related to. Did it mean his solicitors?

the judge asked (and I have suggested above). Mr Bishop said it might mean himself. Things were getting into a muddle.

Mr Bishop said Mr Meacher had not been given time to adopt the statement. The judge then asked whether he could see it. Mr Bishop was (in my opinion, foolishly) reluctant to allow him to have a look. The judge replied, reasonably enough, that he could not rule on severability – on whether the statement should be split up and, if so, in what way – unless he had read it first. Mr Bishop asked the judge to take his word about the contents. He said that if the statement was to be split, only that section which was concerned with, in his word, Mr Meacher's 'schooling' was admissible. If pressed, however, he was prepared to accept the wider field of 'upbringing', but nothing broader than that.

Mr Hartley said that this was not an area where discretion could be exercised. Mr Bishop could not now turn round and say that he had not meant to do what he did. The judge agreed: the question was whether he had done it. Mr Hartley summarised the circumstances: Mr Bishop was seeking to make the point that Mr Hartley had suggested that Mr Meacher was lying. He went on to say that he could prove that he was not. He then read the sentence from Mr Meacher's proof of evidence. It was 'absolutely in because otherwise my learned friend gets the best of both worlds'. As to whether it contained parts that were severable, only his Lordship, Mr Hartley went on, could decide when he had seen it.

His Lordship replied that all kinds of damaging material and hearsay evidence might be contained in the document. Suppose Mr Meacher's colleagues in the Labour Party had suggested that he was wasting his time and should not pursue the action, and that this was in the statement. Should it 'go in', that is, become part of the furniture of the case? If so, it would be to 'open the gates very far'.

The judge ruled: The plaintiff was cross-examined by counsel for the defence on the basis that an interview with 'a certain journalist' (Robert Taylor) had left the impression that he could not have – this was the phrase used by judge and counsel throughout the exchanges – 'gone to public school' unless he had won the scholarship. The relevance was that it went to the allegation of whether the plaintiff was 'falsely bolstering his humble origins in order to curry favour with members of his own party or the electorate'. The question was whether, in re-examination, privilege was waived. Counsel for the plaintiff said that the witness (Mr Meacher) did not adopt: so the question did not arise. However, it seemed clear to the judge that Mr Meacher had adopted 'by implication if not expressly'. ('If not' is one of the most ambiguous of phrases. In this example, it could mean either: 'Certainly by implication, though not expressly' or: 'Certainly by implication, and possibly expressly as well.') It was clear to the judge from the witness's answer that he was indeed saying that he had discussed the matter of the scholarship 'with people before'.

Mr Justice Hazan was a noted criminal lawyer and considered by his colleagues to be a master of the law of evidence. Nevertheless, it seemed to me – as it does still – that Mr Meacher had been given a raw deal. There was no reason for Mr Hartley or the judge to be charitable towards Mr Bishop. As they said, if he had done it, he had done it. But it was not at all clear that Mr Meacher was prepared to live with the consequences of his counsel's catastrophic legal error. Suppose an 'officious bystander' (that favourite fictitious character in the law of contract) had said to him: 'You do realise what this means, don't you? Unless you refuse to answer Bishop and tell him to shut up, your statement to your solicitors, or part of it, will become public property, and you will have to go into the box again to be examined on it by Hartley.' Mr Meacher, in those hypothetical circumstances, would surely have said to learned counsel: 'Stop this tomfoolery at once, you great booby, because you are getting me into serious trouble.'

He went like a lamb. Why should he do anything else? He was not a lawyer. Despite this understandable ignorance, however, Mr Meacher, throughout the trial, seemed surprisingly uninformed about other aspects of the law which, I should have thought, would be part of the ordinary mental equipment of any intelligent public figure.

Having ruled on the admissibility of the statement, the judge adjourned the proceedings so that he and Mr Hartley could read it. Mr Bishop argued that his question had concerned, in his own word, 'schooling' and that disclosure should be confined to that topic. Mr Hartley argued that the true subject-matter was broader, 'upbringing'. He did not want Mr Meacher's observations to his solicitors on the subject of Mr Moonman to come out. That was a separate topic. Mr Justice Hazan agreed. Everyone was relieved. The Moonman allegations had already proved to be one of the more intractable parts of the case. No one could understand them, except those who were directly involved or possessed an unnatural interest in district health authorities.

The judge ruled: It had been suggested by counsel that the document (Mr Meacher's proof of evidence) contained distinct subject matters. If that was the situation, the document was severable. He had come to the conclusion, 'having regard to the pleaded meanings of the matters complained of' – that is, what Mr Meacher said I said about him – that the whole of his proof concerning his family background was admissible, and the sentence about his mother and the scholarship could not be isolated from the rest. At some time Mr Meacher would have to be recalled, and copies of his statement found for the jury.

New matters disclosed

Mr Meacher's statement disclosed several matters which had not emerged during his evidence.

> My grandfather must have had some private income. I believe this side of my family had connections with breweries in Hertfordshire and my

grandfather must have had some inherited money. I do not know the year he retired. When he did retire, he purchased the house at 320 High Street, Berkhamsted, where I was brought up. My understanding is that he retired there with my father, my father's sister and a maid.

This was the first anyone had heard of breweries in Hertfordshire or of a maid – incandescent word to the English! The statement continued, after some details about family moves and removals:

My father died in 1969. He left an estate worth around £40,000 which passed to my mother. My mother died three months later and that money then passed to me. My understanding is that whatever money my father inherited he put into War Loan stock and we lived off the income from that stock. (Mr Meacher added to the typewritten statement, which he had dictated, the following in his own hand: The interest from the stock was part of the income on which our family lived. Further income was derived from renting part of the family house, which I shall refer to later. I have always assumed that the income was important to my parents as there was no other reason for the letting [of the] first floor.)

The £40,000 was significantly higher than the £26,000 which had emerged during Mr Meacher's evidence. Nevertheless, whatever capital and income his father may have enjoyed, the family had led a frugal life:

In the 20 years in which I had lived in the house, I can never remember my parents entertaining any persons outside the family, with the exception of a couple who lived five doors away with whom they regularly played bridge on one evening a week.

In his evidence, certainly, Mr Meacher had never claimed that his father was a farm worker in any real sense at all. What he had claimed, with increasing indignation as the trial went on, was that he was not – could never have been – an accountant. All snobbery apart, one is more likely to come across a bridge-playing accountant than a bridge-playing farm worker. One reason why Mr Meacher insisted that his father could never have followed the profession of accountancy was that he was, in Mr Meacher's words, nervous, dependent and inadequate. But playing bridge regularly required a degree of mental agility and application which, from Mr Meacher's oral evidence, was lacking in him. After some account of the setting and arrangements of the Berkhamsted residence, there was the sentence which Mr Meacher's counsel had quoted so fatally:

I do recall my mother saying that if I had not won the scholarship they could not have afforded to send me to the school.

The family never had holidays, Mr Meacher said, except at his mother's brother's house in Kent, which he would visit about twice a year. There were, however, two exceptions:

I remember that the last two summers which I spent at home included going with my parents for a tour in Wales by car and then on another occasion by car to Scotland. These are the only holidays we had away from home. They had a Ford Prefect which even my mother called a 'bone breaker'. I remember at some point that was exchanged for a Volkswagen Beetle.

In the 1940s and early 1950s, however, the ownership of motor-cars was largely confined to the middle classes. Not all schoolteachers had cars. My own father did not have one, though more out of a combination of parsimony and conservatism than out of poverty. The proof of evidence continued:

> Whenever I have been asked, I have always said that my father worked on a farm. I have always described him as a farm worker. I have always spontaneously supplied the further information that he worked on a farm which was owned by my grandfather.

This differed markedly from what Mr Meacher had told Mr Hartley in cross-examination on Thursday 19 May:

> I don't think that I have ever said, in answer to the question: 'What was your father?' 'He was a farm worker.' I don't think that I have ever said that. I have always given the fuller explanation that I have given now.

All the evidence in our possession showed that Mr Meacher had given a full explanation only to Mr Howard, at the first lunch in 1983, at the second lunch in 1985 and during the radio interview (when the action was well under way) later in 1985. He had given a partial but by no means full explanation to Lewis Chester in 1983. To both Robert Taylor and John Knight he had said: 'He was a farm worker', 'He worked on a farm' or 'Let's say he worked on a farm'. Mr Meacher evidently thought the last two formulations better expressed the truth; as, indeed, they did. The evidence of those three experienced journalists will be considered in subsequent chapters. The proof of evidence, or the part which the judge had allowed, concluded:

> I am prepared to accept that I have not stated in interviews that my father inherited money and part of the family income was investment income. This does not alter the basic fact that he worked on a farm. If I had been interviewed in depth by any person on this point (which I have not), I clearly would have volunteered the information.

In cross-examination on 19 May he had said:

> It is certainly known that I had inherited wealth. There has been reference to this in the press and, with regard to my father, I was never asked. I would

never have concealed it, but the real fact about my father is not that he was a great monied man who lived in grand style. As I said, the truth is the opposite I'm afraid. He was a sadly inadequate man [this was the second time Mr Meacher had used the word 'inadequate'], who was exceedingly lucky and privileged to inherit money on which he could then live. What he would have done if he had not I do not know.

It was not generally known in the lobby of the House of Commons – at any rate among lobby journalists – that Mr Meacher had inherited money. I certainly did not know it. Neither did Mr Howard, a former political correspondent, who knew Mr Meacher much better than I did and had friendly relationships with other members of the Labour front bench. What we both knew was that Mr Meacher senior had not been a farm worker in any meaningful sense. When the case was proceeding, and I was going about my tasks in the House, Joan Lestor[1] told me that Mr Meacher, 'Michael' as she called him, had been embarrassed both by the size of the inheritance and by the ethically questionable investments in which it had come to him. He had, she said, juggled his portfolio to satisfy his conscience (my words, not Miss Lestor's).

To summarise: From Mr Meacher's proof we, the defendants, had caught a glimpse of: the breweries in Hertfordshire; the car; the maid; the weekly bridge evenings; the size of the inheritance; and the discrepancy in Mr Meacher's description of his father's occupation. We had not got hold of it by a trick but by the ineptitude of Mr Meacher's counsel and the harshness of the law. I felt that he did not deserve to be in this position. The luckless Mr Meacher would have to be recalled to the witness-box at some stage: so much was clear. In the meantime we had to hear the rest of his case and the whole of ours. His first witness was, in yet another odd feature of the trial, his solicitor, Sarah Burton.

[1] Labour MP for Slough, 1966-83; Eccles, 1987-. Under-Secretary, Education, 1969-70, 1975-6; Foreign Affairs, 1974-5.

9

Miss Burton's Evidence

A Protestant, if he wants aid or advice on any matter, can only go to his solicitor.

Benjamin Disraeli, *Lothair*

Miss Burton had been Mr Meacher's channel of legal communication with the *Observer* in 1984-5, in the crucial period between the appearance of the column and the printing of the apology, or whatever one chooses to call it. She it was who had dealt with Mr Howard in these months. Indeed, as the case progressed, it sometimes seemed that it should be entitled not *Meacher* v *Trelford and Others* but *Burton* v *Howard and Others*.

Miss Burton was small, very dark, in her late thirties, with a prominent and masterful nose and a discernible though not pronounced New York accent. She looked Middle Eastern. However, everything about her proclaimed the American 'civil rights' lawyer of the 1970s. She went into the box on Thursday 19 May and chose to affirm rather than to swear. This is a courageous action to take even in these times – and even though there is a firm biblical injunction against the taking of oaths: Matthew 5:34-7.

The affirmation apart, her first, oddly skittish words were: 'Looks quite different from up here,' a reference to the prospect of the court from the witness-box as distinct from the solicitors' bench which she would customarily occupy in the normal course of business. The observation, which could have been caused by nervousness, certainly did nothing to commend her to Mr Justice Hazan. He turned his head towards her, to his right, and adopted an expression at once stern and pained, as if preparatory to warning her not to trifle with the court. In the event he said nothing.

Mr Howard and the usher

The other person on whom Miss Burton made an unfavourable impression was the court usher. She too was a small, dark, intense woman. She, in common with Miss Burton, smoked cigarettes, and was not averse to disappearing for a few minutes for a quick drag. Her London accent was stronger than Miss Burton's New York accent. And, it soon became evident, her political views were the opposite of Miss Burton's. I know this because Mr Howard, with his keen eye for the location of power, early cultivated her. She, after all, had charge of the jury; she was their shepherdess. She told us that she had been compelled to reprimand Miss Burton for talking too loudly and moving about too noisily. She also confided that there was one member of the jury who was 'very left-wing' and might accordingly give trouble to our cause. I suspected the youth with the long hair in the front row, though the man with the ear-ring in the back row was also a possibility.

Miss Burton told Mr Bishop that she had qualified in 1980, having been with Seifert Sedley Williams for the previous two or three years. This was an error, as she subsequently admitted: she had qualified in 1982. She had first been consulted professionally by Mr Meacher in that year. In this case she had heard first from his political adviser, Alan Meale. She then received a letter from Mr Meacher dated 11 December 1984. She first met him to discuss the case on 4 January 1985.

Mr Bishop asked her about her method of making notes of telephone conversations – a topic which was to occupy a disproportionate amount of the court's time. Miss Burton replied that when she was talking she would have a pen in her hand and a pad in front of her. The resultant note would either go straight on to the file or be transcribed to go on to it. Which course was adopted would depend on 'a number of factors'. She proceeded to amplify her first note.

Miss Burton's view of Mr Howard

She had telephoned Mr Meacher to check whether he would be willing to meet Mr Howard. Mr Meacher had already spoken to Mr Howard on the telephone. He told her that he had known Mr Howard for a long time and that Mr Howard was trying to help him to get an article into the *Observer*. Mr Howard had asked him what it was all about and he had replied, as he reported it to Miss Burton: 'I told him that I wanted redress for the libel.' Miss Burton was emphatic that it was Mr Meacher who had used the word 'redress', for it was not a word she herself employed. Mr Meacher told her that he had arranged a lunch with Mr Howard for the following day, 7 February 1985. Miss Burton was not at all pleased with this arrangement:

I advised – I mean it is here, so I suppose I will have to say this – Michael basically that I wasn't happy in any way for him to have this lunch with Tony Howard, really for the reasons that we have now discovered: that these discussions, client to client, so often lead to misunderstandings and confusion. It is not very often in my experience that it happens. But, when it does, I have never known a time when it has not led to misunderstanding and confusion. There is a saying in our profession that you don't buy a dog and then bark yourself as well. I was asked by Mr Meacher to represent him and I felt that I was not doing my job if I was saying to him: 'Go ahead and have this lunch', without telling him that I didn't like it and I thought that he shouldn't, but he insisted that he would and he did. I then said to him: 'Please don't agree to anything that Tony Howard says even if it is over which wine you should have. Listen to what he says and then report back to me. Don't agree anything.' And he said that he would do that.

After the lunch, according to Miss Burton, Mr Meacher telephoned her to say that the *Observer* accepted that they had 'misconstrued' his background, having 'false information' on this. Their 'lawyers' had 'dug up' his birth certificate, which had 'retired farmer' on it.

In fact our lawyers had not been brought in at this stage; the birth certificate had been obtained by Mr Millinship. Whether Mr Howard had or had not used the words 'OK – so we got it wrong', as Mr Meacher said he had, the getting it wrong could have related only to the making of *claims* by Mr Meacher about his background. The salient, though not the complete, facts about that background were made known by Mr Meacher to Mr Howard at the first lunch in September 1983 and were supplemented in minor respects only at the second lunch in February 1985.

According to Miss Burton's note or, as she preferred to call it, *aide-mémoire* of the telephone conversation with Mr Meacher after the lunch, Mr Howard had asked him whether he 'really wanted to go for the *Observer* and get into heavy stuff'. (The distinction which she drew between a note and an *aide-mémoire* was that the latter was literally intended to help her memory. Accordingly she would write down only what she thought she might forget or what might otherwise be useful to her rather than make a comprehensive summary.) Mr Howard consistently denied using the words 'heavy stuff', claiming that he did not talk in this way, and that the phrase must have derived either from Mr Meacher or from Miss Burton herself. He denied with equal consistency ever having said to Mr Meacher, as Miss Burton recorded in her *aide-mémoire*: 'If you were talking about £2,000, my attitude would be different.'

Mr Meacher's silence

Miss Burton was clear that she had never seen the original correction written by me and modified slightly by Mr Howard. Nor, she said, had she seen the accompanying letter from him. All she remembered was a tele-phone conversation with Mr Meacher on 15 February 1985 in which he said that this original correction was unsatisfactory to him because it repeated the libel, did not refer to the dreaded Moonman allegations and was not going to go into that week's paper. Mr Meacher said to Miss Burton that he would speak to Mr Howard early in the following week. In fact Mr Meacher did not: Miss Burton supplied no evidence to show that he did. There was no conflict between her and Mr Howard on that point.

Moreover, it squares with my own experience, though I was not asked to give evidence on the matter. If Mr Meacher and Mr Howard had been negotiating about the final form of the correction or apology in the week beginning Tuesday 19 February 1985 (for Sunday newspapers start the working week on Tuesday), I should have expected to be informed, if only about the length of the agreed correction. It was, as I have said, a surprise when I saw on Sunday 24 February what had been agreed. Mr Howard felt that, on the Friday, he had quite enough on his plate dealing with Mr Meacher on the telephone from Euston Station and, later on, with Miss Burton, without bringing me into the negotiations as well. Mr Meacher telephoned Mr Howard; Mr Howard telehoned Miss Burton, who expressed dissatisfaction with the proffered correction; and Mr Meacher later telephoned Miss Burton. He was not best pleased. As usual, he had left things till (almost literally) the last minute, for with the improved technology then existing at the *Observer* my column went 'into the page' on the Friday rather than on the Saturday, as it had in the old days of compositors and linotype operators. Furthermore, he was demanding action within days, while he had stayed his own hand for months.

Nevertheless, Miss Burton was his solicitor, his plenipotentiary, granted full powers to act on his behalf. She had not extracted from Mr Howard that which met with his approval. The fact that we were not, and never had been, prepared to correct, retract or apologise for the Moonman allegations did not matter to him: he remained obsessed by his false inference from my column that he had forced Mr Moonman out of the Labour Party. As far as the father allegations were concerned, he claimed that even in the modified correction cobbled together by Mr Howard on the Friday, we were 'repeating the libel'. What he wanted was some form of words at once vaguer and more comprehensive. This was something which Mr Howard was not prepared to supply.

Mr Howard as peacemaker

It was clear that, while Mr Howard had tried to satisfy Mr Meacher on the Friday, Mr Meacher remained dissatisfied. The court adjourned till two o'clock, which meant, as it always did, five past two. Mr Bishop continued his examination by asking Miss Burton what she wanted to be called.

Bishop: I am sorry – should we refer to you as Miss Burton or Mrs Burton? Or is that your professional name?

Burton: I prefer 'Ms', but if it cannot be used in a court of law –

Judge: I was going to say: do you mind, because you are perfectly entitled to call yourself whatever you like in your social life, but the court is a public place and a vowel sound is a great help.

Burton: I understand that. 'Miss' is correct.

Mr Bishop and Miss Burton then proceeded to clear up a few matters, notably that Mr Howard had not only read out the correction on the telephone but, later on the Friday, sent a copy of it to her by messenger.

Mr Hartley cross-examines

Mr Hartley began his cross-examination by asking Miss Burton about her professional experience. It was at this stage that she corrected her year of qualification from 1980 to 1982. He went on to ask whether she agreed that, in a defamation case, it was essential to make a demand for a correction or apology at once. Miss Burton havered, and had to be prodded gently by the judge, who said that she was being asked her professional opinion. She replied that in general Mr Hartley was right but that in this case there had been 'very good reasons' for the delay. Mr Hartley accused her of making a mystery. Miss Burton replied equally mysteriously:

The reasons are in two stages. The first stage is before I saw my client and the second stage is after that. Before I saw Mr Meacher on 4th January –

Miss Burton could easily have said what she said elsewhere in her evidence: that she was completing some other business for Mr Meacher; clearing the decks preparatory to an engagement with the *Observer*. But she did not proffer that explanation at this stage. She repeated to Mr Hartley that she had received a telephone call of undisclosed date from Mr Meacher's political man of business, Mr Meale. He asked her whether she had seen my column. She replied that she had not, and requested a copy. It arrived with Mr Meacher's letter of 11 December 1984. On 4 January 1985 she met Mr Meacher. On 29 January 1985 she wrote her minatory letter to us. Apart from her claim that she was engaged in other business on Mr Meacher's behalf, she produced no satisfactory explanation for a delay of seven weeks from the day when the matter was first drawn to her attention by Mr Meacher (as distinct from Mr Meale, who had brought it to her notice before then). Mr Hartley then turned to the contents of her letter to us:

Normally, Miss Burton, when one writes in a letter before action that the allegation is untrue, you go on to say that you specify precisely what is untrue and you specify the true facts. Does it surprise you that we did not know, until Mr Meacher gave evidence, whether it was going to be suggested that his father had never been an accountant or near an accountant's office or anything to do with an accountant?

Miss Burton said it would surprise her. Mr Hartley was being accurate as far as he went. What we thought – and what the pleadings said – was that Mr Meacher had falsely exaggerated the humbleness of his origins in order to ingratiate himself with his constituents and with members of the Labour Party. The novel twist which Mr Meacher put on my words was that I was implying that his father had been a rich City gentleman who retired to his country estate to enjoy his accumulated fortune. Such an interpretation had never once crossed my mind. How could it have done, when the salient (though by no means the complete) facts had been known to me since September 1983?

This interpretation, I confess, angered me even more strongly than his interpretation of the words about Mr Moonman. The latter, perverse though it was, could have come about through genuine misunderstanding. The former, more perverse still, could have been a product only of Mr Meacher's considerable intelligence. Time and again, it seemed to me, people connected with the case underestimated his cleverness. His judgment was appalling, his vanity considerable, his ignorance of the legal system comprehensive: but there was nothing wrong with his brain. Mr Hartley turned to Miss Burton's literary style:

> **Richard Hartley, QC:** The letter really comes off a word processor, does it not?
> **Burton:** No, this does not come off a word processor.
> **Hartley:** I am not criticising. It is the way that counsel write them too.
> **Burton:** It does not come off a word processor. It does not come from a draft by counsel. It comes from me.

And then Miss Burton made what was, in the circumstances, an extraordinary admission:

> **Hartley:** You have been in court all through the case, have you not, Miss Burton?
> **Burton:** I have been in and out – mostly in. But I have not been following the documents. I have not had them in front of me.

Later:

Hartley: You were paying very great attention at the times that you were in court, were you not, to what was going on?

Burton: Not all of the time. There have been times when I was not. That is what happens when you are sitting behind counsel and it is not my case any more, remember. I have not been handling this case for some considerable time. One of my partners has.

The partner concerned was Larry Grant. He attended the court every day with Miss Burton. He had taken over the case at the turn of 1987: but afterwards, as I have already pointed out, letters continued to be written by Miss Burton. In any event, six months hardly amounts to 'some considerable time', especially when measured by the time-scale of the legal profession.

However, what was extraordinary about Miss Burton's admission was that she had not been following the documents in the case. I had been following them in two ring-binder files provided by our solicitors. They had been sent to me on the Saturday before the case began, giving me something under two days to absorb the contents as best I could. With some of the material I was, of course, familiar: with what had appeared in the papers in 1983-4 and with much of the correspondence between the two firms of solicitors in 1985-8. Though copies of these letters were faithfully dispatched to me throughout this period by David O'Callaghan, the truth is that I had not paid much attention to them. 'Stick them in the Meacher file, Isabel,' I would say to the secretary I shared with Mr Howard, Isabel Maycock, and move on to more pressing concerns. Accordingly I came to the case with an eye fresher than it might have been, because I had never seriously expected the trial to come on. I still cannot contemplate a row of ring-binder files (which I do not use in my work) without a feeling of apprehension.

Miss Burton had been the plaintiff's solicitor during, effectively, the entire pre-trial period, for little happened in the first half of 1988. And much of her own evidence was documentary in origin, based on her notes of meetings and of telephone conversations. For instance, Mr Hartley put to her that there was nothing in her note about Mr Meacher's saying to Mr Howard that the Moonman allegations were significant. Miss Burton agreed: no, there was not. Surely, Mr Hartley continued, this would be consistent with Mr Howard's evidence – which he had yet to give – that he had persuaded Mr Meacher that the Moonman allegations were unimportant. Miss Burton did not agree:

It is not in my notes. I didn't need to write it down because I knew already. It wasn't something that I needed a note to remind myself of or to remind me to tell the client or – These are what my notes are for. They are *aides-mémoire*. I didn't need that as an *aide-mémoire* because it was very well ingrained in me by them that the Moonman incident was important to my client.

Mr Hartley suggested that Mr Howard had said to her that, as Mr Meacher had not rejected the apology, the *Observer* would publish it anyway. Miss Burton denied this: Mr Howard had never said that at all. She would, she answered, have been so 'stunned' if he had that she would have 'written that down in quotes'. Mr Justice Hazan then intervened. In her experience of dealing with defamation, had she invariably found that, when newspapers published an apology, it was as a result of agreement between the parties? 'Almost invariably,' Miss Burton replied. Would it be 'quite exceptional', the judge continued, for the *Observer*, 'off its own bat', to publish an apology not only without her client's consent but contrary to his wishes? Miss Burton replied that it would not strike her as strange, though it would be unusual.

> **Judge**: Unusual but not strange?
> **Burton**: May I say one thing?
> **Judge**: Surely.
> **Burton**: Because, in certain circumstances, a newspaper will be advised to mitigate damages by publishing a correction as quickly as it can. 'Try and get it agreed. If you can't, publish it anyway.' It would mitigate the damages at a later date and I assumed that that was what their advice had been, because of the way that Mr Howard said to me: 'From our point of view' – in other words, to protect ourselves – 'we will publish this this Sunday'. That was my understanding.

This struck me as quite a good answer by Miss Burton. Whatever the vagaries of her note-taking, this sentence, which was in one of those notes, appeared to me to be exactly what an exasperated Mr Howard (whose many good qualities do not include patience) would have said to her on a Friday evening. In the same note of 22 February 1985, she quoted Mr Howard as saying:

> Very sorry personally that it does not satisfy him. If at any stage he would like to discuss this with me, I'd be happy to do so.

With the proviso about Miss Burton's note-taking in mind, I nevertheless considered that these words effectively disposed of any agreement between the two men. Mr Howard had done his best to meet Mr Meacher's wishes, substantially modifying my original correction. But Mr Meacher was not satisfied. He had told Miss Burton he was not satisfied. Miss Burton had so informed Mr Howard, who had regretfully accepted this state of affairs but nonetheless decided to proceed with the insertion of the correction.

Mr Howard's feelings of personal regret also appeared to me to be consistent and in character. Indeed, throughout the trial and before, we were given to understand that, if there was one feeling which in strength exceeded Mr Howard's regard for Mr Meacher, it was Mr Meacher's regard for Mr Howard. In his evidence and his pre-trial correspondence alike, he blamed chiefly me but possibly also some sinister, un-named anti-Meacher faction at the *Observer* for the words which, he claimed, caused him so much offence. It never fully impinged on him, Mr Bishop or Miss Burton that his conversation with Mr Howard at lunch in September 1983 was the *fons et origo* of all subsequent events. Our counsel asked about the apology or correction.

> Hartley: Well, are you saying that a fair-minded person, reading that – Have you actually seen it [i.e. the apology or correction that in fact appeared] before? You have?
>
> Burton: Yes, I had it sent to me by messenger, just typed out or a carbon version, I think it was.
>
> Hartley: Did you see the newspaper when it came out?
>
> Burton: No, I didn't. No.

Accordingly, Mr Meacher had not seen my offending column when it first appeared but read it five days later. Miss Burton had not seen it either. She had it drawn to her attention by Mr Meacher's man of business, Mr Meale, and actually read it at some subsequent time. Now Miss Burton was telling us that she had not even bothered to glance at the apology which had so exercised her and her client only two days previously in an afternoon and evening of telephones and anger. After all, Mr Howard might have modified the wording again, or decided not to insert the apology at all. How could Miss Burton tell unless she looked at the paper? I was not cast down by neglect, even though it is never pleasant for a columnist to be treated with what the late George Brown used to call 'a complete ignoral'. But I was, and I remain, astonished that so much time, energy and money (nearly £200,000) should have been expended, so much worry, misery and humiliation brought about, by 1200-odd words of mine which, it appeared, none of the aggrieved or interested parties had read.

10

Miss Rouse's Evidence

> Mr Justice Cocklecarrot: Mr Snapdriver, why was this witness ever called?
>
> Mr Snapdriver appeared disconcerted. He consulted his notes and one or two books. Then he whispered to a clerk and consulted another barrister.
>
> J.B. Morton, *The Case of the Twelve Red-Bearded Dwarfs*

Ann Rouse was even smaller than Sarah Burton and appeared considerably more apprehensive. I admired her courage in coming along to give evidence on Mr Meacher's behalf. Miss Burton had testified mainly on our defence of accord and satisfaction; Miss Rouse was to testify on the Moonman allegations. She had been, from 1982 to 1986, a member of the Islington Health Authority. She was also a member of the Islington North Constituency Labour Party (Mr Moonman having been a member of the Islington South CLP). She had been nominated by her local party to the council, which had in its turn appointed her to the District Health Authority.

She was called by Mr Meacher to demonstrate that Mr Moonman had been unpopular with the local Labour Party and with the Labour members of the health authority. By this means, Mr Meacher's side hoped to show that Mr Meacher's questionnaire had been the pretext for rather than the real cause of Mr Moonman's resignation from the Labour Party. Causation is a tricky business. As Francis Bacon expressed the matter: 'It were infinite to judge causes, or the causes of causes.' That was certainly something to be borne in mind. Moreover, Miss Rouse's evidence was likely to lead a bemused judge and a bored jury into the internal politics of the Islington Labour Party. There was, in addition, the ever-present risk of hearsay evidence.

Mr Justice Hazan, himself a master of the law of evidence, was well aware of these rocks, which were not so much submerged as sticking several feet out of the water. Indeed, in his own way he was as apprehensive as Miss Rouse. From the start, he showed a certain impatience, even irritability. He was not annoyed with Miss Rouse but with Mr Bishop, for calling her at all. He was a fair man. Nevertheless, some of his pique fell on Miss Rouse. That could not be helped. Miss Rouse, however, appeared in a state of bewilderment, as well she might. Her apprehension increased. I felt even sorrier for her. She was 33, but a slip of a girl really, and here she found herself, in a Victorian-gothic madhouse off the Strand.

Mr Bishop's examination

Gordon Bishop: Could you tell us what your occupation is?
Ann Rouse: I am a project worker at Islington Mind.
Mr Justice Hazan: Islington –?
Rouse: Islington Mind, my Lord, M-I-N-D.
Bishop: What is that?
Rouse: It is the local branch of the National Association for Mental Health.

Miss Rouse said that, when she started to serve on the health authority, she became aware that the conduct of its meetings was not in the interests of the local community. Other members agreed with her about this. They felt that 'proper discussion' was not always held and that 'important issues' were often brought up at the last minute. There were 'various manoeuvres' by the 'chair', Mr Moonman, to 'force through certain proposals with, we felt, not sufficient consultation'.

Richard Hartley, QC: My Lord, can I ask what relevance this has got to what –?
Judge: What issue does this go to?
Bishop: My Lord, it goes to the question of whether Mr Moonman was forced to resign by the – Whether it was the questionnaire that caused him to resign from the Labour Party or whether it was the situation between him and the Labour Party at that particular point.
Judge: The best evidence of that would be direct evidence, would it not, not secondary evidence from other people who may have views about his motives, which may be right or may be wrong?

Our side had debated – and continued to debate – the wisdom of calling Mr Moonman. He remained available. Indeed, he telephoned Mr O'Callaghan at least once at seven in the morning to find out how the trial was going, and whether he was likely to be called. We decided against calling him (though I played no part at all in the decision). He could have turned out to be a 'wild card' or a 'rogue witness'. I had certainly not been polite to him. However, he was perfectly willing to appear as one of our witnesses. On the other side, Messrs Seifert Sedley Williams could have summoned him by subpoena had they so chosen. Likewise, they did not elect to take this course.

Mr Bishop made various submissions to the judge about the admissibility of Miss Rouse's evidence. Though they appeared to fall on barren soil, he was allowed to continue, in this fashion:

> **Bishop**: Now, you suggested a number of matters there, including the conduct of the chair. Who was the chair or chairman or whatever?
>
> **Judge**: Well, as he was a man, could we please get down to brass tacks and call him 'the chairman'? He is not an inanimate object. He is not a chair. He is a human being. That is a terrible expression.
>
> **Rouse**: The chairman at that time, my Lord, was Eric Moonman.
>
> **Judge**: People look, you know, for all sorts of sexual connotations in things that are perfectly innocent. They look for sexual discrimination where it does not exist.
>
> **Bishop**: My Lord, I could not agree with your Lordship more.

Some 40 years ago the now largely forgotten Professor C.E.M. Joad, a great popular educator famous for his wireless phrase 'It depends on what you mean by ...', described his experiences as a juryman in a weekly column which he wrote in the *Sunday Dispatch*. He said that three aspects of the trial remained in his memory: the way in which counsel bullied witnesses and went unrebuked; the constant deference which the barristers showed to the judge; and the superb courtesy and clarity of the judge in his dealings with the jury. Evidently nothing had changed.

Mr Bishop went on to ask Miss Rouse further questions about her times on the health authority. She said that she and her allies felt they were being 'hectored' by Mr Moonman, because their views differed from his. Mr Bishop asked what she meant by 'hectored'. Miss Rouse replied that Mr Moonman would not give them sufficient time to express their point of view. She turned to privatisation and the differences with Mr Moonman on this subject. Mr Justice Hazan intervened.

> **Judge**: Does it really come to this: there were differences of views and differences of politics. Now, you do not need to go into it, do you, otherwise the jury may feel that they have got to decide which was right? That is something (a) which they cannot do and (b) which is not the issue they are trying.
>
> **Bishop**: My Lord, I would not ask them to do that.
>
> **Judge**: We have got to confine this trial within its proper limits.

Mr Bishop returned to his questioning about the Labour politics of Islington. There had been a motion of no confidence in the health authority which had been supported by Miss Rouse and her allies, but

that had been lost. There had also been a motion in the Islington North
CLP calling for Mr Moonman's expulsion from the party, and that had
presumably been carried, though Mr Bishop did not manage to clarify
Miss Rouse's answers as to the outcome. Miss Rouse also thought – this
was clearly hearsay evidence – that a similar motion had been put at a
meeting of the Islington South CLP, of which Mr Moonman was a
member. Mr Bishop betrayed some confusion of mind about membership
of the Labour Party, evidently thinking that a person could be an
individual member of the party nationally as distinct from locally. But
Miss Rouse's understanding was that Mr Moonman was a member of the
Islington South CLP.

> **Bishop**: I see. As far as you were concerned, in June 1984, when
> things came to a head, at that stage did you have any knowledge
> about Mr Moonman's intentions or – Well, I will take it in stages:
> any knowledge of the atmosphere between members of the Labour
> Party on the health authority and Mr Moonman?
> **Hartley**: My Lord, I do not know how that can be answered
> without –
> **Judge**: I have given you very great latitude, but there are limits.
> **Bishop**: My Lord, I will not ask any further questions.
> **Judge**: I am not going to allow you to expand this.

Undoubtedly this was humiliating for Mr Bishop. He had been not
exactly cut off in full flow – for his ignorance of the Labour Party (which
he shared with Mr Hartley and the judge), together with Miss Rouse's
innocence of what the action was about, not to mention her
understandable nervousness, hardly made for smooth discourse. But he
had been obliged to end his examination-in-chief. Coming after his
mistake in re-examining Mr Meacher,[1] the episode must have
disconcerted him. But barristers are trained to accept adversity and to
suffer rebuffs, even insults, at the hands of judges; and Mr Bishop sat
down, as was his habit, to a shuffling of papers and tapping of writing
instruments on his part, shooting his cuffs and exposing pink wrists
covered with ginger hair. Mr Bishop had the capacity to transform the
simple action of sitting down into a demonstration, sometimes of
hostility, usually of pique. He was rarely content merely to lower himself
into his seat. He would make a clatter, turning an act into a performance.

Mr Hartley's cross-examination

Mr Hartley rose to cross-examine. I was surprised that he was allowed to
do so at such length, covering matters about which the judge had

---

[1] See above, Chapter 8.

previously shown unease. He did, however, manage to clarify that, according to Miss Rouse – the hearsay evidence of Miss Rouse – a motion calling for Mr Moonman's expulsion from the Labour Party had been passed by his own constituency party, Islington South. The only sources that could have supplied definitive evidence on this matter were the Labour Party nationally (for expulsion is a serious business), the Islington South CLP and Mr Moonman himself. None was called. It seemed clear that Mr Moonman remained a member of the party until his resignation in November 1984. Miss Rouse's cross-examination was concluded:

Hartley: Do you know what this libel action is about?
Rouse: Yes.
Hartley: What do you think it is about?
Rouse: I think it is about an article which was written several years ago which Mr Meacher considers to be libellous.
Hartley: And what is the allegation that you have heard? Have you actually read the article?
Rouse: No, I haven't.
Bishop: I have no re-examination.
Judge: Thank you very much.

Miss Rouse withdrew. She had my sympathy, as – up to a point – did the luckless Mr Bishop.

11

Canon Wilkinson's Evidence

A Mr Wilkinson, a clergyman.

Edward FitzGerald, parodying William Wordsworth,
quoted in Hallam Tennyson, *Tennyson*

At the end of Miss Rouse's evidence, Mr Bishop announced that there might be a slight delay. There was a witness whose existence and availability had come to the notice of the plaintiff only on the previous evening. The delay was very slight. All of a sudden, a rangy, bearded, elderly clergyman in a lightweight coat was walking briskly towards the witness box. The press box showed interest; even the jury perked up. This looked like divine intervention. Perhaps God was on Mr Meacher's side after all. Even if He was not, the trial now possessed that final, classic ingredient, the surprise witness. He was Canon Wilfred Badger Wilkinson, Canon Emeritus of Southwell.

Gordon Bishop: Is it Southwell or Southwall?
Wilfred Wilkinson: The high class people call it Southwell; the ordinary people call it S'uthall. Canon Emeritus means that I am an old age pensioner.

A bit of a card

Clearly, the Canon was not a man to be trifled with. Equally clearly, he was – and regarded himself as – a bit of a card. He had a northern accent. It emerged that he had been priest-in-charge of All Saints' Church, Berkhamsted, from 1953 to 1957. He was, Mr Howard (a connoisseur of such matters) established, on the evangelical wing.

Bishop: Would you tell us please, if you would, how you happen to be here today, giving evidence? How did that come about?
Wilkinson: Yesterday afternoon I saw a little cutting in *The Times* when I didn't know anything about this case, because we had been on a caravan holiday for a fortnight in Scotland and had not

had any newspaper. I saw this little cutting in *The Times*, and the first thing that struck me was that Michael had said that his father was 'inadequate' and 'dependent', and I said to my wife, I said: 'That's absolutely true,' and then I read on that the suggestion was that he had, as it were, overplayed a difficult and poor background, and I said to Betty: 'That is not true. They had a real struggle that family, as I well know.'

Michael was a server at holy communion services. His mother came to church regularly but his father not at all, except to occasions such as harvest suppers. The house was at the 'going down' end of Berkhamsted.

Bishop: What were conditions like inside?

Wilkinson: Well, the whole property was run down. I mean, when I first went, I remember so clearly my first visit. I thought what a run-down house it was. I went down this sort of passage; there were a couple of sort of outhouses and then a door. It was quite dark in the living area. I remember how shabby the furniture was and I thought it could do with decorating. The other thing I remember so clearly is that I didn't know what to do about Mr Meacher. He didn't talk. I just felt –

Mr Justice Hazan: Mr Meacher senior?

Wilkinson: Yes, my Lord.

Judge: So he did not talk? He was rather withdrawn?

Wilkinson: Yes, yes, he was.

Bishop: Did you see Mr Meacher senior on occasions after that?

Wilkinson: Yes, I saw him sometimes. I didn't have a lot of contact wih him. You just didn't get through to him. Really I felt that he was in a real situation of breakdown, and it just went on and on with never any change; and really my only relationships were with Michael's mother and with Michael.

Canon Wilkinson paid tribute to the mother, who 'carried the whole family' and was 'quite a remarkable person'. Mr Meacher's eyes filled with tears.

Bishop: What about Michael himself? What did you think of him at that stage? Did you see anything of him at that stage?

Wilkinson: I saw a lot of Michael. I think I have hardly ever thought as highly of a boy as I thought of Michael, and as I watched him at school. He was a tremendous boy in the life of our church. He was so real, he was so sincere and honest, and he had such guts. He really was first-class. This is the reason I am here today. I knew nothing about this until I saw this in *The Times* yesterday, and I said to Betty, my wife, I said: 'I couldn't live with my conscience,

Betty, if I don't do something about this.' And I rang the House of
Commons to find out how I could get through to Michael. I thought
the case might be over and I couldn't do anything. But I had to do
what I could because of what I had thought of him.

It was a terrific performance by the Canon. Not only did he dominate
the court: he appeared quite at ease as he was doing so. This was not
surprising when you came to think about it. In Court No. 14 the
witness-box is in the top left-hand corner as you look towards the judge.
The judge is on a slightly lower level. The witness turns left to speak to
the judge, then right to face counsel for the defendants, who is diagonally
opposite him but below him in elevation, and then right again to face
counsel for the plaintiff, who is likewise below him. This particular
witness-box – the one in Court No. 13, which is also used for libel cases, is
less satisfactory in several respects – resembles a pulpit. Canon
Wilkinson was at home.

Mr Hartley began his cross-examination by treating Canon Wilkinson
as an expert witness on marriage certificates; as, indeed, he was; he
overwhelmed learned counsel with his knowledge and experience. All
the various certificates, it may be remembered, described G.H. Meacher
slightly differently. In his own marriage certificate, he was called a
gentleman; in his son's birth certificate, a farmer, retired; and, in his
son's marriage certificate, a farmer. In none of the documents was he
described as a farm or agricultural worker or labourer. Mr Meacher had
hazarded, in his evidence, that he thought that, on his own marriage
certificate, 'farmer' had been inserted by his future wife's parents, most
probably by her mother, because her father was listed as an 'executive
manager' – which, as Mr Meacher explained, was a somewhat exalted
way of describing his future father-in-law.

Our counsel took Canon Wilkinson through the procedure leading to
the issue of a marriage certificate, which began with the completion of a
form by the engaged couple or their relations and ended with the signing
of the register. I quote the following exchange at length not only because
it is instructive and amusing in itself but also because it illustrates the
Canon's capacity for taking hold of the court by the scruff of its neck, as if
the unrighteous were being confronted by a minor prophet.

Hartley: Thank you. Right. I do not think we need worry any
more on that document. Would I be right in saying that, when you
came to Berkhamsted, which I think was 1953 –?
Wilkinson: Please, my Lord, I need your guidance. I don't know
anything about courts. But there is something I would like to say
about this form, if I may.
Judge: Yes, certainly. Yes?
Wilkinson: The other thing, in reading this little column from *The*

Times yesterday, was that there had been a criticism of the fact that Michael's father was listed as a farmer, and that therefore, according to this little part in *The Times*, showed that he had not been a poor man, that he had been a farmer. Now if I may say this, from my very wide experience: you often find that it may come either from a young man's parents or from the in-law's parents, that they want this form to look as good as possible. And, to give you an example, I had a form brought to me by the son of the college porter at Clifton College of Education, and it had on: 'Father's rank or profession: major retired.' Well, of course he had been a major during the war. But what was that? About 20 years ago. And I said to the couple: 'Look, you have got to put what your Dad is.' Well, the next day the girl's parents came round and absolutely went for me. Or again, very often a chap would come to me and he wouldn't put 'bank clerk' here, he would put 'banker'. I never had anybody who put 'unemployed' and I never made anybody. I used to say: 'What is your father?' 'Well, he's a plumber.' I said: 'Well, let's put "plumber", because that is what he is even though he is out of a job at the moment.' One of the things I felt so deeply against was the suggestion that Michael Meacher's father must have been, sort of, quite a well-off-and-responsible-job kind of person, because I know he was not, from my meeting them from 1953 to 1957. I hope you will forgive me. I know you didn't ask for that, but I felt so deeply about that yesterday, you see.

The Canon takes control

But Mr Hartley had indeed asked for it, by bringing up the subject in the first place, so allowing the Canon to embark on his discourse on the theory and practice of marriage certificates. The jury were evidently enthralled; partly, I suspect, because the witness used words and examples which they could understand. Mr Hartley, I considered, mishandled the Canon. Jurors have a respect for clergymen and for doctors (and in Scotland and Wales, though not in England, for schoolmasters as well) which they deny to lawyers, to politicians and, above all, to journalists. Moreover, Mr Hartley was a particularly racy kind of lawyer, a bachelor, fond of ladies, gambling, horses and golf. The jury were not to know this, of course: nevertheless, the dialogue did have undertones of a contest between metropolitan smoothness and provincial virtue.

And Mr Hartley went on far too long. The longer the Canon was kept in the witness-box, the more favourable and the more lasting was the impression which he made on the jury. Mr Hartley should, in my opinion (which I expressed at the time to Mr Howard, though not to Mr Hartley), have said something on these lines:

Good morning, Canon. It is very good of you to come along to the
court at such short notice, and I am sure we are all delighted to see
you looking in such excellent health. But perhaps you could assist us
on one matter. When you knew the Meacher family, was Mr
Meacher at any stage a farm worker?

Canon Wilkinson would presumably have replied:

Farm worker? But I've just told you, he hardly went out of the house.

The Canon might then have embarked on a further description of hard
times in the High Street, but he could reasonably have been cut off by Mr
Hartley. Instead of this, he decided to treat the aged cleric more
aggressively. The clergyman had the better of every exchange by being
able to return each time to what he had seen with his own eyes of the
deprivation in the Meacher household and the saintliness of Mrs
Meacher.

> **Hartley**: Did you know that he was the son of three generations of
> tenant farmers? Did you know that?
> **Wilkinson**: No, no.
> **Hartley**:Does that come as a surprise to you?
> **Wilkinson**: No, no. I mean I just didn't know anything about the
> earlier background.
> **Hartley**: And Michael's father –
> **Wilkinson**: I didn't talk a lot because Mrs Meacher was sensitive,
> and I didn't try to find out why he was like he was, and so on. Mrs
> Meacher was very sensitive about it. It was part of her stress, the
> load she was carrying.

It was a masterly reply. But our man did not give up easily. He
established that the Canon did not know that G.H. Meacher had inherited £6,000. (The amounts various members of the Meacher family had
been left in wills caused trouble, and some confusion, throughout the
trial; Mr Justice Hazan joked at one stage that, if the parties wanted him
to construe a will, they had better send for a Chancery judge instead.) Nor
was this inheritance the sole aspect of the Meachers' relative affluence,
according to Mr Hartley.

> **Hartley**: And they own the lease of their house, do they not? Did
> you know that?
> **Wilkinson**: I didn't know that. But one thing I did know was – and
> this is hardly the word to use but I don't want to use the word 'poor'
> – they were hard up. She was struggling to do more for her son than
> she really could manage to do, and I used sometimes to worry about

her. She longed for him to go to university. I couldn't see any hope of them having the money. And I don't know a thing about what Mr Meacher senior had inherited. But, so far as I am concerned, she wouldn't be letting one floor of the house off to lodgers, and working at the local doctor's, and the whole place be obviously run down and hard up – I've no explanation for it, but that is what I saw and what I lived with as their parish priest, that they were so hard up and they were struggling.

Nor was the Canon prepared to allow the QC's inference that, because Michael had been sent to the preparatory school as a fee-payer, accordingly the family must have had some money.

Hartley: And yet, with some inherited wealth, they were able to send their son to a public school and pay for it for three years. Does that not surprise you?

Wilkinson: That was before I was at Berkhamsted, so I know nothing of it. I don't know what the fees were in 19–. What would it be, 1949 in the prep? I mean if you say that to me I feel, well, by Jove, Mrs Meacher must have gone through it to do that. But I can imagine she would. I was sometimes surprised she didn't have a breakdown because of the way she worked and skimped in all sorts of ways.

Once again, the Canon succeeded in bringing his answer back to Mrs Meacher's industry and selflessness. And, like the fine verbal boxer he was, he started to take the fight to his opponent on the principle that the best form of defence was attack. In so doing he almost over-reached himself, but quickly recovered his balance.

Wilkinson: Look, I want us to be accurate about this. The one thing I feel convinced of is that they could never have paid for him to have been in the senior, main school at Berkhamsted School. For them that would have been impossible if he had not got a scholarship. How they managed in those earlier years, when I wasn't there, at the prep – the prep fees were always a lot lower than the main school – I just can't think how they managed that. But I do know that, if he had not won a scholarship to the Berkhamsted main school, he would never have got there.

Hartley: Just let us look at that. How do you know that?

Wilkinson: Because I know, from all sorts of things, the struggling, poor level at which they lived. That is how I know. I know the kind of people who were able to pay for their children to be in the main school at Berkhamsted. And they were totally different,

the Meachers and those other people in Berkhamsted. That is why I
say I know it.

Though the Canon had recovered his balance, this came close to bluster
– to swinging wildly and failing to make his punches connect. After all,
G.H. Meacher was himself an Old Berkhamstedian. That was admitted
on all sides. His wife had been a schoolteacher. That was admitted
likewise. The Meacher household may have been poor, even bizarre: but
it was indisputably not a working-class household. The Canon, having
said that he thought very highly of the Meacher family, ended his
evidence by bringing the house down.

> **Hartley**: You think very highly of them indeed?
> **Wilkinson**: Yes, but I don't want you to think from that that I
> have got my head in the clouds, because I have not. And I don't want
> you to think that I am here to talk of somebody who is rather to the
> far Left of the Labour Party (*Laughter*), because I am not. I am a
> Social Liberal Democrat (*Laughter*).
> **Hartley**: Well, Canon, if you wanted to take on a new job, I am
> sure he would employ you as his agent (*Laughter*).

Throughout his evidence, Canon Wilkinson continued to suggest a
division along class lines between, on the one hand, his church, All
Saints', and its parishioners – who numbered the Meacher family among
them – and, on the other hand, Berkhamsted School. The school and the
parents were, he implied in answer to one question, more the province of
his Rector.

After the case was over a correspondent in Berkhamsted kindly sent
me a copy of the school magazine, the *Berkhamstedian*, for the Lent Term
1956. In the list of subscribers to the school's appeal fund, alongside an
Admiral, an Air Marshal, several Brigadiers, numerous Colonels and Dr
Raymond Greene (whose brother Graham was not, however, listed), was
the name G.H. Meacher. His son appears as a house prefect. There is also
a tribute to Canon Wilkinson.

> We are very much indebted to the Revd W.B. Wilkinson, priest-in-charge of
> All Saints', Berkhamsted, for the stimulating and memorable addresses
> given by him during Lent on the theme 'The Christian in the World'. His
> enjoinder in his last address, that Christian worship should always be
> enjoyable, characterised his whole series, and his lively presentation
> ensured a receptive congregation.

The Canon had not, after all, been so remote from Berkhamsted School as those of us listening to his evidence had supposed. At its end, Mr Howard passed a note to Mr O'Callaghan saying: 'He has sunk our case.'

Part Three

The Case for the Defendants

12

Mr Watkins's Evidence

'I'm afraid I have serious news, old man,' I said, in a hushed voice.
'Serious news?' said Ukridge, trying to turn pale.
'Serious news!'
I had warned him during rehearsals that this was going to sound uncommonly like a vaudeville cross-talk act of the Argumentative College Chums type, but he had ruled out the objection as far-fetched. Nevertheless, that is just what it did sound like, and I found myself blushing warmly.

P.G. Wodehouse, *Ukridge*

Mr Hartley began by announcing that he did not intend to make an opening speech. Our case, he said, had already emerged through the cross-examination of Mr Meacher and his witnesses. He would therefore call me without further delay.

I was wearing a black pinstripe suit, a blue-green silk shirt and a black silk tie with small white spots. On succeeding days I wore a dark blue suit and a Garrick Club tie. Altogether I tried to present a respectable and tidy appearance. Whether I succeeded I do not know. Adam Raphael (next to William Keegan, the most assiduous attender at the court from among my friends and acquaintances) told me that I looked like a *louche* actor-manager. What I did know, however, from my experience of observing the Law Courts, was that journalists – anyway, writing as distinct from television journalists – were, with the shining exception of Mr Raphael in the Archer case, prone to present a mean, furtive and seedy appearance in the witness-box. Somehow the air went with, was almost a consequence of, the clothes worn.

In this case Mr Howard, Mr Taylor and Mr Knight did us proud both with their appearance and with their demeanour in the box. After the trial was over, my friend Frank Johnson (another regular attender) told me that for the first time in a court he had felt proud of his profession.

It is easier to don a nice suit than to simulate a nice nature. This was what I was told was required of me, not by our professional advisers – for no 'coaching' of any kind took place – but by friends and well-wishers. Gerald Bermingham, a Labour MP and solicitor-turned-barrister, told me that it was my function to appear in the third act of the play as a good rather than a bad guy. What counted was the general impression one made. The most dangerous error was to say too much. Mr Howard advised perhaps more usefully that, whatever else I did, I must on no account lose my temper; must not say things on the lines of: 'I didn't come here to be insulted.' A woman friend advised similarly in different words, saying that there must be no 'X-ray eyes', a reference to their bulging appearance when I was angry. She added that I must not behave like 'a demented schoolmaster'.

All this advice was entirely well-intentioned, mainly good: it was obviously necessary to be in control of oneself all the time. But it nevertheless hinted that I should try to appear as a different kind of person. This did not strike me as good advice. After 55 years, I knew myself well enough to realise that, beneath a physical indolence which often appeared as an easygoing tolerance, and which I had inherited from my father, there was a layer of combativeness, which I had likewise inherited from him.

Friday morning

Mr Hartley took me through my examination-in-chief. The substance of most of the questions and answers has already been summarised in Chapters 2 to 5. There was one omission by him. This concerned my re-reading of the articles written about Mr Meacher in 1983 by Mr Knight, Mr Taylor, Mr Chester, Mr Costello and Mr Winder. It was this re-reading (or, in some cases, reading for the first time, as I had not noticed Mr Knight's and Mr Costello's articles when they had first appeared) which had convinced me that Mr Meacher had indeed claimed to be the son of a farm worker. Hence his assurance to Mr Howard during the lunch of February 1985 was false, and my consequential apology or correction misguided.

Mr Hartley could not, however, be blamed for failing to tell the story fully. I had omitted to do so myself in my proof of evidence. Somehow the usually conscientious David O'Callaghan and I had grown weary of the tale. Barristers proceed on what their solicitors tell them.

The new element of the case, which had been introduced by Mr Meacher's solicitor just before it began, was the allegation of malice against me. Inevitably the louse and the flea came into this. One part of me was sorry he had ever heard of Dr Johnson; another part said that, if it was libellous for a political columnist to produce one of the best-known quotations from one of our greatest writers, it was a poor look-out both for political journalism and for the law. Mr Hartley asked me to explain why I had put it in.

Alan Watkins: I put that in as a joke, as a literary joke, as an allusion or quotation from Dr Johnson – well-known eighteenth-century figure.

Mr Justice Hazan: It is not very flattering to either of them.

Watkins: No. The point raised by Mr Bishop in his opening address – that it was clear that it was Mr Meacher who was the louse and Mr Moonman the flea – is not so at all. The whole point is that they are interchangeable.

For the first but not the last time, the good Mr Justice Hazan helped my evidence along, enabling me to make a point which I wished to make. Mr Hartley returned to the question of malice, as demonstrated – or not, as the case was here – by the desire to injure.

Richard Hartley, QC: Did you have it in your mind: 'How can I get at Mr Meacher? How can I write an article defaming him?' or anything like that?

Watkins: No, no.

Judge: This is dealing with the question of malice, is it?

Hartley: Yes.

Watkins: No, he had a small walk-on part. He wasn't the star of the production.

Judge: In the article?

Watkins: In the article, yes.

Hartley: The article that you were commenting on was the article in *The Times*, was it not?

Watkins: Yes.

Mr Hartley had been quick to emphasise that most of the words complained of had been comment by me on the *Times* leader.[1] The judge was equally quick to take the point. Both Mr Meacher and Mr Bishop were less perceptive, Mr Meacher, I think, through a misreading and a consequential sense of outrage, and Mr Bishop, I suspect, through a desire to muddy the waters in what he conceived to be his client's best interests. But Mr Meacher had not demonstrated any outrage at the time, in November 1984. Mr Hartley asked whether he had approached me.

Hartley: Were you able to recognise him? Obviously, you knew who he was, did you, physically?

Watkins: Oh yes.

Hartley: Would he have known who you were? You describe how you go to the House of Commons many afternoons a week.

Watkins: I could not say. I would think that he probably had an idea, yes.

Hartley: Anyway, did you hear from him or from anybody that Mr Meacher complained about that article, until we come to what is

[1] See above, Chapter 4.

called 'the letter before action', which is at the end of January, 1985?
   Watkins: No, no complaint whatever, nothing at all.

I should have liked Mr Hartley to go further, and to ask whether
anyone, irrespective of prompting by Mr Meacher, had said anything on
the lines of: 'Golly, you were a bit hard on old Meacher last Sunday, I
must say.' My answer would have been that no such observations had
been made. This question-and-answer may have breached the rules of
hearsay evidence. It may be that this was the reason Mr Hartley did not
ask the question. But I was determined that it should be made clear that
the column (which even I was now beginning to call 'the article') had
created no stir, aroused no controversy. I also, as I explained earlier,
regretted Mr Hartley's omission to ask me about my examination of the
1983 articles on Mr Meacher.
   At lunch I was still being examined by Mr Hartley. David O'Callaghan
and Paul Fox, our solicitors, took me to the Law Society's cafeteria. They
said that this was to ensure that I did not communicate with anyone else
about the case while I was giving evidence. Mr Meacher had previously
found himself in mild trouble for telephoning his former assistant, Alan
Meale, to verify some dates. I could see no harm in this myself if it helped
him to get things right, but Mr Hartley had been indignant and Mr
Justice Hazan disapproving. However, the true reason for Mr
O'Callaghan's solicitude, as I later discovered, was to see that I kept off
strong drink. I would not have touched a drop anyway.

Friday afternoon

Shortly after my abstemious and frugal repast, Mr Bishop rose to
cross-examine. His questioning, I discovered, was all over the place,
because he had insufficiently mastered his brief, because the brief itself
was incomplete and inaccurate (especially over the two lunches and over
my examination of the 1983 articles) and, not least, because my evidence
was interrupted by that of others – Mr Clarke and Mr Taylor – and by
legal argument. Accordingly I had four separate sessions with Mr Bishop.
He tended to go over ground that had previously been covered. One of his
motifs was my alleged reluctance to apologise after having made a
mistake. This derived from a distinction I tried to clarify between a legal
apology, drawn up by lawyers, and a personal correction, made
voluntarily by the journalist himself (or herself). This is a valid and
useful distinction to make: Mr Bishop tried to use it to infer meanness of
spirit rather than generosity.

   Gordon Bishop: But you were not willing to apologise?
   Watkins: I was willing to correct. If you get something wrong, you
correct it. If someone tells me, and Mr Meacher didn't see fit to tell

me: 'Look, Watkins, old son, you did get it a bit wrong last week,' I say: 'Do you want me to correct it?' I am talking for the MP. He is talking to me in the House of Commons. He can say various things. He can say: 'No, let it go. Buy me lunch sometime.' I say: 'OK.'

Bishop: Do you –?

Watkins: Hang on. That is one form of putting it right. Another form of putting it right is that I will write it in my column and he will say: 'Well, I don't want all that, you know, let's forget the whole thing. But you did get it wrong, you know.' So that is what happens.

As our side had withdrawn the correction, apology or whatever in view of later information, this and much else besides was irrelevant, it seemed to me. But Mr Bishop persisted with questions about the circumstances in which the original correction had been made. We are now in early 1985.

Watkins: There was a mound of cuttings about Mr Meacher's contest in 1983. But I thought I had made it clear that what we were looking for was a specific claim by Mr Meacher: 'I am the son of a farm worker.' And no such specific claim had been turned up.

Bishop: In what form did you expect to find it?

Watkins: In the form which I have just indicated to you.

Bishop: Quotes?

Watkins: 'Michael Meacher said: "As the son of a farm worker, I know all about foot and mouth",' or words to that effect. Now, there was nothing of that sort there.

Bishop: Well, would you –?

Watkins: Or: 'As the son of a farm worker, I am very glad to be in turnip country.'

After a few more questions on similar lines, Mr Bishop jumped to the Moonman allegations. He elected to approach them in an oblique manner, which left some observers puzzled about what he was trying to get at.

Bishop: Mr Watkins, you say, I think, that you live in Islington. Is that right?

Watkins: Yes.

Bishop: So you know quite a lot about the affairs of Islington?

Watkins: No, very little.

Bishop: Is there a local paper?

Watkins: Yes.

Bishop: Do you read that?

Watkins: No.

Bishop: You deliberately don't read that?

Watkins: I don't read it. I don't know how you deliberately don't read something.

There were some titters, and a few gasps, from the press box below me on my right. Learned counsel, however, kept his temper.

Bishop: Very good point. You are obviously an expert with the use of words.

Mr Bishop asked me about my reading in 1984. I replied *The Times*, the *Guardian*, the *Sunday Times*, the *Observer*, the *Sunday Telegraph* and the *Spectator*. I added that my reading in 1988 was the same with the addition of the *Independent*. Whether out of curiosity or because he thought I was getting above myself – perhaps a mixture of both – Mr Justice Hazan intervened to inquire whether it was *infra dig* for the correspondent of a national newspaper to read the local press. I replied that I had a lot to get through in the course of my work. This seemed to satisfy the judge. Mr Bishop then asked me at length about how I went about that work, and the light in which I regarded it.

Bishop: So you comment on both facts and opinions?
Watkins: Yes indeed, and rumours.
Bishop: You comment on facts, opinions and rumours?
Watkins: Yes.
Bishop: Do you comment on anything else?
Watkins: I comment on politicians and their personalities.

Mr Bishop took me again through my methods of composition, giving me the opportunity to deliver another blow.

Bishop: Was that draft that you write out from 10.30 onwards, for three-and-a-half hours, essentially the body of the article?
Watkins: It is the article. It is not the body of the article. It is the article. It is what appears.

I explained that my jokes arose naturally, and that sometimes they did not arise.

Bishop: Sometimes there are not any of these insults in your columns?
Watkins: Well, you call them insults. I would call them jokes, sallies.
Bishop: Sallies?

Watkins: Sallies.

Bishop: Jokes?

Watkins: Yes.

Bishop: Just funny?

Watkins: Yes, I hope.

Bishop: Sorry?

Watkins: I hope, funny.

Bishop: Do you accept that some people might not find them funny when they are in relation to them?

Watkins: Well, there are always people without a sense of humour.

Bishop: You mean some people without your sense of humour?

Watkins: Some people without my sense of humour or any sense of humour.

This was very much like the Argumentative College Chums cross-talk act referred to at the beginning of this chapter. More was to follow, when Mr Bishop quoted again Dr Johnson on the louse and the flea, a reference of which I was by now becoming thoroughly sick.

Watkins: Yes, literary allusion.

Bishop: Literary allusion?

Watkins: Yes, joke. Joke at this point.

Bishop: Joke?

Watkins: Joke.

Bishop: Purely joke?

Watkins: Purely joke.

Bishop: No comment on them?

Watkins: Yes, the comment that they were not particularly important people.

Bishop: Anything more than that?

Watkins: And that the dispute was really not worth bothering with too much.

Bishop: And them not worth bothering with too much?

Watkins: Certainly not major politicians.

After some more questions, Mr Bishop went on to make a serious error in cross-examination. He asked a question expecting one answer, and got the opposite. He asked whether I knew who the louse and the flea were in eighteenth-century Grub Street. I did know, and told him. Michael Toner of the *Sunday Express*, and several other colleagues in the press box and in the seats at the back of the court, thought that this was the turning-point, not perhaps in the case, but in Mr Bishop's cross-examination. His confidence had received a nasty blow from which it never properly recovered. Their view, contrary to that of Mr Hartley and

Mr Nathan, was that the jury were enjoying the fight – as, by now, I was. Throughout my period in the box there was a conflict between the barristers and the journalists. The latter, with a few exceptions, thought I was right to be myself and to attack. The former thought I was being altogether too cocky and risked prejudicing the jury. This conflict I learnt of only afterwards. While I was in the box I spoke to nobody.

Bishop: Do you know to whom Dr Johnson was referring?
Watkins: Yes, I do.
Bishop: You do?
Watkins: Yes.
Bishop: Who were they?
Watkins: The two poets were Samuel Derrick, who was an Irishman, and Christopher Smart, who was a ne'er-do-well often incarcerated in lunatic asylums, but a poet nevertheless.
Bishop: And the first one?
Watkins: Derrick, yes. Derrick was a friend of Dr Johnson's and, indeed, he helped Johnson with his 'Life of Dryden' in the *Lives of the Poets*. He wrote several miscellaneous volumes and Johnson thought that his volume of *Letters* would have been better received if Samuel Derrick had been better known. He thought that he was quite a good general writer but not much of a poet.
Bishop: You see, that was thrown in just as an insult at the end of the piece, was it not, to Mr Moonman and Mr Meacher?
Watkins: No.
Judge: You seem to have intended this as a literary joke. Do you think that the element of vulgar abuse comes into it?
Watkins Yes. It is a very well-known quotation.

That it was a very well-known quotation did not mean that it was vulgar abuse. But I recognised that the judge had thrown me a lifeline. 'Vulgar abuse' is a legal term of art: such language is not defamatory. I doubt whether I would have picked this up as general knowledge. I knew it because I had spent some six years of my life studying English law. Had I not known it – not realised that the judge was trying to be of substantial help – I might have responded more combatively, even though I had enough sense to treat the judge with some respect.

Nor was this respect feigned. I was astonished at how little of the evidence escaped him. Miss Rouse, for instance, had, through no fault of her own, muddied Islington's Labour waters even more thoroughly, contriving to suggest that Mr Moonman had not resigned but been expelled. Mr Justice Hazan now firmly established from Mr Bishop that he had resigned. Mr Bishop could have cleared this up with Miss Rouse during her evidence, though it is fair to say that his examination-in-chief had been cut off by the judge. Mr Bishop and I were by now again in the thick of the People's Party.

Watkins: I think that the 'hard Left' was a flag of convenience which Mr Meacher flew in 1981, when he was backing Mr Benn. But by 1983 he was rather making his peace with Mr Kinnock. And, indeed, he voted for Mr Kinnock in the election. Is it helpful to go into internal Labour politics, my Lord?

Bishop: No, not at all. But I thought that you accepted earlier in your evidence when being examined by my learned friend [Mr Hartley] that the main reason that Mr Moonman left the party was because of what was going on in the party in Islington?

Watkins: No, I had no knowledge of this whatever. I was not apprised of what was going on in the party in Islington.

Judge: He did not say that, Mr Bishop.

Bishop: I am sorry, my Lord, I thought –

Judge: I think that you may have misunderstood.

Bishop: I may well have done. I will check. So (*addressing the witness*) you say that the only reason that he resigned was this questionnaire?

Watkins: No, I certainly don't say that it was the only reason. It was the proximate cause.

'Proximate cause' seemed to me a good jurisprudential phrase which Mr Justice Hazan, at any rate, would understand and which had the merit of accurately summarising what had happened over Mr Moonman. I was also anxious to establish, in my answer about the 'hard Left', that Mr Meacher was as much a conniving politician as the rest of them. I nevertheless had an odd respect for him.

Watkins: I have always regarded Mr Meacher as a decent man.

Bishop: What do you mean by 'decent' in that respect? A man of integrity?

Watkins: Integrity, yes, integrity.

Bishop: But you disliked him, did you?

Watkins: No.

Bishop: Disliked his views?

Watkins: No, not necessarily. I agree with some of them. I mean, I agree with his views on elections to health authorities, for example. But we don't want to go into that. There are all sorts of views of Mr Meacher's that I agree with.

Mr Bishop was, yet again, trying to push malice, and not making much progress. To the same end, he quoted once more my sentence on Mr Meacher's claims about his father's occupation.

> **Watkins**: Very interesting fact about Mr Meacher, most interesting.
> **Bishop**: Very relevant to the piece that you were writing?
> **Watkins**: Most relevant. No doubt, if I had you by my side when I was writing my articles, they would be much better afterwards.

This piece of cheek on my part was a straight lift of Randolph Churchill, being cross-examined in his successful libel action (the 'hack' case) against the *People*. However, it succeeded in making Mr Bishop cross.

> **Bishop**: This is a serious matter, Mr Watkins.
> **Watkins**: I rather doubt that. I rather doubt whether it is a serious matter.
> **Bishop**: You doubt if it is serious?
> **Watkins**: I doubt whether it is serious.
> **Bishop**: You think that we are here because of one of your little jokes, do you?
> **Watkins**: I think that you are here because you have got into something which you probably wish you had got out of.

Mr Howard told me afterwards that at this point he experienced feelings of apprehension. He thought I had gone too far. I thought so too. Accordingly my final answer was a substitution for what I had originally intended to say, before second thoughts asserted themselves: 'Much ado about nothing, if you ask me.' This was exactly Mr Justice Hazan's view, as he was to express it in his summing-up. But whether he would have welcomed it from me at that stage is another question. Mr Bishop tried again.

> **Bishop**: It was a vicious, nasty thing to do, was it not, Mr Watkins?
> **Watkins**: No.
> **Bishop**: You followed that up with your little joke of the quote from Dr Johnson?
> **Watkins**: Yes.
> **Bishop**: Would you agree that a 'louse' means a 'mean, unpleasant person'? Forget about this particular context of the quote, which you say makes a difference to it. Would you agree that, otherwise, a louse is an unpleasant, mean person?
> **Watkins**: A louse is a louse. It is an insect.
> **Bishop**: And it is also used of people, is it not?
> **Watkins**: Yes, it is. I would never use it.
> **Bishop**: You would never use it?
> **Watkins**: No, but it is used.

Bishop: So you would not say of a person: 'He is a louse.'?

Watkins: No, certainly not, I would not say it. I know that other people say it, but people don't say: 'He is a flea.'

Bishop: Because 'a flea' is not usually used of people in that way.

Watkins: Yes, absolutely. 'A louse' is used as a hostile term and 'a flea' is not. I don't think that this gets you very far.

Bishop: Well, do not worry where it gets me.

At this point learned counsel erroneously thought I was exchanging pleasantries with the reporters in the box below me to the right, and took it upon himself to rebuke me.

Bishop: If you have some asides to make, let us all hear them. I am sure that they are very funny.

Watkins: I am frightfully sorry. What asides?

Judge: He did not say anything.

Bishop: I thought that you said something just now to the reporters below you which the rest of us did not hear, and if I am wrong I apologise.

Watkins: Oh, thank you.

Bishop: Right, I apologise.

It had been an exhausting afternoon for both of us, and perhaps for others as well. In next day's, Saturday's, *Daily Express* there was a long article by Michael O'Flaherty which depicted me favourably and cheered me up greatly.

Monday morning

When we re-assembled on Monday morning Robin Young, who was covering the case for *The Times*, told me that, while I had been given a 'good show', as he put it, in the *Express*, Mr O'Flaherty had by no means reflected the unanimous view of his colleagues on the press benches. This did not strike me as the most helpful thing for Mr Young to say in the circumstances. Mr Bishop began by reverting to my mistake about Mr Moonman's having resigned from the Islington District Health Authority as well as from the Labour Party. This again went to malice – recklessness as to the truth, though it was Mr Moonman, not Mr Meacher, who was involved. The charge of malice, which I considered grotesque, was playing an altogether larger part in Mr Bishop's advocacy that I had anticipated.

Bishop: It is right, is it not, that you have little concern for the facts when you are writing your piece?

Watkins: Not so. Wrong.

Bishop: You said earlier, in answer to one of my questions to you: 'I am quite happy to comment on rumours'?

Watkins: Yes, a rumour is a political fact. A rumour in Westminster is part of the fabric of politics.

Bishop: And you are happy to repeat it?

Watkins: Indeed, yes, making clear that it is a rumour. 'People are saying that Geoffrey Howe is going to get the heave-ho.' Now that is a rumour.

This was the period when the future of the Foreign Secretary was being discussed, as he was thought to have caused offence to the Prime Minister. The woman in the back row of the jury laughed. So did the large, jolly, ginger man sitting next to her. Even the long-haired youth in the front row smiled. I had, over the Saturday and Sunday, consciously decided to try to be more demotic in speech, to talk about the heave-ho rather than the proximate cause. My next noteworthy exchange with Mr Bishop, however, was amusing to the press benches only. The jury understandably did not know what to make of it. It concerned the famous 'Pendennis article' of 1983, which had preceded my own column by over a year. I had forgotten it when I wrote my column.

Bishop: It was by Mr Hillmore. Is that right?

Watkins: Yes.

Bishop: But when you came to write your article in 1984, you must have remembered that it had appeared, what you were putting in your article about Mr Meacher?

Watkins: No, I didn't. Oddly enough, I didn't. I just remembered my conversation with Mr Howard.

Bishop: Of 14 months earlier?

Watkins: Yes. The conversation with Mr Howard was rather more memorable than a paragraph by Mr Hillmore.

Monday 23 May was a particularly well-attended day. Not only friends and colleagues from the *Observer* were present, but Frank Johnson of the *Sunday Telegraph*, and Christopher Silvester and Richard Ingrams of *Private Eye*. Mr Ingrams was standing next to Mr Johnson at the back of the court and kept up a running commentary on the proceedings. Mr Silvester was sitting in the press box and laughed loudly at this sally, later reprinting it in *Private Eye*. The *Eye* referred to Mr Hillmore as 'Peter Pisspoor', under which name he made frequent appearances. After this diversion, Mr Bishop came to the crux of the case, and quoted again the sentence – of which I was by now as sick as I was of the louse and the flea – about Mr Meacher liking to claim that he was the son of an agricultural labourer.

Bishop: Now you agree, do you not, that that statement is untrue?

Watkins: No, it is true. That statement is true. Why do you think that I agree that it is untrue?

Bishop: Well –

Watkins: Just answer. May I interrupt you, because what is at issue is whether he claimed it. The statement as it stands I now support. It is a true statement.

Bishop: You stand by that statement?

Watkins: I do.

Bishop: Let us look at it part by part. The sentence starts: 'Mr Meacher likes to claim ...' Is that right?

Watkins: Yes.

Bishop: Now, when you say he 'likes to claim', do you mean that he is given to claiming or he frequently claims?

Watkins: He finds it convenient to state, which is what Mr Meacher told us, after all. He said: 'If someone asked me: "What did your father do?" I say: "He was a farm worker".' This is what Mr Meacher said in his evidence.

In fact Mr Meacher had said this in his proof of evidence, saying something different in his evidence to the court. No matter. If Mr Bishop had intended to show an intention on my part to injure Mr Meacher – hence adducing evidence of malice – he had let the chance slip from his grasp. He had dropped the ball not with my answer but with his question, which should perhaps have been along the lines: 'Likes to claim? Isn't that a form of words which suggests that Mr Meacher is lying to serve his own ends?' I should still have replied in the same way, but counsel would have made his own point first. Mr Bishop returned later to trying to show an intention to injure.

Bishop: An allegation of this kind was likely to injure Mr Meacher, was it not?

Watkins: No, no.

Bishop: You think not?

Watkins: No.

Bishop: You say that you raised it at this time because it was just an interesting little matter that you had at the back of your mind?

Watkins: Yes, a currant in the suet pudding.

The older members of the jury laughed at this. The younger ones perhaps did not know what a suet pudding was. This was one of the homely phrases that I had thought of on the Saturday and Sunday. It had the merit of answering a question which not only Mr Bishop but occasionally, and more dangerously, the judge was prone to ask: what was the purpose of bringing this up in this way, in this article, at this particular time?

Bishop: Something rather spicy in the suet pudding?

Watkins: I said: 'A currant in the suet pudding.'

Bishop: Even if there is any excuse for raising it in 1983, that has disappeared completely by November 1984, has it not?

Watkins: I don't need an excuse for mentioning a Labour politician. What do you mean by 'excuse'? If I choose to write about Michael Meacher or Roy Hattersley or Neil Kinnock or Geoffrey Howe or Margaret Thatcher, I don't need an excuse for it.

Bishop: No.

Watkins: Well, thank you.

This was sheer bluster on my part which, however, went unrebuked by the judge. Mr Bishop tried to recover.

Bishop: But this particular part was totally irrelevant?

Watkins: Oh no, it wasn't irrelevant. It was a little aside.

Bishop: A little aside to give it a little spice?

Watkins: A currant in the suet pudding.

We next embarked on the question of whether Mr Meacher's father had or had not been an accountant. I said I had already explained that I knew he had trained as an accountant and suffered a nervous breakdown but that I had decided to call him an accountant.

Bishop: Which is false, is it not?

Watkins: Well, when is an accountant not an accountant? Inasmuch as he was anything, he was as much an accountant as he was a farm worker, because it does not seem to me that he could have been a very good farm worker ... What I knew about him was that he started off to train as an accountant and had suffered a nervous breakdown. And I didn't want to bring in his nervous breakdown. It is Mr Meacher who has dragged his father through the Law Courts, not me.

This was another line which had occurred to me over the weekend. Nor was it produced for effect merely. I reprobated Mr Meacher's description of his father as 'inadequate' and a 'dependent person'. Mr Bishop then proceeded to whether Mr Meacher had or had not retired. As I have explained, the hypothetical sequence ' ... rich accountant ... City man ... retired to enjoy himself on the family farm ... ancestral estates ...', which had never occurred to Mr Howard or me before the case began, now assumed greater and greater importance to Mr Meacher's cause as the trial went on.

Bishop: He did not retire, did he?

Watkins: Yes, he did. If you go to bed and say: 'I'm retiring to bed for the night,' it does not mean that you are going to spend the rest of your life in bed.

Monday afternoon

We adjourned for lunch. I went to El Vino's, did not talk to anyone, and had mineral water and a sandwich. I was losing weight rapidly. After the adjournment, Mr Bishop returned to the topic of Mr Meacher senior's retirement.

Bishop: I have suggested to you that 'retired' to work is the incorrect word to use because it gave a false impression and you disagreed, because you said that you 'retired' to bed.

Watkins: Yes.

Bishop: But saying that someone who at the age of 18 did a short course of training and then went off to a farm, that he 'retired to the farm'?

Watkins: Yes, he retired to the farm. He went off to the farm. He rusticated himself.

Mr Bishop started going round the houses once again, on the 'relevance' of Mr Meacher's claim that his father was a farm worker.

Bishop: That was relevant?

Watkins: Yes, indeed. It is relevant to know that an MP says his father was a farm worker when he wasn't a farm worker. That is a relevant piece of information. It is not relevant that the father suffered a nervous breakdown.

Bishop: It is relevant also to know that he claims his father is a farm worker, when in fact he was an accountant?

Watkins: He was an accountant (failed).

Bishop: A failed accountant?

Watkins: A failed accountant. He tried to become an accountant and gave up.

Mr Bishop read the passage yet again, and came to the line about 'matters not, as the barristers say'. In his opening speech he had doubted whether barristers said it.

Watkins: Yes, I remember who the barrister was who kept saying: 'It matters not,' if you are interested.

Bishop: Well –

Watkins: Because you said that barristers didn't say it and I remember the barrister who kept saying it.

    Bishop: Perhaps you would like to tell us whether it is a barrister who is practising in the near or distant past?

    Watkins: He is a member of the House of Lords (*Laughter*).

The peer was Lord Wigoder. The case to which I was referring was the unsuccessful Official Secrets Act prosecution in 1971 of the *Sunday Telegraph*, Jonathan Aitken and others, where one of the defending counsel had been Basil Wigoder, QC.

    Bishop: Well, we will not ask for any more details. 'But this by the way ...'?

    Watkins: Yes.

    Bishop: 'By the way' in the sense of 'Oh, by the way, have you heard ...?'

    Watkins: Yes. You are probably too young to remember Max Miller, but he used to say –

At least three members of the jury perked up.

    Bishop: You flatter –

    Watkins: 'Here's a funny thing, here's a funny thing.' Here's a funny little thing about Mr Meacher. That is a 'by the way'.

    Bishop: Funny little thing?

    Watkins: Yes, this is a little account about Mr Meacher.

    Bishop: A little bit of gossip about Mr Meacher?

    Watkins: It is not gossip, certainly not gossip at all. It was gone into very thoroughly by Mr Howard and me.

Mr Bishop once more took me over my method of writing my column and the role of Mr Howard. He was like a child asking for a familiar and loved story to be told yet again. Learned friends said sapiently that he was on a 'fishing expedition', hoping for some indiscretion.

    Bishop: Let us go on to that, then, shall we? Having written the article in longhand –

    Watkins: Yes.

    Bishop: You then took it to Mr Howard to look at?

    Watkins: No, I explained this already. Mr Howard, although he can read my writing if he tries, does not look at my article in longhand at all. I write in longhand.

    Bishop: Sorry, you did. You are quite right.

    Watkins: Thank you.

    Bishop: It is typed up and then Mr Howard saw it?

    Watkins: It is typed. I do not know what you mean by 'typed up'.

This was a piece of pedantry by me which succeeded in annoying Mr Bishop and landed him in mild trouble with the judge on the following morning.

> **Bishop**: You know what I mean. You are just being clever, are you not, Mr Watkins? ... What time would you have started writing?
> **Watkins**: My Lord, I did explain my methods of work.
> **Bishop**: Yes, you did. I just want you to repeat that part, if you would.
> **Watkins**: 11 o'clock.
> **Bishop**: About 10 o'clock?
> **Watkins**: 11 o'clock.
> **Bishop**: Thank you. And would you carry on writing it until it is finished?
> **Watkins**: Yes, once I start I carry on writing until it is finished. I would have finished it at about 2 or 2.15.

Mr Ingrams, at the back of the court, asked Mr Johnson whether he had noticed that I seemed to do all my work in the morning.

> **Bishop**: You go out for a quick lunch or something like that?

Mr Howard shook his head vigorously. Mr Ingrams said that learned counsel was trying to imply that I had been drunk in the afternoon.

> **Watkins**: No, no. I go straight in, straight in to the *Observer* office from Islington, where I live.

Mr Justice Hazan concluded the afternoon's proceedings by saying:

> Mr Bishop, as this court sat at 10 o'clock this morning [to hear legal argument about the admissibility of Mr Meacher's proof of evidence], I want to try and help the jury with their arrangements. I think that I will pause there, as far as the evidence is concerned, and invite you to take stock of the situation.

The last eight words cheered me up a lot. The judge obviously thought Mr Bishop was not getting anywhere. Indeed, he had long ceased taking notes.

Tuesday morning

But Mr Bishop had not finished yet. On the following day, Tuesday 24 May, he allowed me to return to the difference between 'typing' and 'typing up'.

Bishop: Mr Watkins, you are usually very meticulous in your use of the English language?

Watkins: I try to be.

Bishop: I am sorry?

Watkins: I try to be.

Bishop: Yes. You point out, for example, that it should be 'type' a letter rather than 'typing it up'.

Watkins: Yes, because typing up suggests that you are –

Bishop: Sorry –

Watkins: No, you just raised it. You have raised this.

Judge: You might let him answer.

Bishop: I am sorry, my Lord.

Watkins: 'Typing up' implies that you have a rough collection of notes and you are typing from the notes. You are typing it up.

Bishop: Yes.

Watkins: 'Typing' means that you are making an exact copy of what is written down.

Bishop: Very well.

Watkins: That is what I mean.

Bishop: I am happy to be corrected in relation to it, Mr Watkins.

Watkins: Not at all, not at all.

Mr Hartley re-examined. He established that I was someone who was prepared to say 'sorry'. He asked whether I had ever been sued for libel before. I said I had not. The re-examination was brief. This, I thought, was a good sign: it established that Mr Bishop had not produced much (or, indeed, anything) to clear up during cross-examination. It was only later that I learnt that Mr Hartley considered me a dangerous witness who had already done our cause enough damage with the jury – and that he wanted to get me out of the box as soon as he could.

13

Mr Howard's Evidence

Lady Bracknell: Untruthful! My nephew Algernon? Impossible! He is an Oxonian.

Oscar Wilde, *The Importance of Being Earnest*

It was part of Mr Howard's function to undo some of the damage which I may have done in the witness-box. I had been not only cheeky to Mr Bishop but hard and unforgiving to Mr Meacher. Why should I, I thought to myself, be compelled to submit to this ignorant and impertinent questioning by a ginger-haired gentleman in a wig?

Mr Meacher's friend

Mr Howard approached the case, not necessarily more humbly, but differently. He had been, he claimed he still was, a friend – anyway, a good political acquaintance – of Mr Meacher's. The industrious, the puritanical, even the prefectorial side of the Labour Member's character was congenial to Mr Howard, whereas to me it was comic when it was not repulsive. As a consequence of these amicable feelings, Mr Howard had tried to settle the action. He considered that he had been frustrated in his endeavours by Sarah Burton. In his evidence he referred to her several times as 'the architect of this action'. Afterwards I ventured the criticism that he had perhaps overdone it and referred to her too often in an uncomplimentary manner. He replied that he would not have done so unless he had thought, as he did, that she had gone down badly with the jury.

Mr Howard was wearing a smart blue suit and a yellow silk tie. After Mr Hartley had established his journalistic credentials, he drew the attention to his own and the *Observer*'s political position.

Richard Hartley, QC: Does it tend to take a slightly left stance than a right stance, or how would you describe it?

Anthony Howard: I would say it is not the Conservative Party's favourite Sunday newspaper.

Hartley: Have you yourself been a member of the Labour Party for some 35 years?

Howard: Yes, I have. I would guess a little longer than Mr Meacher, but I make no point about it. I am a few years older than he is.

Clearly, Mr Howard was saying, this was not a case of a man of the Left persecuted by a newspaper of the Right. He told the court of accepting articles from Mr Meacher at the *New Statesman* and of trying to publish his articles in the *Observer*. He went on to the lunch of September 1983 and the first conversation about Mr Meacher's background.

Hartley: Now, can you go slowly on this, because maybe we will want to take a note. Can you just tell us first of all how that arose?

Howard: I can't say with absolute conviction, because I haven't got a note of the lunch, but my memory is that I said at some stage – it was a very agreeable lunch – 'Come on, Michael, tell me something about your background. What about all these things I read all the time about your being the son of a farm worker?' I ought to say, if it is not a nuisance at this stage, that I had always had a little bit of difficulty with this, because I somehow found it difficult to reconcile what I believed and what I had read with the impression that Michael created. I couldn't quite see how the two blended together.

The judge is put out

Donald Trelford was spending part of the morning in court on his way to Sir Denis Hamilton's memorial service. He turned to me, sitting near to him – I had already completed my evidence – and whispered that the judge was put out. Mr Howard was trying to say what we had both long thought, well before the election for deputy leader in 1983: that Mr Meacher was a poseur.

Mr Justice Hazan: What do you mean by that? What impression are you referring to?

Howard: Well, I just had difficulty – and this is a delicate area, my Lord – I just thought that –

Judge: By anything that he said or did, what impression did he convey to you, rightly or wrongly?

Howard: Well, if you had said to me – he has been dead many years – that Ernest Bevin was the son of a farm worker, I would have had no difficulty in accepting it at all. He was a rugged individual as Foreign Secretary. You know, he spoke with a West Country accent and he looked like the son of a farm worker. Michael,

I am afraid, in my eyes – maybe I was wrong – was not so obviously the product of that background. That is all I can say.

This seemed to satisfy the judge. Anyway he did not pursue the matter. Mr Howard went on to give an account of Mr Meacher's telling him about the migration to London, the nervous breakdown, the return to the farm and the fear of thunderstorms. He had assumed, from the bath in the kitchen and the outside lavatory (by now, though Mr Howard did not say so, as much standard props of the case as the louse and the flea), that Mr Meacher, invalid father notwithstanding, had been brought up in a farm worker's cottage. The house at Berkhamsted did not impinge on him until after his wireless interview with Mr Meacher in Summer 1985.

Hartley: Mr Howard, once he explained about the family farm and that his father had gone up to London to try to become an accountant, and his other answers, did that then fit in with the impression you had of Mr Meacher?

In my own evidence I had compared Mr Meacher with Roy Hattersley, whose father was a local government clerk who had previously been a Roman Catholic priest. Mr Howard adopted this comparison.

Howard: Yes. It is very difficult. I mean, it solved everything for me. Now, suddenly, everything fell into place which I had had some difficulty with before. If I can give the analogy that has been used before – maybe it is not germane; stop me if it isn't – but when I found out from Roy Hattersley that his father had been a Roman Catholic priest, that explained to me why he was so well-read. Hattersley has got an extremely well-read mind. Obviously there were books at home that a former Roman Catholic priest would have and that normally, in the 1920s and 1930s, a local government clerk would not have, which was the job Mr Hattersley senior took after leaving the priesthood on getting married. It is a snobbish, difficult area, but there is something there that you suddenly see: 'Ah, that fits. I now understand.'

The judge is helpful

Mr Hartley then turned to the by now famous 'Pendennis article' by Mr Hillmore. This led to a helpful intervention by Mr Justice Hazan.

Judge: And, well, I hope I can say quite clearly – it appears that a different interpretation may be given to almost any group of words – but it would seem, would it not, Mr Howard (though I appreciate you are not responsible for this article, in the sense that you did not write it), but it would certainly seem that the writer is making quite clear that this assertion of Mr Meacher and his supporters about coming from working-class stock was a last-ditch attempt to win support? That must have been to win support in the deputy leadership election?

Howard: Yes.

Judge: And then he blatantly, well, he quite bluntly says: 'It's nonsense. Meacher's father was not a farm worker or agricultural labourer, as is often claimed.' So he is quite baldly asserting –?

Howard: Yes ...

Judge: Now, we have heard what Mr Meacher himself has had to say about this article. In view of the fact that the article embraces his supporters as well, after this was published on Sunday 2 October 1983, did you, in the sense of the paper, did the *Observer* receive any complaints or comments from any of his supporters for the deputy leadership, saying: 'We have never claimed any such thing on his behalf,' or anything like that?

Howard: Nothing at all, not a squeak.

Hartley: Not from Mr Meacher and not from his supporters. It is fair to point out that Mr Meacher said he never read the [Pendennis] article.

Judge: That is why I thought it fair to ask about the supporters, since they are included in the wording as well.

Howard: I mean, Mr Meacher had a very active campaign manager. Maybe I used the term loosely, but we heard, I think, from him about a gentleman called Mr Alan Meale, who is now a Labour MP. Mr Alan Meale, in my view, was the main propagator of all these exaggerated claims about how he was going to win, and obviously, if Mr Meacher did not read this, Mr Meale could have written and said: 'This is a very damaging thing. We have never claimed working-class stock or anything like that.' But not a squeak came from anybody.

Perhaps it was a small point in Mr Meacher's (or Mr Meale's) favour that by then it was too late, because the election had come and gone, and Mr Meacher had lost. Mr Hartley came to Mr Howard's conversation with me.

Hartley: Did you tell Mr Watkins about your lunch meeting with Mr Meacher in September 1983?

Howard: Yes, I certainly told Mr Watkins, long before I told Mr Hillmore. We are engaged in roughly the same vineyard and when he comes into the office we frequently have a chat ...

Hartley: When you read that article, did you have any reason to

think that anything there was either false or defamatory of Mr
Meacher?

Howard: It didn't cross my mind.

Mr Howard confirmed what I had said in my evidence about the
disagreement between us over whether it was Mr Meacher senior's
father's farm or his brother's farm, and about our compromise on 'the
family farm'. He confirmed also my difficulty about mentioning the
nervous breakdown.

Hartley: During the next week and the weeks that followed, up to
Christmas, first three or four weeks of January 1985, did anybody –
either Mr Meacher himself or anybody on his behalf – tell you that
any objection was taken to anything in that article?

Howard: Not a soul.

Mr Howard is bewildered

Mr Howard told the judge, answering his question, that he had received
Mr Meacher's article before the solicitors' letter.

Hartley: What was your reaction on reading this letter, having, as
you have already told us, received earlier in the week this letter
from Mr Meacher enclosing an article for publication?

Howard: Total bewilderment. I couldn't believe my eyes.

Mr Howard added that at first he did not take the solicitors' letter with
'tremendous seriousness' because he could not believe that any 'rational
human being' would behave in this way. The only issue was whether he
had made the claim that his father had been a farm worker. Mr Howard
accepted his word that he had not, though he told him that he had been
remiss in allowing the impression to be created. He persuaded Mr
Meacher, after some discussion, to drop the Moonman question. The
agreement that I should 'weave in' a correction or apology (at which I
later jibbed) was proof of the dropping of Moonman.

Howard: It can't be true that even he could possibly have foreseen
that in the body of copy of 1,250 words the whole history of regional
and district health authorities, the role of Mr Moonman, going on to
a reference to Mr Meacher's own family background – there is no
way it could be done. It is just impossible.

Hartley: So the weaving-in that you were suggesting that you
hoped Alan Watkins would do would be solely relating to the
background?

Howard: It is the proof that at the end of the lunch we had come to an agreement ... which pushed Moonman out of the way ... And, of course, what I have learnt in this case – and I thought it was very revealing, and I am not sure it may not have been one of the most revealing sentences in the whole case, when Miss Burton told us that she had strongly advised against Mr Meacher's having lunch with me and that she had said, no doubt as a joke – but sometimes jokes can be revealing – 'If he makes even a suggestion from the wine list, do not agree to it.' So that was really why this agreement slipped away, in my view. And it was never intended by Miss Burton, whom I regard as the architect of this action, that we ever should reach an agreement.

Mr Howard proceeded to excoriate Miss Burton's note-taking and to deny that he had ever offered or even mentioned £2,000 during the February 1985 lunch, as sums of money (certainly of that size) lay outside his sphere of authority as deputy editor. Mr Justice Hazan then asked a question, interrupting counsel for the defendants.

Judge: I am so sorry, Mr Hartley, but you will appreciate why I need to know this for the purpose of my note. (*To the witness*) Are you or are you not saying that any concluded agreement had been reached between you at that lunch about what was to happen?

Howard: No, no concluded agreement at all. We both left – and here Michael and I are at one; I think he said so – and my mood walking down Soho to get a bus or something was: 'We have now the basis of an agreement.' But no more than that, one reason quite clearly being that he would be entitled to see how we were going to put in the correction. And, if it was in the body of the article, he would clearly be entitled to see the whole article.

Judge: So it was subject to his approval of the correction?

Howard: Absolutely.

Mr Howard thought he had admitted too much at this stage. But it was difficult to see what else he could have said. In truth his evidence did not demonstrate – and could not have demonstrated – 'accord and satisfaction' but, rather, that he, I and the *Observer* had, initially, gone out of our way to try to accommodate Mr Meacher. Miss Burton (with whom I had no dealings, and on whom I did not set eyes until the trial) was more difficult to satisfy. However, it was by keeping in the defence of accord and satisfaction that we forced Miss Burton into the box, where she did not (Mr Howard at any rate considered) create a good impression.

On two occasions during my own evidence I thought I was losing the sympathy of the judge. The first was when I said that, if it had been considered proper to send out the questionnaire (as I did not consider it to be), the correct originating source was not Mr Meacher but the Labour

Party in Walworth Road. Mr Justice Hazan could not grasp the distinction I was trying to make between Labour as a national organisation and the party's front-bench spokesman in Parliament. The second occasion was when I recast the words complained of to involve Roy Hattersley and his father, the former priest, rather than Mr Meacher and *his* father. I somehow sensed that the judge did not like it, though he did not say anything.

Mr Howard adopted the Hattersley analogy, in the context of something which also caused the judge some unease: his saying that Mr Meacher had somehow never struck him as the son of a farm worker. Later in his evidence, Mr Howard was asked by the judge why he had consented to interview Mr Meacher, who by now was joined in legal combat with the *Observer*, in the Summer of 1985. This was the occasion when Mr Howard settled, or thought he had settled, the action for £500 and a further apology, though it is difficult to see what the apology could have said.[1] Mr Hartley excluded this agreement, or near-agreement, from our case.

Judge: Mr Howard, you have criticised Mr Meacher for sending an article to you to be published just before his solicitors write to say he is probably going to sue for libel, saying that you find that an incomprehensible attitude. And yet, here you are in the Summer, in August 1985, after all this has started, when you are being sued for libel, cheerfully interviewing him. Is it not a little bit odd both ways?

Howard: It is a nice debating point, my Lord. But it is not actually, if I may say so, quite right, in that I, in my freelance capacity, am an employee of the BBC. The BBC said to me –

Judge: So you are wearing another hat?

Howard: I am wearing another hat, and the BBC say to me: 'Look, would you like to do "Talking Politics" during the Summer recess?' I say: 'Yes, I am not going on holiday. I can fit it in.' They then make the approach to Mr Meacher. They find out, they choose, whom I am going to interview. I am just a hired hand.

Hartley: Did you have a perfectly friendly conversation with Mr Meacher, during the interview and indeed after?

Howard: Perfectly friendly, yes indeed. I thought it was the best of the five interviews I did that Summer, and I think the BBC thought the same.

Hartley: And you walked around the garden afterwards?

Howard: Walked around the garden afterwards, and I took the opportunity to say: 'Come on, one last try, really.'

Hartley: Well, I think that is beyond any date of agreement. Although I would be happy for that to be gone into, I think it is probably for my learned friend.

[1] See Chapter 5.

Mr Hartley concluded by asking Mr Howard his view of the questionnaire. He thought it was a 'pretty shabby episode' and re-emphasised the point which I had made: that no one had rallied to its defence at the time except Mr Meacher.

Mr Bishop rose to cross-examine. He had observed that Mr Howard had taken his own file of documents with him into the box. Mr Howard said he was 'getting on in years, you know' – at the time of the trial he was 54 – and it was 'a help to have actually the thing in front of you'.

On taking notes

Gordon Bishop: Difficult to remember details of what happened a long time ago?

Howard: No, not necessarily. I mean, I can remember details vividly. You know what the difference is. But on things like dates, you suddenly find, I think: was that 1984 or 1985? It is quite different from remembering the atmosphere of a conversation and what was said.

Bishop: The atmosphere of a conversation, yes. Did you make any notes at the time?

Howard: No, I didn't make any notes. It has never been my custom, unlike some journalists, who come back from lunch and spend the whole of the afternoon writing up an account of the lunch; and it is a profitable practice, I suppose, a conscientious one. My first editor always did it, Alastair Hetherington. I have never done it, and there is no exception in this case. I have always said, OK, I can take on board what was interesting of it, and I don't make any notes.

Bishop: The two lunches you had, you did not make any notes during them?

Howard: No. Nor did Michael.

Bishop: When I say the two lunches you had, I mean the two lunches with Mr Meacher.

Howard: Quite. No, neither of us. I would have thought it was a very unfriendly act. We once had a Cabinet Minister come to lunch at the *Observer*, and he brought his Press Officer with him, who started getting out a notebook and writing everything down. It does not seem to me to be civilised behaviour.

Bishop: So you took no notes of any of the matters you have given evidence about today. Is that right?

Howard: Perfectly right.

Judge: We are learning some interesting things.

Mr Justice Hazan was clearly referring not to Mr Howard's omission to take notes but to his recollection of the lunch with the Minister. Libel barristers are obsessed with note-taking by journalists. Partly this is because of genuine concern with the law of evidence. Partly it is because of a desire to embarrass a defendant or a witness. But partly it is because of ignorance about the way in which journalists – certainly political journalists – do their work. Barristers seem to think, or anyway choose to think, that journalists perform their tasks much as police detectives perform theirs. But, as Mr Howard said, a journalist entertaining a politician at a restaurant and writing things down in a notebook would rightly be thought guilty of uncivilised behaviour. (A meeting, at a Minister's request, in his own room raises different considerations.) A journalist entertaining a politician at his club and taking out a notebook would be reprimanded by the secretary. The lobby correspondents themselves prohibit the taking of notes within the lobbies and corridors of Westminster.

The practice of circulating accounts of a lunch or other meeting raises different considerations again. It has always seemed to me a betrayal of confidence, in that the politician believes he is talking to the journalist and not to the journalist's colleagues in the office. As a habit, it seems to me to be the reverse of conscientious. The maintenance of a private file (such as some journalists, notably gossip columnists, compile) is different from this. It may be seen by other members of the column's 'team', if there is one, but it is not an internal office memorandum. Even so, I think it is a sneaky practice.

Bishop on pleadings

Mr Bishop went on to cross-examine Mr Howard on the pleadings – the statement of the case, and its defence, expressed in lawyers' language. This also seems to me a sneaky practice, though it is allowed by judges. Even legally qualified witnesses and defendants such as Mr Howard and myself are unfamiliar with the technicalities of pleading. We certainly were in this case. I escaped relatively lightly. When Mr Bishop reproached me over not amending our defence until 1987, I replied that I was not responsible for what our legal advisers did. He was more persistent with Mr Howard – who made the same reply as I had – partly, I surmise, because he knew that Mr Howard was a qualified barrister, whereas he did not seem to realise that I was one too. But Mr Bishop did not do himself much good with Mr Justice Hazan. He made a technical point about the pleadings. Mr Justice Hazan was growing impatient.

Judge: I think that you have got better points than that, have you not?

Bishop: My Lord, I have, yes ...

But Mr Bishop went on, reading the pleadings about the correction which was offered and the different one which in fact appeared. The pleadings went on to say that Mr Meacher had misinformed Mr Howard about his never having claimed to be the son of a farm worker.

> **Howard**: Just before you leave, Mr Bishop, as you put it to me, it is perfectly true that that is part of our case, and it has to be part of our case. But can I tell you what would have happened otherwise? I would have been perfectly content to leave that correction and that retraction on the record, without this case, and I will tell you why: because, if I have to err, I prefer to err on the side of generosity, and we have been driven into making this claim by your persistence in bringing the action.

This was correct. If Mr Meacher had taken his costs after the 1985 correction, I should not have examined the files on that wet Friday afternoon and decided, from the evidence of the interviews with and articles about him, that he had indeed claimed to be the son of a farm worker. Mr Howard said that this had been the hope. Mr Bishop ploughed on about whether there had been a concluded agreement (Mr Howard had prevailed upon him to substitute 'concluded' for 'binding').

> **Judge**: It may be a matter of law what the point pleaded is, but you may rest assured I have more than grasped the point, Mr Bishop, long ago.

The court adjourned for lunch. I deliberately stayed away from Mr Howard. We were both conscientious about not speaking to each other when we were in the witness-box. Obeying the rules made life easier.

The afternoon's proceedings were less technical. A good deal of ground was traversed again. Mr Howard said that he took in the Meachers' address in the High Street, Berkhamsted (as opposed to an address at or near a farm) after the broadcast interview rather than at the lunch: 'I don't go about my social occasions in the same way as my professional occasions of doing a radio interview.'

> **Bishop**: But you got the impression from what Mr Meacher told you during that lunch – well, he told you that his father had worked on his father's farm?
>
> **Howard**: That is right, yes. I am not sure about the 'had'. I think he said: 'My father worked on his father's farm.' What I am saying is that it is rather odd, it seems to me, to say that you are the son of a farm worker if, through the whole of your youth, your father had not been anywhere near a farm. And that is the case with Mr Meacher. I might just as well say, if I was applying for a job, let us say, at the National Secular Society or the British Humanist Association, that I was the son of a schoolmaster, when in fact my father was a

schoolmaster before I was born. When I was brought up he was a clergyman, but it might suit me to put 'schoolmaster' if I was looking for a job.

With this answer Mr Howard compendiously implied disingenuousness on Mr Meacher's part and both frankness and paternal respectability on his own. The cross-examination then turned to whether Mr Howard had any suspicion that I had libelled Mr Meacher. He had already said he had not. He had probably laughed on reading about the louse and the flea. Mr Bishop ploughed the accountancy furrow.

Bishop: Why an accountant? An accountant is wrong, is it not, on any basis whatsoever? Whatever the defendants' case may be, Mr Meacher's father was never an accountant.

Howard: Mr Meacher's father went to be an accountant. He went to London to become an accountant, and it is perfectly true that he never qualified as an accountant.

Mr Howard added that, in any case, he did not see that it was defamatory to call a man's father an accountant. It was obviously technically untrue to write that he was an accountant. He never qualified. But, Mr Howard said, if he saw an estate agent, did he know whether he was a qualified estate agent? The person who built the new *Observer* building across Chelsea Bridge was always referred to as an architect, whereas in fact he was a developer.

Bishop: ... You knew also that it was wrong to say that he had retired to the family farm?

Howard: Well, I am not sure about that. I mean, a lot of weight is put on this word 'retired', as if he had made a pile in the City and then sort of went to live in the country. I am afraid I find that quite incredible. But in fact he did, in my view, retire because he had proved to be honourably ineligible for the struggle of life.

The last seven words were a quotation from Cyril Connolly's *Enemies of Promise*,[2] describing the young Lord Home (then Lord Dunglass) as a boy. Mr Howard was proud of summoning it up from his mind at this point. Mr Bishop proceeded to bare the confusion at the core of Mr Meacher's case: he could not remember having told Mr Howard virtually everything about his family background at the first lunch, in September 1983. If Mr Meacher's recollection was correct, neither my column of November 1984 nor – even more telling – the 'Pendennis' paragraph of October 1983 made sense: Peter Hillmore and I must have made up the story, or derived it from some source or sources other than Mr Howard. Of course, we had

2 (1938, Penguin edn 1961), 245.

not. Mr Howard and I each tried to explain the course of events, time and again.

We started on Wednesday with Mr Howard still in the box. There was more from Mr Bishop on the pleadings in the case and on Mr Howard's qualifications as a barrister.

Bishop: Mr Howard, you know, do you not, that a vital part of the case that has been put forward on the defendants' behalf is that there was a binding agreement settling this matter?

Howard: We went into that yesterday.

Bishop: Yes. You know that, do you not?

Howard: Well, I am prepared to accept it from you. I am not an expert on pleadings.

Bishop: Mr Howard, I would have been willing to forgive you in relation to that if it wasn't for the fact – and you have admitted it – that you were called to the Bar.

Hartley: My learned friend should not say: 'I am willing to forgive' people. It is not the sort of comment that is helpful in this case. He is being cross-examined, of course, on pleadings which have been drafted by lawyers, albeit on instructions. But really as to whether there was an agreement or not, that is a matter of law for your Lordship to decide.

Judge: That is true. Of course you are entitled to cross-examine about any difference between the evidence and the pleadings, in so far as you think it may assist you on an issue of credibility. But the question whether there is a concluded agreement or not is finally a matter of law for me to decide.

In the end Mr Justice Hazan decided that there was no such agreement. But Mr Howard had been an impressive witness, conveying competence on his own part, confusion on Mr Meacher's and intransigence on Miss Burton's. Mr Bishop could not leave alone my description of Mr Meacher senior as an accountant, my statement that he 'retired' to the family farm and Mr Howard's qualification as a barrister. All three were combined in the last part of his cross-examination.

Bishop: You were satisfied that the rest of the sentence was correct?

Howard: The rest of?

Bishop: The rest of that sentence: ' ... though I understand that his father was an accountant who retired to work on the family farm because the life suited him better.'

Howard: Yes, we have been round the bushes on that, you and I. I don't think there is any point in doing it any further.

Bishop: What is your occupation, Mr Howard?

Howard: My occupation? I am a journalist.

Bishop: You are a journalist, are you? If someone asked you what you did, you would say a journalist?

Howard: I would say a journalist, yes.

Bishop: Why, if that part of the article is correct, when you are asked what you do, do you not describe yourself as a barrister who retired to journalism because the life suited you better?

Howard: I really don't think there is any point in answering that question, my Lord.

Mr Justice Hazan indicated concurrence. Mr Bishop sat down in what appeared to be a fit of pique, breathing heavily through his nose, slamming shut his file, and making a great clatter with his pens. Mr Hartley asked one question only in his re-examination. In this question he took something of a risk.

Hartley: Mr Howard, there is only one matter. You were cross-examined about the use of the word 'accountant' to describe a person who had gone to London to train as an accountant and had become an articled clerk. You mentioned architects and the like. Are there different kinds of accountants, in your mind?

Howard: Well, there are. I have never known, when dealing with my tax affairs, whether the man who rings me up with what seem to be rather trivial questions for a large firm of accountants – I have no idea whether he is an accountant or not. He may well be an articled clerk. He is dealing directly with me as a client. In fact I have got a suspicion, oddly enough, that he isn't an accountant.

Counsel had taken a risk, and the witness had turned up trumps.

14

Mr Clarke's Evidence

Mr Justice Cocklecarrot: Is it necessary to call all these people?
Mr Bastin Hermitage: I believe so, m'lud.
Cocklecarrot: But surely they cannot all be connected with the case. For instance, I see here the name of a Cabinet Minister.

J.B. Morton, *The Case of the Twelve Red-Bearded Dwarfs*

In May 1988 Kenneth Clarke was Chancellor of the Duchy of Lancaster and Minister for Trade and Industry. He had joined the Cabinet in 1985 as Paymaster-General and Minister for Employment. In 1984, when he had a dispute with Mr Meacher about the questionnaire and the introduction of a party caucus system into health authorities, he was Minister of Health, outside the Cabinet. It was later in 1988 that Margaret Thatcher split the Department of Health and Social Security, reverting to an older pattern (as she did also by detaching Transport from the Environment). Mr Clarke became Minister of Health in the Cabinet, in which capacity he was rarely absent from the nation's television screens, at one minute pronouncing on nurses' pay, at another reassuring the public about the consumption of eggs.

Even before this, he was quite well-known, being one of those Ministers who are forever popping up on television to announce 'initiatives' of one kind or another. Indeed, despite a chubbiness of appearance and a negligence of dress, he was a politician who was regarded as being 'good on television'. He was moderate in his language and reasonable in his views. These were attributes which he shared with Sir Geoffrey Howe (another barrister who, like Mr Clarke, quite lacked legal pomposity). But he had, or appeared to have, more life in him than Sir Geoffrey.

Accordingly, he was something of a catch for our side. Though his evidence concerned health authorities and the Moonman allegations – matters which were tedious for the reporters, difficult for the judge and, I imagine, incomprehensible for the jury – his appearance lent weight to our case. It was not so much that he was a Cabinet Minister as that he was a television performer, even if in a small way of business. Beside him, Mr Meacher was obscure. He was probably better-known than Mr

Howard as well. We were anxious not to lose Mr Clarke. He was, with the permission of the judge, fitted into my evidence on Monday 23 May. He went into the witness-box having travelled down from his constituency.

Mr Clarke explains

He began by explaining to Mr Hartley the method of appointment of members of health authorities. As Minister of Health he was responsible for the appointment of all members of regional health authorities. In theory they were the Secretary of State's appointments (Norman Fowler at that time). In practice they were his. He appointed all the members of the regional authorities but only the chairmen of the district authorities. The appropriate regional authorities would appoint the other members of the district authorities. He did not have complete discretion in his appointments to regional authorities. Certain people had in effect to represent certain interests. There had to be so many people from local government, from the trade unions and from the medical and nursing professions.

> **Richard Hartley, QC:** Can you tell us, please, how important, if at all, the political stance was of a potential member?
> **Kenneth Clarke, QC, MP:** Well, it was something that I would be advised of, when we were looking at a list of possible people, if it was known what their politics were. But certainly I did put the ability of the person in question first, whether I thought he or she was up to the job, before I paid any regard to their politics; and many people I appointed without having the first idea of what their political affiliation was.

He had reappointed the chairman of the Anglia Regional Health Authority. He was a local man, the chairman of Norwich City Football Club, and he had been a very active member of the Labour Party. Indeed, he had been one of David (later Lord) Ennals's right-hand men in the Norwich Labour Party. Lord Ennals, a former Labour MP for Norwich North, had originally appointed him when he was Secretary of State for Health and Social Services in a previous Labour Government. Mr Clarke reappointed him because he was a 'very good chairman' who had a 'lot of clout' in his area and 'ran his authority well'.

> **Hartley:** In November 1984 did you come to learn about a questionnaire that came from Mr Michael Meacher?
> **Clarke:** Yes, I did, because I began to receive copies of it. What happened was that actually – in plain sealed envelopes, as it were, with the covering letter – copies of the questionnaires began to turn up at the House of Commons addressed to me. I can't remember

exactly how many, but I got about three which I assumed had come from irate members of the authorities who had received them and decided to send them anonymously to the Minister.

Mr Hartley then read out the extract from *Hansard* which is given in Chapter 3. He concluded his reading by asking Mr Clarke what his general view was about the sending out of the questionnaire.

Justification and fair comment

Gordon Bishop: My Lord, I am not sure that Mr Clarke's view of it is of great assistance to anybody in court. Either it has to be proved to have been shabby, as a justification, or it has to be Mr Watkins's fair comment, and what Mr Clarke thinks about it is –

Mr Justice Hazan: There are two issues – are there not? – justification and fair comment. How do you put the expression of this witness's views?

Hartley: My Lord, the difficulty we are in is this: Mr Meacher, in his cross-examination, agreed with me that 'admittedly shabby' was a comment. It is fair to say that Mr Watkins, in cross-examination, by my learned friend, said: 'No, it is a statement of fact.' Obviously this is going to be for the jury to decide, whether that is comment or fact or a mixture of the two. In so far as there is comment, it is, in my submission, perfectly proper for me to ask this witness what his view of this questionnaire was, to see if he had the same view of it.

Judge: Well, have you not really covered it by that extract?

Hartley: My Lord, I have, and I am happy with that.

Apart from Mr Meacher's – or Mr Bishop's – waiver of privilege and the consequential recall of the plaintiff,[1] perhaps the most interesting aspect of the case from a *legal* viewpoint was whether 'admittedly shabby' was fact, comment or a mixture of both. In my cross-examination, as Mr Hartley correctly and fairly stated, I had differed from him and said it was fact. Mr Bishop nevertheless made much of what I had said to Mr Howard and Mr Millinship when we first received the letter from Miss Burton. This was that the author, whoever he (I did not then know it was a she) was, did not seem to understand the law of fair comment. Mr Bishop later made several derisory references to my supposed expertise on the law of fair comment. I said that 'admittedly shabby', as applied to 'episode', was fact partly out of perversity but partly also because I was – and still am – in some doubt. Afterwards, when I retailed the episode to him over a glass of wine in El Vino's, Louis Blom-Cooper, QC, gently

---

[1] See Chapters 8 and 18.

rebuked me for mental sloppiness. 'Admittedly shabby' was, he said, clearly comment.

I am not so sure. Whether a political episode is or is not shabby is clearly a matter of opinion. Whether even a coat is shabby is often a matter of opinion: a garment which is decent to me may be shabby to someone who is of a dressier disposition. But whether a political episode is admittedly shabby is, it seems to me, a matter of fact; just as whether a coat is admittedly shabby is a matter of fact likewise. We are saying: the vast majority agree that the episode (or the coat) in question is shabby. It is a matter of general admission on all sides. We are stating a fact about the state of public opinion. Mr Hartley went on to quote Mr Clarke's remarks, reported not in *Hansard* but in a contemporary news-story, that Mr Meacher was conducting 'a shabby little political exercise'. He was referring both to the questionnaire and to Mr Meacher's wish to introduce a caucus system into health authorities, as demonstrated by the document entitled 'Guidance for Labour Members of Health Authorities'.

The fugitive paper

This paper made fugitive appearances in the case, being wholeheartedly embraced by neither side. It had been 'disclosed' – it was one of the 'agreed documents'. But it was not in the 'bundle' referred to by counsel in conducting the case. When, just before my evidence, I asked Mr Nathan why this was so, he replied that Mr Hartley had 'taken it out'. I decided, off my own bat, to put it back in again, for it appeared to me that he had thrown away a valuable piece of ammunition. Accordingly I referred to it in my cross-examination by Mr Bishop.

This perplexed the judge, who became irritated not with me but with Mr Hartley and, especially, Mr Bishop. Mr Justice Hazan, following the intervention of a weekend, and still a lack of any proper explanation from either counsel as to the document's provenance and status, was not content to leave the matter alone. Little escaped the acute judge. After Mr Clarke had told how he had received copies of the questionnaire at the House, he intervened.

Judge: Did you get something else as well that is not in here?

Hartley: Yes, my Lord, I think in fact he has got a copy of it in the –

Clarke: A note called 'Guidance for Labour Members of Health Authorities' that circulated at the same time.

Hartley: That is the thing, my Lord, that Mr Watkins referred to. It has been disclosed and it is not in the bundle.

Clarke: My comments arose from putting them together. It is obviously a difference of opinion between myself and Michael, no more than that ...

Mr Clarke referred to Mr Meacher as 'Michael' throughout and, like Mr Howard, appeared to hold him in warm personal regard.

> **Clarke:** ... but I did not want, myself, the health authorities to start organising themselves on party political lines, in party political groups. Whatever their party political views, I thought they should put them on one side and act as a body, once they were responsible for a health authority for their region or district.
>
> **Judge:** Well, now, Mr Clarke, that is what I would like you to help us about. There was a time, was there not, when men and women of good will, of all political persuasions and none, were prepared to sink their political preferences by serving on boards or other public bodies for the benefit of the public at large? Now, has the appointment of health authorities now become so politicised that all that has gone by the board, by which I mean – and you will appreciate I am not trying to make any party points – does each party try to get its own nominees on?
>
> **Clarke:** Well, no, they do not. I think that most of the business of a health authority ought not to divide people on party political grounds. Ninety per cent of their business – 99 per cent of their business – ought not.

A high-minded judge's question had been followed by a politician's high-minded answer.

Mr Bishop's cross-examination

Mr Bishop began his cross-examination by asking Mr Clarke whether he was prepared to accept that Mr Meacher had not written the mysterious 'Guidance ...' document. Mr Clarke replied that he had never said he had. Mr Bishop went on to ask him whether he was prepared to accept that the document had not originated from Labour Party headquarters, which he referred to as 'Central Office'. (Throughout the trial, the lawyers' ignorance of politics and political journalism was even more apparent than Mr Meacher's innocence of the law.) Mr Clarke was not prepared to concede that the party had had nothing to do with the circular: to him, it bore all the marks of an official document.

Counsel for Mr Meacher tried a different tack. Did he agree that, when he was Minister of Health, the authorities became 'more political' owing to the policies of the government? No, Mr Clarke did not agree: every government had its own national policy. Then followed an interesting (to me, at any rate) dispute between counsel and the Minister as to whether contracting-out various functions within the health service was part of the more general policy of privatisation. Mr Bishop, echoing his client, suggested it was; Mr Clarke contended that privatisation and contracting-out were different concepts: 'I think privatisation means that you change the ownership.' The questioning-and-answering went on to whether there had or had not been 'cuts' in the health service. Mr Justice Hazan sensed a political argument: 'We need not go into merits.'

Mr Bishop repeated his question about the government's policies' turning the health authorities into the 'political animals' which they had not previously been. Mr Clarke replied that he did not know the politics of large numbers of members of the health authorities. He was reasonably sure that some of the people he appointed were not Conservatives. He could not recall asking a member of a health authority what his or her party politics were: 'that would have got in the way of the relationship between me and the chairman or me and the member'.

Bishop: But you and the chairman, you are saying, was a fairly close relationship?

Clarke: Certainly.

Bishop: And you tended to appoint people who shared your views?

Clarke: I increased the number of businessmen. I did increase the number of people who, in my opinion, had experiences of responsibility of this kind, running their own business, perhaps. I was attracted by the kind of characters who had made a success of running a large business and organising these kinds of sums of money, these kinds of numbers of people, with all the bureaucracy on the one hand, and the industrial relations problems on the other, that the health service has ... Most of those turned out to be Conservatives, it is true, because a feature of British political life is that quite a high proportion of British businessmen vote Conservative.

Bishop: That is right. And those people, I think: would they not give the impression of supporting Thatcherism, supporting privatisation?

Clarke: I don't know. Some of them get very indignant indeed if you call them Thatcherites (*Laughter*).

Mr Bishop in trouble

Judge: You are now getting into the political arena again, which is the area of political debate.

Bishop: Well, my Lord, I am trying to avoid that.

Any sympathy for Mr Bishop which Mr Justice Hazan may still have retained was draining away like the dregs of the bath-water. And yet, Mr Bishop was, as he perhaps somewhat plaintively maintained, doing his best to keep party politics out of his cross-examination of a Conservative Cabinet Minister. It was not his fault.

Nor was it our fault for calling the Minister on our behalf: we were trying to present as persuasive a case as we could. In turning up as he did we were duly grateful to Mr Clarke, who was not a special friend of the *Observer* or of anyone else involved in the case. Nor was it Mr Meacher's or even his legal advisers' fault for trying to make what they could of whether or not Mr Moonman's resignation from the Labour Party as a result of Mr Meacher's questionnaire was a shabby episode. They in their turn were trying to make the most of what they had.

But the truth is that the 'Moonman allegations' were non-justiciable *unless* party politics were allowed to be taken into account by the jury. The trial would have been simpler – certainly more comprehensible both to the jury and to the newspaper reporters – if the Moonman allegations had been eliminated at its beginning, or even before then.

Mr Hartley had no re-examination. Mr Clarke went off to his Ministry, having, it was generally agreed, 'made a good impression'.

15

Mr Taylor's Evidence

A reasoning, self-sufficing thing
An intellectual, All-in-all!

William Wordsworth, *A Poet's Epitaph*

I had first met Robert Taylor at the *New Statesman* in the early 1970s, when Mr Howard was the newly appointed editor of that paper. He was not on the staff but attended editorial conferences (sometimes grandly and inaccurately called 'the editorial board'), lending his knowledge of industrial and trade union matters and of the Labour movement generally. He had also worked for the *Economist* and *New Society*; in 1976 he joined me at the *Observer*, where he became Labour Correspondent. In 1984-5 he had a brief, unsatisfactory period at the *Sunday Times*; early in 1985 the *Observer* welcomed him back as Political Correspondent, as number two to the Political Editor, Adam Raphael.

Of all the journalists covering the election to the Labour Party's leadership and deputy leadership in 1983, he had been the one most favourably impressed by Mr Meacher's chances. Mr Howard, the deputy editor, thought he over-estimated them. He thought this not only because of his friendship with Mr Meacher's opponent, Roy Hattersley, but also because his political 'nose' told him that Mr Taylor was wrong; for Mr Howard had, after all, been in and out of this Labour Party world (more in than out) since 1958, when at 24 he became Political Correspondent of the now defunct *Reynolds News*. In particular, he considered that Mr Taylor was being misled by Mr Meacher's man of political business, Alan Meale – another of those characters, such as Eric Moonman and William Millinship, who flit in and out of this story without ever putting in an appearance on the stage. This occasioned much banter on Mr Howard's part which was essentially good-natured, even though it had a certain edge to it.

However, Mr Taylor was far from being sympathetic to Mr Meacher's brand of Labour politics. If Mr Howard stood in the solid Centre of the party, with an inclination towards the old *New Statesman* Left as represented by Barbara Castle and Richard Crossman, Mr Taylor belonged to the revisionist Right who had looked to Anthony Crosland for salvation.

Mr Taylor was of a recognisable but now scarce type: the scholar-journalist. He had taken a First in History at Oxford; assisted Randolph Churchill with the life of his father; taught at Lancaster University; and published a life of Lord Salisbury. He was of slightly below medium height, well-covered, with dark, curly, unruly hair, spectacles and a round face. He could have passed for a Welshman. He wore his collar unbuttoned beneath his tie and, as the day progressed, his shirt outside his trousers.

In the witness-box he looked unwontedly neat and tidy. He had made an effort. He had made an effort in coming at all, for he had recently become Nordic Correspondent of the *Financial Times*, based in Stockholm. He had in fact arrived in London at the end of the previous week. I was grateful to Mr Taylor for turning up as he did; we all were.

Mr Grant's conversation

Shortly after his arrival Mr Taylor was seen talking to Larry Grant of Seifert Sedley Williams in the corridor behind Court No. 14. In the frequent intervals that occur in trials, the parties, with their barristers, solicitors and, often, witnesses form two groups and talk in low and grave voices. The sound of laughter is rarely heard. Mr Grant had indicated to Mr Taylor that he wished to talk to him. Mr Howard was concerned at this incident, and contemplated intervening to break up the conversation, but desisted.

Mr Taylor began by explaining that Mr Meacher was a 'fairly unknown political figure' at the time of the election. Accordingly he had interviewed Mr Meacher with a view to doing a 'Man in the News' feature in the news pages of the paper, something shorter than a full-scale 'Profile'. Mr Meacher seemed pleased and happily agreed to the interview, which took place in the House of Commons on the Thursday or Friday before the article appeared.[1]

> **Richard Hartley, QC**: Well, now, you have not kept the notes of the interview, have you?

Libel barristers, as I have already mentioned, are obsessed by note-taking on the part of journalists. Here the question was friendly: Mr Hartley knew from Mr Taylor's proof of evidence that he had not retained his notes.

> **Robert Taylor**: Alas, it is five years ago, and I did not think that the interview was of such great significance that it would warrant keeping the notes with the expectation of appearing in the High Court, frankly.

[1] See Chapter 2.

Hartley: Understood. I just wanted to explain to the jury that there are no notes of the interview.

Taylor: Of course.

Hartley: Can you recall in that conversation that you had with Mr Meacher going into his background at all?

Taylor: ... I always ask, as a stock question, when I meet someone for the first time, something about their background and, particularly, what their father did for a living. Perhaps it is a prerequisite of being a labour correspondent. One tends to be involved in the world of work. It is a natural question to ask. It wasn't an important question to me, in the case of Mr Meacher or anybody else, but it helps to shape the environment in which an individual grows up. And it seemed to be important to know that, particularly as Mr Meacher had a very distinguished academic career at Oxford and public school.

Mr Hartley then read out that part of the article which dealt with Mr Meacher's background. Libel barristers – indeed, all barristers – have a liking for reading out loud documents which have been read already and are, in any case, before judge, jury, counsel, solicitors and parties. Usually they are too long, too involved or both for the recital to be of any great value to the public. Here, however, the reading was short, and to the immediate point. Mr Hartley confirmed that all the biographical facts (including the spending of a year with the Danilo Dolci Trust) had come from Mr Meacher.

Mr Justice Hazan: Where did you get, particularly, the expression 'son of a farm worker'? When you asked him about his father – what he did, 'what did he do?' – what, as far as you can recall, did he, Mr Meacher, say to you about his father?

Taylor: He said his father worked on a farm.

Judge: Those were the words, were they, as far as you –?

Taylor: As far as I can recollect.

Judge: Not necessarily the exact words, or what?

Taylor: I have to say it with some hesitation that he said this. But he said: 'Let's say my father worked on a farm.'

Judge: So that is why you put 'farm worker'?

Taylor: That is why I put 'the son of a farm worker'. Somebody who works on a farm is a farm worker (*Laughter*). I have to say also, in addition to that, that at no stage of this interview, and certainly not when dealing with that particular point, which is only a very minor point and not of great significance to me, did he refer to his father having been a trainee accountant or having a nervous breakdown etc. I only learnt of that much, much later on.

It was a sign of the good Mr Justice Hazan's largeness of spirit that he did not seem at all annoyed at Mr Taylor's having raised a laugh, it might have been thought, at his own expense. But Mr Taylor was not trying to be funny. He clearly considered that he was stating the obvious: that someone who worked on a farm was a farm worker. Throughout the case, however, the judge gave great latitude – even, on occasion, some encouragement – to displays of wit and humour by witnesses. It may be that this was because he was, by training and experience, a criminal lawyer. Mr Hartley, who took up his examination of Mr Taylor from the judge, was perhaps more conventional in this respect.

> **Hartley:** If he had said that his father was a farmer, or a tenant farmer, or his grandfather had been a tenant farmer, what would you have put then?
> **Taylor:** I would not have put that he was the son of a farm worker. I would have said 'the son of a farmer'.
> **Hartley:** You say he did not tell you anything about having gone to London to train as an accountant?
> **Taylor:** No, he didn't. But it was not relevant to the interview. I wasn't interviewing Mr Meacher about his father. I was interviewing Mr Meacher about the deputy leadership of the Labour Party, and it seemed to me to be totally irrelevant.

This was possibly a dangerous answer. 'Totally irrelevant' smacked of what Mr Bishop had been putting to me, over the Monday morning and the previous Friday, about the words complained of in so far as they concerned Mr Meacher's father. Later, in cross-examination, Mr Taylor clarified his views, saying that, whereas he would have included the abortive effort at accountancy in his article if he had known of it, he would not have included the nervous breakdown. Mr Justice Hazan now intervened briefly on the latter.

> **Judge:** And you would not have been interested in the state of his father's health?
> **Taylor:** No, I wouldn't. Indeed, I later thought that is the reason why he didn't declare that at the time, understandably. If my father had had a nervous breakdown, I would not have wanted it to be known to the newspapers.

Mr Taylor is unshaken

Mr Taylor had given strong testimony. Mr Bishop tried to shake it by implying, through his questions, that he had forgotten some of what Mr Meacher had told him. There was the usual barrister-and-journalist exchange about the absence of notes which it would be tedious to recapitulate. Mr Taylor agreed that the notes which he took were of about twice the length of the article that appeared.

Gordon Bishop: And, when it comes to remembering precisely what was said, you have to rely upon what actually ends up within the article itself. Is that right?

Taylor: Well, I can also recollect from my memory, which is not entirely faulty.

Bishop: Yes, I appreciate –

Taylor: I am not absent-minded when it comes to these matters, and I have to say I stand by everything I wrote in this article.

Mr Bishop asked Mr Taylor to confirm that Mr Meacher was not 'sort of playing down his background'. Mr Taylor refused, replying that 'he was not honest about the origins of his father'.

Taylor: He was slightly hesitant about that. I do recollect that. He said: 'Let's say that my father worked on a farm.' ...

Bishop: Hesitant?

Taylor: Hesitant, hesitant, hesitant, hesitant.

Bishop: Hesitant. And he said?

Taylor: I mean, I have to say that I wasn't pressing him. I mean, it wasn't an interrogation.

Bishop: No.

Taylor: It was simply to shape up the article. So we agreed on a form of words.

Bishop: Yes.

Taylor: Well, I mean to say, he said: 'Say my father worked on a farm.' And I said: 'Fine. I'll call you the son of a farm worker.'

Bishop: Are you sure he didn't say: 'My father worked on his father's farm'?

Taylor: No, I don't recollect that.

Bishop: Because I think a Mr Grant of the plaintiff's solicitors asked you a question about it a couple of days ago. Is that right? Do you remember that?

Taylor: Well, he collared me in the corridor, yes (*Laughter*). I wasn't quite sure how proper or improper that was, but still. He wanted to ask me what questions I was going to be asked in the witness-box.

Bishop: Do you remember saying to him that Mr Meacher said he was a farm worker: he worked on his father's farm?

Taylor: No, I didn't recollect that. I do not recollect saying that on Thursday afternoon. No. He's the son of a farm worker; his father worked on a farm. That's what I was told by Mr Meacher in 1983. I take exception to the idea that I should be tricked in the corridor.

Bishop: It is not a question of being tricked by anyone, Mr Taylor.

Taylor: Well, I am sorry. It is not true. I did not know that it was his father's farm, when I wrote this article in 1983.

This was, it seemed to me, pretty low-grade stuff from Mr Bishop, as it had been earlier, in the corridor outside Court No. 14, from Mr Grant. Naturally I was biased in Mr Taylor's favour. Moreover, I was at this time in the middle of my own cross-examination by Mr Bishop, Mr Taylor having been allowed to interrupt my evidence on account of his journalistic duties in Stockholm. I was not disposed to look charitably on counsel's endeavours to do the best he could on his client's behalf. That is not how these matters appear when you yourself are actively involved in a case.

But whereas I, unlike Mr Howard, was quick to anger, Mr Taylor was equally quick to take offence. He was reminiscent of the late Alan Melville's running joke: 'And now we will take a little umbrage.' Mr Taylor took more umbrage later on when Mr Bishop pointed out to him that Mr Meacher had not spent a whole year working in Sicily for the Danilo Dolci Trust, as Mr Taylor had stated in his article, but a few weeks only. Mr Taylor expostulated that Mr Meacher had indeed spent a year working for the trust and that the trust was indeed based in Sicily. The error – for Mr Meacher had spent the year working for the trust mainly in England – was, Mr Taylor rightly maintained, a trivial one. It certainly did not justify Mr Bishop in casting doubt on the rest of the article.

Mr Taylor may have overdone the injured tones, but he was patently a witness of the utmost integrity: 'a most impressive witness, you may think', as Mr Hartley was later to put it to the jury in his barrister's language. Manifestly Mr Bishop had quite failed to dent his evidence on what Mr Meacher had actually said to him in 1983.

16

Mr Chester's Evidence

O thou of little faith, wherefore didst thou doubt?

Matthew 14:31

Mr Hartley and Mr Nathan had between them mounted a legal *coup* in compelling Mr Meacher's recall to the witness-box, which would come about after our witnesses had completed their evidence. That I considered this a bit hard on Mr Meacher made no odds. Nevertheless, Mr Hartley thought we were going to lose. I asked him why. He replied by in turn asking me when a newspaper had last won a libel case. (The right answer, I think, was when the 'Moonies' had unsuccessfully sued the *Daily Mail*.) Some 40 cases had gone by, Mr Hartley said; the plaintiff had won every one. His suggestion, which may have come from Mr Bishop – if it did, Mr Hartley did not let on – was that we should ask for half our costs to date and, in his words, 'call it a day'.

Mr Hartley was, of course, famous as a plaintiff's man. That was the way he looked at things. On this occasion, however, he was supposed to be a defendants' man. Mr Howard – who, at the trial, was in reality representing the first two defendants, Mr Trelford and the *Observer* – told me he thought Mr Hartley should, to use the old Bar turn of phrase, get on his legs and carry on. Mr Hartley, however, wanted to settle. Mr Howard promised to put this to the *Observer's* managing director, Nicholas Morrell, which he duly did. Mr Morrell replied that, as we had come so far, we were not going to withdraw now.

Lewis Chester gave his evidence on the morning of Wednesday 25 May. He was a journalist of much experience and some distinction, having grown up in Harold Evans's *Sunday Times*. He was the co-author of several books of an investigative nature. His article on Mr Meacher in 1983 had been the longest and, in some respects, the fullest. In 1988 he had thick dark hair, heavily-rimmed spectacles, five o'clock shadow at eleven in the morning. Unlike the rest of us, he had made no attempt to modify his appearance or to dress up for the occasion. Indeed, there was a hole caused by a cigarette (or a burn of some nature) on the left thigh of his trousers. I noticed this when he sat down on my right, behind Mr

Nathan. Nonetheless, I was grateful to him for appearing. Journalistically he had had his ups and downs lately.

> **Richard Hartley, QC**: Are you presently working as a journalist with the *News on Sunday*?
> **Lewis Chester**: The *News on Sunday* went out of business last November.
> **Hartley**: Yes. I was rather wondering about that (*Laughter*). Where do you work now?
> **Chester**: I am a freelance journalist. I work mainly for the *Illustrated London News*.

Mr Chester explained that in 1983 he was working on the *Sunday Times*. The interview with Mr Meacher took place some time in August and lasted about two hours.

> **Hartley**: Can you tell us what your general practice is when you interview someone, and I am asking you specifically about the taking of notes?
> **Chester**: Well, if I would have an interview with a leading politician for an article of this type, I would usually write up my notes on the following day. The reason for this is because there would be this time lag between the time you interviewed the person and the time you wrote the article. And, as my notes are usually illegible after about 24 or 48 hours – they are all right for football matches, but they won't be very good for complicated matters over a long period – I'd write my notes on the same day or the next day at the latest.

Mr Chester's notes

At last, notes, the holy grail of libel barristers! There was much toing-and-froing about bundles, pages, copies: finally everyone was satisfied. Mr Hartley read them out. Mr Chester had certainly not been idle:

Meacher – born 1939. Only child. Father 56. Mother 36. Father had been a farm worker most of life, but hardly worked at all as he was growing up. Lived in Berkhamsted. Outside loo, bath in kitchen. Mother who worked as doctor's secretary was the force in the family. All except a second cousin were Conservative voters. Remember father when he aged nine reflecting on Attlee government: 'If we go on like this, we will all be bankrupt.' Life was modest. He'd study in cold front room with electric fire and hot water bottle on lap. Family took *Express* and *Telegraph*. Day boy at school, and had a straightforward career. Idea of becoming a priest strong aged 15 to 20. Mother important in this. Got divinity scholarship as ordination candidate

– Anglican. Involved with Pusey House. Still has friends from churchmen of this period. In last year thought not cut out to be a priest ... Went to 'Crime and Challenge' meeting and directed to probation.

The judge intervened. Mr Chester had written: 'Father had been a farm worker.'

> **Mr Justice Hazan**: Do you recall whether he actually used that word, or is it a description you wrote down of what he was telling you his father did?
> **Chester**: I mean, I don't recollect any word that was said at that interview. I mean, it is impossible. I've tried to do so, and it's not feasible. But, I mean, I do remember the main heads of what was talked about, and this is my best record of what was talked about that was almost contemporary – I mean, within a day or two. So this is, in a sense, better than anything I can ever recollect.

A distressing witness

Mr Chester was proving a distressing witness, both to our lawyers and to those of us who had known him for over 20 years. He mumbled. He had to be asked to speak up. Worst of all, he could not – he haltingly admitted he could not – remember a word that had been said at the interview with Mr Meacher. Mr Hartley tried again and was reinforced by Mr Justice Hazan.

> **Hartley**: What impression did you get of his father's background from what he told you?
> **Judge**: What did you gather his father had been or had done?
> **Chester**: Well, sorry, yes. There were two things about this. The thing I was interested in was what it was like for him growing up – that is, Mr Meacher. I wasn't really terribly interested in his father. But naturally his father very much comes into that aspect of the matter. But I do not think I asked a question like: 'Tell me about your father.' I would have said, you know: 'What was your upbringing like?'

Mr Hartley took Mr Chester through his article, presumably hoping he would sooner or later hit a more promising seam. In a way, he did: but Mr Chester was immediately overcome by doubts.

> **Hartley**: Having interviewed Mr Meacher in the way you have described, what was the impression you formed of his background?
> **Chester**: I formed the impression that he was the son of a farm worker. Since – I mean, this is not – I can't remember, you know – I

think there must have been some things that I don't have in my notes, because when it came out that it was his father's farm – I think it was in this case – or something like that – I did remember that. So he must have told me that at the time – that his father was working on his father's farm. So that must have been one of the things that he told me at the interview. I also seem to remember him mentioning some breakdown his father had had early in his life, but I was unable to – which was, in some way, the reason why he was a farm worker. But I didn't think he was other than a farm worker. I mean, I didn't think he was, as it were, continually unwell. I mean, I thought, you know, that his father had, as I have said in my notes, worked for most of his life on the farm.

Hartley: Did he say anything to you at all about his father having gone to London to train as an accountant?

Chester: That I don't recall.

Hartley: If he had said it, do you think you would have written it down?

Chester: I think I would have done, but I can't be sure, it is too far away to remember. When stories about his father being an accountant came up, I was surprised by them, because I thought – well, I was a bit sorry that I hadn't got them myself, as it were.

From our point of view, Mr Chester was turning from being a distressing witness into a potentially disastrous one. Mr Hartley concluded his examination-in-chief here. Quite enough damage had already been done.

On the one hand, Mr Chester confirmed that he had formed the impression that Mr Meacher senior was a farm worker who had spent most of his life on a farm. But, on the other hand, he hazarded that Mr Meacher must have told him that it was his father's (Michael Meacher's grandfather's) farm. This was what Mr Meacher, through his counsel, had unavailingly suggested to Mr Taylor. Mr Chester further guessed that Mr Meacher had told him about the nervous breakdown which had caused his father to take up working on a farm.

Yet neither of these pieces of information which Mr Meacher had allegedly divulged – that it was his father's farm and that he was working there because of a nervous breakdown – was in Mr Chester's rewritten or finished notes or in his *Sunday Times* article of 1983. True, Mr Chester did not know that Mr Meacher's father had been an accountant, or a trainee accountant. But, as it was part of Mr Meacher's case that his father had never been an accountant of any description, this omission was unimportant: indeed, if anything it strengthened Mr Meacher's case.

Mr Bishop's work is done

Though it was not Mr Hartley's fault, Mr Bishop's work had been done for him. He easily established from Mr Chester, first, that not everything in his original, rough notes was in the document (the rewritten, finished notes) which the court had before it. He established, second, that not everything said at the interview was in even the original, rough notes; Mr Chester said that they were not a transcript.

After that, Mr Bishop had little more to do. He had established – or, rather, Mr Chester had established for him, in his examination by Mr Hartley – that Mr Meacher may indeed have given Mr Chester that 'full explanation' which he claimed always to have given, provided he had the time and opportunity. Mr Chester could not remember, though he now remembered some things which were neither in his finished notes nor in his published article.

Gordon Bishop: Your note actually says: 'Life was modest.' So that is obviously the conclusion you gained – was it not? – that life was modest. Was that the word that Mr Meacher used, or was that the impression you gained in relation to that?

Chester: I could not say. I mean, I can't remember.

Bishop: Thank you very much, Mr Chester.

17

Mr Knight's Evidence

You cannot hope
to bribe or twist
thank God! the
British journalist

Humbert Wolfe, *The Uncelestial City*

I had known John Knight for nearly 30 years, ever since I had first
become a journalist. For a time, in 1968-9, we had worked for the same
paper, the *Sunday Mirror*, to which I briefly contributed a freelance
political column in addition to my regular work at the *New Statesman*. He
was a Fleet Street friend. We did not visit each other's homes and I knew
nothing of his domestic circumstances, any more than he, I fancy, knew
anything of mine. But when we met we almost always had time for a
drink and a chat. We both patronised El Vino's in Fleet Street, and had a
good working knowledge of the other licensed premises of the
neighbourhood.

He had an educated voice which nevertheless contained a hint of
menace. He was of medium height, pale, even, some might say, pasty, but
with an underlying strength. He regularly wore a suit. He could have
been connected with show business or boxing; there were times, indeed,
when he seemed to have stepped straight out of a 'B' film of the forties or
fifties. In fact he was a popular journalist of much experience and some
dedication. He was not cynical about his writing, nor did he aspire either
to imitate or to transfer himself to the heavy press. He was a
conscientious craftsman whose work, as we shall see, Mr Bishop made
the mistake of seeming to patronise.

A welcome witness

I was glad to see him on the morning of Wednesday, 25 May, and not only
because it is always fortifying to see an old friend in time of trouble.
Whereas Mr Taylor had been as solid as a prop, Mr Chester had not
exactly been steady on parade. We counted ourselves fortunate that we
still had Mr Knight to come.

There was another consideration. Of all the newspaper articles and
other documents painstakingly, and sometimes painfully, read out by
learned counsel in the course of the case, it was only Mr Knight's article[1]
which had given manifest pleasure to the jury. While my reference to
advising Mr Meacher to jump off the Terrace into the Thames raised an
appreciative smile, Mr Knight's numerous sallies had them laughing out
loud. And they carried on laughing through numerous readings; for, as
we have seen,[2] it is a principle of English jurisprudence that anything of
importance must be repeated at least three times. When he appeared, the
jury were clearly interested in this journalist who had provided them
with so much innocent enjoyment. Indeed, their concentration was
palpable: they were listening to every word.

Mr Knight told Mr Hartley that the interview with Mr Meacher had
lasted from an hour-and-a-half to two hours. Mr Hartley was taking him
through his article and came to Mr Meacher's quotation: 'It's all open. But
from my contacts I believe I have a very good chance.'

Richard Hartley, QC: Did he say something on these lines?
John Knight: Yes, he did. I tape recorded part of the interview
with him, and that would be a direct transcript from my tape.
Hartley: Is that still in existence – the tape?
Knight: The tape is, yes.

Mr Knight had created a small sensation. A secret tape! I knew about
it, whether from conversation with him or from reading his first
statement to our solicitors of July 1987. His second statement, made just
before the trial, contained no reference to the tape. Why it did not refer to
the tape, and why it was thought necessary for Mr Knight to make a
second statement at all, I do not know. But I did know that the tape was
not specially helpful to our case, for the recording had ended after
three-quarters of an hour or so and contained most of the overtly political
material on which the article was based. The information about Mr
Meacher's background had come later, in more relaxed conversation
between him and Mr Knight. Mr Hartley had either forgotten or not been
properly briefed.

Hartley: You have the tape?
Mr Justice Hazan: It might not be in dispute. I do not know. It
may not be in dispute.
Hartley: My Lord, that has come as a surprise to us, that a tape

[1] See below, pp. 228-30.
[2] Patrick Devlin, op. cit.

is – We did not know there was a tape.

Judge: Well, I mean, we will see what happens.

Mr Justice Hazan was demonstrating his refusal to become excited about tapes. They might be relevant or they might not: we should just have to wait and see. That was what the learned judge was saying. I thought subsequently – it did not occur to me at the time – that, if this course were allowable under the law of evidence, the recording could perhaps have been replayed to demonstrate Mr Knight's reliability as a reporter. But Mr Hartley soon progressed to what had not been recorded and had produced, in the article:

> Meacher has an immaculate background which appeals to Socialist romantics. His father was a farm worker (outside lavatory and bath in the kitchen), and his brainy son won a scholarship to a public school and went on to get a First at Oxford.

Hartley: Now, first of all – if I do not ask you, I know my learned friend will – those words are not in inverted commas.

Knight: No. This is something that he told me, but I didn't quote him directly about saying that.

Conventions of the libel bar

The libel bar, a lucrative closed shop, have, like other similar bodies, their own customs and practices. I have already referred several times to their belief – or pretended belief – that journalists spend most of their time dashing about with notebook in hand.

Another convention, which they cannot possibly believe, is that reporters write their own headlines. This did not come up in this case. I freely admitted having written 'Neil should get his retaliation in first' over the offending column. Nothing turned on this. But it is rare either for columnists or for reporters to compose their own headlines. Libel barristers must realise this. But, for their own purposes, they pretend otherwise. Let us suppose that a young lady is suing the *Daily Brute* in respect of a story by some wretched reporter that she spent a night with a famous England cricketer. The reporter is being cross-examined by Mr Silk, QC.

Silk: Mr Seedy Hack, could you tell us, please, why you chose to write 'My night of sin with England star' over your article?

Hack: Well, I didn't write it.

Silk: You didn't write it? But (*in tones of astonishment*) it's got your name on it.

Hack: I know. But they do that back in the office.

Silk: I see (*in tones of scorn*), in the office. And what else do they do in the office? Insert lies, I suppose? Let me ask you: did you attempt to check this article in any way whatsoever? Did you go back to the office?

Hack: No I didn't.

Silk: But surely, Mr Hack, you could have done? What was so difficult about it?

Hack: Well, we don't normally do it. We leave it to the subs.

Silk: I see. You are happy to leave it to someone else. Thank you very much, Mr Seedy Hack.

Yet another convention of the libel bar was now being displayed before our wondering eyes: that, in newspapers, anything of importance is enclosed by quotation marks, indirect speech being an inferior and even suspect form. Mr Hartley was not being unfriendly to Mr Knight but trying to anticipate objections by Mr Bishop on this score.

Hartley: Did he say his father was a farm worker?

Knight: Yes, he did.

Hartley: Those specific words?

Knight: Yes. I can remember him saying that …

Hartley: What about 'outside lavatory and bath in kitchen'?

Knight: Well, my recollection is that he volunteered this information, because I asked him. I said: 'What did your father do?' And he said: 'Farm worker, outside lavatory, bath in kitchen, that sort of thing.' He briefly dismissed it within that sentence.

After learning the history of the tape recording, which I have already retailed, counsel returned to the outside lavatory and the bath in the kitchen, which, in the examination of Mr Meacher's evidence, were assuming the same importance as the louse and the flea in mine. Would Mr Knight ever have known about them, Mr Hartley asked, if Mr Meacher had not told him?

Knight: It would be inconceivable, unless I had had some aberration and totally invented it.

Hartley: Did in that interview Mr Meacher say at the time that after school his father went to London to train as an accountant, or became an articled clerk, or anything like that?

Knight: I have no recollection of him doing so.

Hartley: Anything about his father having had a breakdown or an illness?

Knight: No. He seemed to want to get rid of that part of it quickly.

It was very clipped. I asked him a straight question, and he gave me a short, straight answer.

The jury pay attention

Mr Knight was clearly making a tremendous impression on the jury, who were giving him their complete attention. Even the young man with the long hair in the middle of the front row had abandoned his customary somnolent yet cynical expression, and was sitting up and taking notice. Mr Bishop clearly had a difficult task in cross-examination.

His best course, I thought when I came to consider the case afterwards, would have been to bring out more clearly what Mr Knight had already admitted: that at no stage had Mr Meacher made any attempt to play up or, if you prefer, play down his background. 'Playing up' and 'playing down' were confusing terms throughout the case. What was agreed was that Mr Meacher had not emphasised – not made a big production of – the modesty, deprivation or even poverty of his youth. He had dismissed the subject in a few words. That, indeed, was the reason Mr Knight still remembered those words after almost five years had elapsed. Mr Taylor had given evidence to precisely the same effect.[3] Instead of trying to make a virtue out of this agreed reticence, Mr Bishop elected to impugn Mr Knight's memory as well as his journalism. He suggested that Mr Meacher had really told him more. Maybe he was inhibited by the 'pleading', which stated that Mr Meacher had told or tried to tell the full story to anybody who asked.

At all events, Mr Bishop began badly by muddling the date of the article. He claimed – he even tried to insist to Mr Knight – that it had been published in April 1983. Mr Knight, after some toing and froing, prevailed upon him to accept that 7 August was the correct date. So it was, Mr Bishop agreed; he now remembered; Mr Knight had stated in his examination by Mr Hartley that the interview with Mr Meacher in Highgate had taken place on a fine day.

This was pretty inconsequential stuff from learned counsel. In a British August, it might just as well have been a rainy day. The month could not have been April because it would have been too far distant from the month of the Labour Party elections in which Mr Meacher was a candidate, October. As it was, Mr Knight was one of the first journalists in the field with his profile-interview. Not for the first or last time during the trial, Mr Bishop was demonstrating a shaky grasp of chronology. He turned to the article itself.

Mr Bishop is patronising

Gordon Bishop: The article itself – I do not mean any slight to you in relation to this at all – is a somewhat trivial little article, is it not?

[3] See Chapter 15.

Knight: I would not have thought so, no.

Bishop: You would not. Right.

Knight: Quite the contrary, Sir.

Bishop: It is different – Can I put it this way? As I say, I do not want to – It is in a different sort of mould from one you might find in one of the more serious daily papers or Sunday papers?

Knight: Oh, possibly. But it is in a more conversational tone. It is bringing to a very large readership something about a man that they probably know very little about. And we are telling them about him, and we are also telling them – the readers – about the deputy leadership contest, and we are explaining what all that is about, and trying to do it with some entertainment as well, I hope.

Bishop: Right. Yes, quite. But it is slightly different – or the paper is different, is it not, and the article itself is different – from one you might find in the *Observer*, or –?

Knight: Not particularly, I wouldn't have thought. I could have seen this published in a more serious journal. It depends on your point of view.

This was surely folly of a high order in a professional advocate. Not only was he patronising Mr Knight's work as a journalist for the purpose of casting general doubt on the article: he was also casting doubt on the standing of the newspaper for which he worked and in which the article had appeared. Yet, though one can never be sure about these things, the jury looked more like *Sunday Mirror* than *Observer* readers to me. They were listening to Mr Knight with an attention which they had not shown to any other witness, not even Canon Wilkinson. They had clearly enjoyed the renditions of his article.

They had been particularly taken by the picture of Mr Meacher with his poodle, Oscar, which had illustrated the article. And now, here was Mr Bishop, bringing in the dog to demonstrate the triviality of Mr Knight's approach.

Bishop: I mean, you were interested that he had a poodle –

Knight: Yes.

Bishop: – because that would make a nice picture?

Knight: Yes, there's Oscar.

Bishop: You were interested in his family background?

Knight: Oscar is on the left (*Laughter*).

Bishop: Yes. Quite right. Michael Meacher would – But you were interested in these matters. You thought these were the sort of matters which might be of interest to your readership?

Knight: Absolutely.

Bishop: What one might describe as slightly more peripheral matters so far as a politician is concerned?

Knight: Absolutely.
Bishop: But of interest to the readership?
Knight: Yes, absolutely, Sir.
Judge: The canine-loving English public?
Knight: Absolutely, yes.

Mr Knight is unmoved

And so, Mr Bishop proceeded, he asked Mr Meacher about his background, and one of the questions was what his father did.

Bishop: And are you seriously telling us that what he said was simply: 'Farm worker, outside lav, bath in kitchen, that sort of thing'?
Knight: That's right. I can remember.
Bishop: Dismissed it in one sentence of about ten words?
Knight: I remember it because he dismissed it so quickly.

I thought at the time that both Mr Bishop and Mr Hartley were sloppy in the way in which they used 'lavatory', 'lav', and 'loo' promiscuously, the last being Mr Hartley's preferred word, while Mr Bishop favoured 'lav'. Mr Knight was consistent in using 'lavatory' both in his article and in his version of Mr Meacher's words to him. The various words are important ('toilet' and 'w.c.' did not, as far as I can recall, occur) not so much for Mitfordesque reasons as because they went to the accuracy of the witness's recollection. This Mr Bishop proceeded to question in another way.

Bishop: You suggest he said nothing further at all in relation to that?
Knight: No. He seemed to want to get rid of it. I mean, I am now, possibly, putting some interpretation on it, at this very late stage. But, looking back, he seemed to want to deal with it quickly. I mean, it was the opening gambit – you know, a question which he could have elaborated on far more, if he had wanted to. But I felt by the tone of his voice that he didn't want to. Maybe he had an appointment, and he wanted to get rid of me as quickly as possible, and that was the end of the interview.

Mr Bishop then put to Mr Knight that 'outside lav' (his preferred phrase) and 'bath in kitchen' did not 'really go with farm worker'. One was to do with his father's occupation, the other with the conditions under which he grew up. Mr Knight replied that the two phrases amounted to 'a sort of code'. Mr Bishop suggested the word 'shorthand', implying a certain sketchiness on Mr Knight's part. Mr Knight replied that he had inherited the shorthand from Mr Meacher. Mr Bishop suggested that, in the absence of the article which was before him, Mr Knight would not have remembered anything at all about the interview. Mr Knight denied this.

> Bishop: Well, perhaps you would remember the pet poodle, would you?
> Knight: Probably (*Laughter*).

Mr Bishop was leading the poodle in once more. Perhaps he wished to emphasise Mr Meacher's credentials as an animal-lover. That was certainly a consideration to be borne in mind. Whenever he mentioned the dog, the jury laughed. But manifestly it was Mr Knight rather than Mr Meacher who was the popular pet. Mr Bishop implied that Mr Knight might have omitted salient matters from his article because, as a Sunday journalist, he had been granted some leisure for its composition.

> Bishop: You had two or three days to write the article?
> Knight: No. As far as I can recall, I saw him in the morning, and I wrote the article in the afternoon.
> Bishop: Right.
> Knight: So it was red hot from the presses of my mind.

Mr Knight's vivid phrase – or the procedure which it expressed – added to the weight of his evidence. Mr Bishop, showing that ignorance of the ways of journalists which all libel barristers seem to evince (sometimes deliberately, sometimes not), had assumed that, for a Sunday paper, the article would have been composed on the Saturday. But feature pages, on which Mr Knight's article appeared, in those days went to press from Wednesday or sometimes Tuesday onwards. I was impressed and a little surprised by Mr Knight's dispatch, even though it may have been rendered necessary by the paper's production schedule. I should have written the article on Friday; at the earliest on Thursday evening, in case some political development had supervened, despite the month's being August. Mr Knight had written it in mid-week, immediately after seeing Mr Meacher.

> Bishop: And you would not have had much time, in the meantime, to look up reference books, or anything of that kind?
> Knight: I would have looked those up beforehand.

One direct hit

The principal reference books consulted about MPs are *Who's Who, Dod's Parliamentary Companion* (in the 1980s, alas, in a changed, larger format, no longer pocket-size), *The Times House of Commons* and Andrew

Roth's *Parliamentary Profiles*. The last, as it happened, described Mr Meacher's father both as a 'farmer' and as an 'accountant'. Presumably Mr Knight had not consulted this work. Nonetheless he had been diligent. Yet, oddly enough, his very industry now enabled Mr Bishop to score his one direct hit of the cross-examination. He was referring to a sentence in the article.

> **Bishop**: You see, it said there: 'His brainy son won a scholarship to a public school.' Is the scholarship something you say was in record books? Because I would suggest it is something which does not appear in the record books. The school might be mentioned in *Who's Who*, or something of that nature, but not the scholarship.
> **Knight**: I might have read that in an article about him, then.

Mr Bishop was undoubtedly correct. While scholarships to colleges or universities are usually recorded in *Who's Who*, those to schools (with a few exceptions, such as King's Scholarships) are rarely put down by the entrants, though there is nothing to prevent the inclusion of the information if the person concerned thinks it worth conveying or is sufficiently vain. Certainly there was nothing in the main reference works to indicate that Mr Meacher had won a scholarship to Berkhamsted. It followed from this either that Mr Meacher had told Mr Knight about the scholarship or that he had, as he said, found out about it by reading the 'cuttings'.

I had learnt about the scholarship some time – I do not remember precisely when – before August 1983. Indeed, it was this knowledge which had first aroused my suspicions about Mr Meacher's *bona fides* as the son of a farm worker. But I lived in this political world daily – had lived in it for nearly 30 years. Mr Knight was even more experienced as a journalist. But, like John Wesley, he took the world as his parish: he was not a political specialist. The trickle of references to the scholarship became a torrent only later, in August 1983 and September, as the Labour elections approached. Mr Knight had certainly been diligent in his research – or Mr Meacher had told him.

Mr Bishop could have persisted in his questioning. What article, precisely? Did Mr Knight remember? Was it an article relating to the deputy leadership, or some earlier 'profile'? And so on. But he let the matter drop.

Mr Bishop rebuked

Mr Justice Hazan now intervened to rebuke the unfortunate Mr Bishop for not putting specifically to Mr Knight a matter which had been pleaded, namely, that Mr Meacher had told Mr Knight that his father had worked on his father's farm.

Bishop: My Lord, I thought it was clear, from Mr Meacher's [meaning Mr Knight's] answers.

Judge: Yes. I am sorry: it is not clear to me.

Bishop: Mr Knight, I would suggest to you that Mr Meacher went into more detail in relation to this, that is, so far as saying what did his father do? [sic.] In answer to that question, he said he worked on his father's farm.

Knight: That is not my recollection.

Mr Knight had done us proud. He was, in a sense – certainly in the sense that the jury liked and were amused by him – our answer to Canon Wilkinson, who had caused so much despondency in Mr Hartley. For the first time since the case had started eight working days before (ten in all), I felt reasonably confident of winning.

'You're the star,' I said to Mr Knight as he sat down solidly beside me on his release from the box.

And I meant it. Mr Knight sat on for a few minutes.

'Time for drinkies, I think,' he said, gesturing towards the exit and inviting me to join him.

It was twenty to one. I declined, because Mr Howard and I were taking our secretary, Isabel Maycock, to her farewell lunch at a nearby restaurant in Chancery Lane. Moreover, we were about to witness the most dramatic event of the entire trial: the recall of Mr Meacher to the box.

18

Mr Meacher Recalled

I'm getting married in the morning!
... get me to the church on time!

Alan Jay Lerner, *My Fair Lady*

Mr Justice Hazan may have been trying to be kind, but he treated the jury as children over the recall of Mr Meacher. Certain questions, he said, had been asked of Mr Meacher. He had made certain replies to those questions. Owing to those replies, it was now necessary to question him further. Accordingly he was being recalled to the witness box.

This was all very well as far as it went, but it did not really explain why Mr Meacher's ordeal was being renewed. To begin with, to be sure, he had brought that ordeal upon himself, by bringing the action – though, as the case progressed, it became increasingly evident that he had possessed little notion of what bringing an action for libel in the Queen's Bench Division of the High Court of Justice entailed. To this extent I had no sympathy with him: either for bringing the action or for not knowing what the trial of the action would be like. A man in his position, of his intelligence, ought to have known.

His recall raised different considerations. His counsel had asked a legally foolish question about what he had told his solicitor, and he had given a trusting answer to his counsel. Waiver of privilege and the doctrines of adoption and severability are no doubt difficult matters.[1] Should Mr Justice Hazan have tried to explain them to the jury? It is tempting to answer: 'No: they would not have understood a word.' But they had already, in Mr Bishop's opening speech, had to endure an exposition of the law of libel which would have secured his instant unpopularity in any course of legal education on account of its tedium. The jury were later, in the judge's summing-up, to have to listen to a livelier but still mentally taxing account of the same branch of the law. Could they not now have been told – necessarily in broad and simplified form – the legal reasons for Mr Meacher's re-appearance in the box?

[1] See Chapter 8.

In my opinion, the attempt should have been made. Leaving the matter as Mr Justice Hazan did conveyed to the jury that Mr Meacher had already been found guilty of some form of sharp practice or of deceiving the court in some way. That was not so. Certain inconsistencies might now be discovered in what he had already told the court and what he had previously told his solicitor. That was a different matter, and was for Mr Hartley to elucidate. Mr Hartley had before him Mr Meacher's statement to his solicitor. The crucial sentences in this were:

> Whenever I have been asked, I have always said that my father worked on a farm. I have always described him as a farm worker. I have always spontaneously supplied the further information that he worked on a farm which was owned (as I then thought) by my grandfather.

Mr Hartley did not read this out yet, but put his first question in the form of a summary of what Mr Meacher had already told the court about his background. When asked about what his father did (Mr Hartley suggested), Mr Meacher had always said that after leaving school he trained for a short time as an accountant in London, and shortly afterwards suffered a nervous breakdown, or a severe illness, which forced him to return to work on the family farm, helping his father, for the next 25 years. He was a nervous, inadequate man. For example, he would only walk around the farm in circles, so as not to lose sight of the farm building.

He had never said that his father was a farm worker. He had repeatedly said that the background was complicated. He had always given the fuller explanation because he realised that 'farm worker' did not convey the full flavour. Neither 'farmer' nor 'farm worker' gave the true impression. But, if a single word was to be used, 'farm worker' was more accurate than 'farmer'. He agreed, however, that he had acquiesced in his father's being described as a 'farm worker'. He agreed further that 'farm worker', 'farm labourer' and 'agricultural labourer' were the same.

Was this a reasonably fair summary? Mr Meacher said it was, though he disagreed about 'agricultural labourer'.

Michael Meacher: 'Farm worker', as I said, I would not demur at in respect of my father.

Richard Hartley, QC: But you said, in answer to me in cross-examination – and if there is any doubt about this we will have to get the transcript – you said more than once: 'I have never said that my father was a farm worker.'

Meacher: I have never said that my father was a farm worker, full stop. I have always gone on and I have indicated the fact that he worked on his father's farm. That is the important point.

The crux of the case

It was indeed the crux of the case as far as the father or background allegations were concerned. The evidence was that he had not given this additional information to Mr Taylor or Mr Knight. He may or may not have given it to Mr Chester, who could not remember. He had certainly given it, and more, to Mr Howard. This, as both Mr Hartley and Mr Meacher were to say, several times – drawing different morals from it – was 'one of the ironies of the case'. Mr Meacher was to urge it as proof of his openness, if given the time to be open. Mr Hartley would say that, if it had not been for Mr Meacher's revelations to Mr Howard at the first lunch, Mr Hillmore in his 'Pendennis' column and I in my political column would not have been able to indicate the truth about Mr Meacher's upbringing.

Even so, we were now to hear more about this period and before. They were not strange or surprising facts, in themselves: they were commonplace, given that we were all talking about things that had happened a long time ago. But they put the Meacher family in a different light, more prosperous and even odder than Mr Meacher had already indicated in his evidence. He now cast doubt on his account of his father's having gone to London to train as an accountant. And he introduced a maid into the Meacher household.

> **Meacher**: I thought that my father had bought the house [in High Street, Berkhamsted]. Apparently his father, my grandfather, bought the house and moved into it with my father and my father's sister and a maid. This maid was the person who brought up my father when he was a little boy. As I say: later, she must have been getting on in years. But, anyway, she was known to the people I rang up [about the Meacher family history]. She knew everything about my father that there was to be known, and when I asked her whether she – her name was Fanny – had ever made any reference to the question of my father going up to London, she said she had no knowledge of it. I said: 'Well, are you sure?' And she rpeated it again: 'She [presumably, Mr Meacher senior's sister] never mentioned it to me.' Now that is all that I can say. I therefore am not absolutely certain that this event, round which this whole trial revolves, ever actually happened.

I never thought that the trial revolved, or ought to have revolved, on whether Mr Meacher's father had gone to London to train as an accountant or on whether he could fairly be described as an accountant. My case was that Mr Meacher had claimed that his father was a farm worker and that he had never been one in any meaningful sense, either when Mr Meacher was growing up, which was admitted, or in the period following the return from London, which was still somewhat mysterious as far as Mr Meacher senior's way of life was concerned.

Throughout the trial, however, Mr Meacher and his counsel emphasised my charge that Mr Meacher senior had been an accountant. Mr Howard said in evidence that he did not see that it was defamatory to call a man's father an accountant. Nevertheless, in private he took a gloomier view – it was gloomier than mine – saying to me that he thought we could 'go down on the one word "accountant" '. Mr Meacher had till now stated, despite some hesitation in his main evidence, that his father had gone to London to train as an accountant, suffered a nervous breakdown, returned to Berkhamsted and worked on the family farm. He was changing the accountancy part of the story.

> **Meacher**: All that I can say is that I do have a recollection of my mother saying it, and that is why I have always said it when asked.
> **Hartley**: You understood from your mother that he went to London to train as an accountant? He then had a nervous breakdown whilst he was training as an accountant?
> **Meacher**: Well, that he had a nervous breakdown, there is absolutely no doubt about that.

But how neurotic, how remote, how (to use Mr Howard's phrase, which he had picked up from Cyril Connolly on the young Lord Home) ineligible for the struggle of life had Mr Meacher's father really been? The evidence so far, from Mr Meacher himself and, perhaps more notably, from Canon Wilkinson, was that 'he was very nervous, had lost all his confidence and clearly he was unable, for whatever reason, to proceed with any career'. This was what was in Mr Meacher's proof of evidence. It was what, in substance, he had told the court. But by its side, in the proof, he had written: 'On reflection, I think this is over-stated. He was not at all as neurotic as this seems to imply.' The judge now took up Mr Meacher senior's neurosis, if that is what it was.

> **Mr Justice Hazan**: Whether you regard it as neurotic or not, you see, you will recall that Canon Wilkinson, for example, said that if you were to speak to him you could not get a reply out of him.
> **Meacher**: Yes, and he said he was a broken-down man. Yes, I mean, all of that is true, absolutely, perfectly true. It was just that when I read those words I thought they conveyed a slight over-statement and I just simply wanted to put it right.

Mr Hartley now indulged in a libel barrister's quibble, which did, however, serve a purpose.

Hartley: Well, it is more than a slight over-statement, is it not? You have put: 'I think this is over-stated.'

Meacher: Well, all right, yes. I think it is over-stated.

Hartley: But can you help us now any more with what your father did do on the farm all the years that he worked?

Meacher: No, I can't. I don't think there is anyone alive who knows the answer to that question.

It was now apparent: we did not know what, if anything, Mr Meacher senior had done on the family farm. Mr Hartley tried to show that the picture which Mr Meacher and Canon Wilkinson had painted in their evidence of Mr Meacher senior was something of a caricature.

Hartley: I suggest to you that you have, in your evidence that you have given before we saw this statement, suggested that your father really, after the nervous breakdown when he trained to be an accountant, he was – you have not used the words, but in effect – almost a zombie. He could not play any useful role in the farm.

Mr Howard and I were horrified at Mr Hartley's use of 'zombie'. It was not that it was inaccurate; it did not misleadingly summarise what Mr Meacher (and, even more strongly, Canon Wilkinson) had told the court earlier. But it was a coarse and insensitive word to use. Mr Howard and I were similarly exercised by Mr Hartley's use of the phrases 'low class' and 'lower class' to categorise the occupation of farm worker. These phrases, along with 'working class' tend to arouse hostility. But the use of the word 'zombie' illustrated a wider difficulty under which we laboured.

To defend the case properly, we had to introduce matters concerning Mr Meacher senior's health and the family's finances: matters which any jury might reasonably consider to be private. That Mr Meacher had introduced them himself – it was he, after all, who had described his father as inadequate and as a dependent person – made no difference to the impression which we, in our turn, might create. I had tried to forestall this objection by saying in cross-examination by Mr Bishop that it was Mr Meacher who was dragging his father through the courts, not I: but the risk of seeming to invade the Meacher family's privacy was one which we inevitably ran. Mr Meacher denied, however, that his evidence justified Mr Hartley's interpretation of it.

Meacher: No, I disagree with you. I don't think I have said anything that remotely justifies the use of a word like 'zombie'. I mean, that again I would utterly repudiate. My father wasn't like that at all. He was – there are people who are disabled to the point that it is accepted they can't work. They nowadays get a non-contributory invalidity pension. Well, I should have said my father was probably similar to that.

Hartley: But he could not work?

Meacher: I don't think one wants to exaggerate. It would be easy for me to exaggerate but I am trying not to. I am trying to be balanced and fair.

Hartley: Mr Meacher, what I am saying to you is that before we got this statement, and it is a statement which you were reluctant to let us see, is it not?

Meacher: Would you like me to tell you why?

Hartley: You can do.

At this point Mr Meacher appeared to me and others to be in danger of breaking down. His voice was cracking, the veins on his forehead stood out and he seemed on the verge of tears. The spectacle and what had led to it – the inept question by Mr Bishop, Mr Meacher's answer to it, the objection taken by our side, the legal argument, the disclosure of the statement and the consequential recall of Mr Meacher to the box – all illustrated the cruelty of the law.

Meacher: I will tell you why. I was indeed very reluctant for this statement to come into court and I will tell you exactly why. You had me in this witness box for three-and-a-half days and I make no grumble about that at all. And I thought that if this comes back into the court and I am cross-examined by you – and for all I know this is exactly what is going to happen – it could easily take another day or more. I am getting married on Friday, this Friday. I was absolutely desperate that my marriage and my honeymoon is not wrecked by a libel trial hanging over it. That is why, and that was the sole reason. There is nothing here that I am not perfectly willing to answer on. That was the sole reason.

Hartley: Mr Meacher, of course I appreciate and accept that you are getting married on Friday, but you have known about this libel trial being due to start last Monday – your libel trial – have you not? It has been fixed for months.

Meacher: It was fixed for months and I was told it was five to seven days.

Judge: It is not his fault if an underestimate has been given by somebody.

As often happens in the law, cruelty had in minutes turned into comedy. Mr Meacher must have been the first litigant to ask the court to get him to the church on time.

It would be tempting to write that the rest of Mr Meacher's further cross-examination was an anti-climax. So, in a sense, it was: but we were not to realise that at the time. There was no knowing where it would end. Mr Hartley turned to the breweries in Hertfordshire: Mr Meacher denied that his grandfather had been rich but confirmed that his father had left £40,000 in 1969, which had gone first to his mother and then, in a few months, following her death, to him. Mr Hartley pressed him, and produced what I thought subsequently (though not at the time) was the most significant passage of Mr Meacher's recall to the box.

Hartley: Yes, but connection with breweries and also owning the farm – it is a different picture that one might have from the one you gave in court.
Meacher: Well, if someone asked me, sat down with me and said: 'Right, let's go over your family background. I want to do an interview with you on your family background,' all of this I would say. But as the journalists who have appeared before this court, I think two of them at least – and particularly, I think, Robert Taylor made this point – the fact is that it was a matter of the merest insignificance.

Mr Meacher, I observed throughout the trial, combined exceptional intelligence and acuity with extreme unwordliness and naivety. Here he was demonstrating the former qualities. I had also noticed Mr Taylor's answer at the time, and been slightly worried by it.[2] Though Mr Taylor was a witness of integrity, there was an inconsistency – or apparent inconsistency – in his evidence on this matter. On the one hand, he said that, as a labour correspondent, the world of work was paramount in his mind, and that accordingly he would naturally ask the occupations of his subjects' fathers. On the other hand, he said that this was a question of little or no importance. The conflict was easily resolvable: Mr Taylor liked to get things clear in his mind and then move on. But there was no doubt that Mr Meacher had scored a small point. His answer continued.

Meacher: When they asked me what my father did or what my background was, they wanted one word. They didn't even want a tedious paraphrase going into the complications of my father's background. If I had gone into my grandfather – I mean, they would have thought that I was mad.
Hartley: But you have always said that you gave a full answer when asked what your father did, and didn't just stop at: 'Oh well, he was a farm worker.'
Meacher: That is right.

[2] See Chapter 15.

Hartley: In fact, you said before that you have never ever said that he was a farm worker?

Meacher: I have never said, in answer to the question: 'What was your father?' 'Farm worker,' full stop, by itself, nothing added. I have never said that. I have always said: 'Worked on his father's farm,' but if someone used the phrase – because, as I said, what they wanted was a single phrase, just to place me – I would not demur at the use of 'farm worker'. I think it is probably the single most accurate word that you can find to describe my father's situation ...

Hartley: You know what this libel action is all about – is it not? – the suggestion, on your background, that you liked to claim that your father was an agricultural labourer. That is what it is all about, is it not?

Meacher: Absolutely, and I have nothing to hide ...

There was now a clear conflict of evidence. Mr Meacher had never actually used the phrase 'agricultural labourer'. So much was common ground. But had he allowed that impression to become current? Mr Meacher's version was that he would say: 'My father was a farm worker. He worked on his father's farm', or: 'My father worked on his father's farm' or: 'My father worked on a farm. It was his father's farm.' However, both Mr Knight and Mr Taylor were positive that they had heard no mention of his father's farm. 'Farm worker' or 'He worked on a farm': that is all *they* remembered.

Mr Hartley reverted to the Meacher household's maid. The jury had heard nothing about her before from Mr Meacher, had they? Mr Meacher replied that that was because no one had asked the relevant question. That again was 'telling half the story', Mr Hartley suggested. Mr Meacher said that he could not seriously be expected to give a sociological dissertation on his father's family every time he was interviewed.

Mr Meacher was challenged next on the lodgers in the small house at Berkhamsted. The whole first floor had in fact been let off as a flat. This, Mr Hartley said, was rather different from taking in lodgers; it was a different kind of arrangement. Mr Meacher replied that this was 'splitting hairs' and an 'absolute quibble'.

The importance of bridge

The bridge-playing activities of Mr Meacher senior were more important to our case. This was so not because bridge is regarded as a pastime engaged in by the middle classes (though the word 'bridge', like 'maid', no doubt had its emotive effect) but, rather, because doubt was now cast on Canon Wilkinson's evidence, and Mr Meacher's too for that matter, as to the hopeless condition of Mr Meacher senior. Mr Meacher's proof of evidence described his parents playing bridge weekly with neighbours.

Hartley: That is your father and mother regularly playing bridge, is it not?

Meacher: Yes.

Hartley: But again, how does that fit in with a picture of your father, which I think Canon Wilkinson supported, of in effect not being able to communicate – and bridge is quite a complicated game, is it not?

Meacher: My father was very good at bridge.

Hartley: He was able to play it?

Meacher: Absolutely. And that is precisely why I didn't want to exaggerate in the other extreme when you were leading me on to suggest that he was extremely neurotic. I never said any such thing. He was an extremely good bridge player.

Hartley: Well, you did not mention that, unless –

Mr Meacher now displayed filial affection and pride. It was rather moving; also rather sad. He was, however, fully in control of himself, as he had not seemed to be earlier, speaking of his impending marriage.

Meacher: I mean, he was interested in watching cricket as well. He liked – because he had led his whole life in the countryside – he liked going out in the countryside. He liked telling me about flowers, about trees, about birds, about farm crops, on which he was extremely knowledgeable. I didn't mention it.

Judge: So he was not wholly cut off within himself?

Meacher: No, no, I don't use that phrase and I don't think that is quite –

Judge: Canon Wilkinson's evidence. I see.

Hartley: Do you think that Canon Wilkinson's evidence was a little exaggerated?

Meacher: No, I don't think he exaggerated at all.

This last passage was to be echoed in the judge's summing-up. It remained for Mr Hartley to deal with the Meacher motor-car, first a Ford Prefect, then a Volkswagen Beetle. It was Mr Howard who emphasised to Mr Hartley the rarity of cars in the 1940s and early 1950s. To own a car in those days was an indication of relative prosperity, of middle-class aspiration or of both. Mr Howard was correct to point this out. Throughout the case, it seemed to me, lawyers, parties and witnesses judged the past by the standards of the present: thus, for much of this century, an outside lavatory was not a sign of impoverishment, and a maid, such as my own parents had before 1940 (a local girl who came into the house to help five or six days a week), was no sure indicator of affluence.

Mr Justice Hazan ended the day's proceedings by discharging a juror.

We were now at the Wednesday before Whitsun, and he, a coach driver by occupation, was due to drive a party on the Continent. Neither he nor his employers had expected the case to last so long. (Mr Meacher had not expected it either.) If he failed to fulfil this obligation, the driver, so he had told the judge, would lose his own summer holiday later in the year. Mr Justice Hazan regarded this as a serious matter for the driver. He was accordingly discharging him. Our solicitors pointed him out to me as a sensible-looking man in the front row. We regretted his departure. We thought he would have proved a counterweight to the youth with the long hair and the sleepy yet cynical expression, whom we had early categorised as a potential loose cannon. Still, there it was. The Easter Term ended in Court No. 14.

Mr Meacher is married

There remained Mr Meacher's marriage. His future wife had been the subject of much speculation throughout the trial. She was said to be South African, rich and paying for the case, as far as Mr Meacher's costs were concerned. I was able to correct the first two statements and to cast doubt on the last. My source was an old friend from Cambridge days, John Macdonald, who was now a QC, who had been Liberal candidate for Wimbledon and whose chambers in Lincoln's Inn I visited one morning when I had arrived too early. The future Mrs Meacher, he told me, was 'a very nice woman' who was not South African but had spent some time in the country and was opposed to the regime there. Her first husband had been his agent in the constituency. She was not rich, as far as he knew: she was a physiotherapist and masseuse who specialised in the treatment of old people in their own homes. Her brother was a merchant banker in the City.

As the case went on, she kept turning up at the court and sitting next to Mr Meacher. She was neat, and seemed composed, but occasionally she would cast sidelong glances of hatred towards me. It was a disconcerting experience, the like of which I had not undergone since youth: but I did not dislike her reciprocally, even though I considered that any reproach ought more properly have been directed at her consort. It was he, after all, who had brought these sad and comic events about. But I realised that this would be asking too much of anyone, certainly of any plaintiff's fiancée.

They were married on the Friday. In the register, in the space for his father's occupation, Mr Meacher wrote: 'Farm worker'. In all the various certificates produced and examined during the case, it was the first time this precise phrase had been used of him.

Part Four

The End of the Case

19

Closing Speeches

Let the long contention cease!
Geese are swans, and swans are geese.
Let them have it how they will!
Thou art tired; best be still!

Matthew Arnold, *The Last Word*

We reassembled for the Trinity Term (minus the discharged coach driver) as if we were a school coming together again after the half-term break. It was now June; summer might be beginning shortly. Mr Howard asked our friend the usher whether she had had a good holiday. 'My mother died,' she replied. Even Mr Howard's social skills were not adequate to responding to that, except with: 'I'm terribly sorry.' Later in the day I expressed my condolences myself. The usher blamed the hospital.

Among those turning up again was Mr Delaney. He has not figured hitherto in this narrative. Mr Delaney was, apart from the new Mrs Meacher, Mr Meacher's solitary faithful supporter, who would arrive virtually every day. He was thin and middle-aged, and had an air of fanaticism. He wore a track-suit, a tee-shirt and, usually, a woolly hat. I thought I had seen him somewhere before. Where was it? A Labour Party conference?

One day he turned up wearing a tee-shirt urging support for Tony Benn. I hesitated no longer. I approached him and introduced myself, which was unnecessary really, as he had been in court almost as much as I had. 'Delaney', he said, holding out his hand. He confirmed that he was indeed an attender at party conferences. He would arrive at the court, making a good deal of noise if he was late – he had the knack of drawing attention to himself, quite apart from his curious garb – and would sit directly behind Mr Meacher, proffering advice or comment and, on his departure, wishing the plaintiff good luck. In October 1989 we met again at the Grand Hotel, Brighton, during the party conference. He greeted me with cordiality, but revealed his true name as Mick Priggen: 'I use the name Delaney when I'm not sure who I'm talking to.'

Legal argument

On the Thursday before the adjournment the court had heard legal argument. Even before this interlude, it had already been agreed by counsel and judge that two simple questions should be put to the jury: first, did they find for the plaintiff or the defendants and, second, if they found for the plaintiff, how much the damages should be. The other principal matter concerned the allegation of express malice on my part – which I had not taken seriously when it was first made but which had assumed a certain importance as the trial progressed.

Mr Hartley argued that there was no evidence to support it; it was the thinnest case of malice he or any court had ever heard; and, accordingly, it should not be put to the jury. No evidence, Mr Hartley contended, had been produced to show that I had any intention to injure Mr Meacher. The judge replied that the jury were entitled to infer such an intention from the words used – thus the matter ought to be left to them. I was, I must confess, a little despondent at this ruling. Our lawyers told me not to be. Mr Justice Hazan was, as they put it, 'trying to make the case appeal-proof'. The Court of Appeal might possibly decide, in the event of an appeal, that the issue of malice should have been left to the jury. Hence the judge's decision.

Mr Hartley's speech

'Long time, no see,' Mr Hartley said to the jury with a certain dated colloquialism twelve days later, at the start of his closing speech. They could be forgiven for having forgotten much of the evidence after an interval of almost two weeks. That meant he was bound to take a considerable time reminding them of that evidence. He had mentioned on several occasions that there were numerous ironies in the case. It was one of the few libel actions where the result was far more important for the defendants' reputation than for the plaintiff's. It was 'at the bottom of the league tables' of libel actions. Even if the plaintiff did win – though Mr Hartley suggested he would not – the damages would be very small.

By contrast, the reputations of the *Observer*, Mr Howard and myself were 'on the line'. We were accused of publishing statements which we knew were untrue or about which we were reckless as to truth. The plaintiff's advisers knew that, if the jury found that the words came within the defence of fair comment, the plaintiff lost, unless he could prove a high degree of express malice. Why, Mr Hartley asked, had it taken three years to introduce this charge of malice? Mr Meacher conceded that politicians had to 'take a lot of flak'. Yet he launched a libel action on the strength of a few words in my article. He accused me in effect of being a dishonest journalist.

When the jury retired they would be asked two questions: whether they found for the plaintiff or the defendants and, if they found for the plaintiff, how much they awarded in damages. They would not, however, have to decide whether there was a legally binding agreement following Mr Howard and Mr Meacher's lunch of 7 February 1985. For his Lordship had ruled as a matter of law that no such agreement had been made.

The first question was whether the words complained of by Mr Meacher were defamatory of him. The jury must make up their minds, first, what the words meant. What was the natural and ordinary meaning? They should look at the words and any 'reasonable inferences' which could be drawn from them. The test was that of the 'reasonable reader'. On a fair reading of the passage, the 'real sting, real criticism' was directed at *The Times* for 'drawing false distinctions' in the dispute with Mr Moonman. I was dismissive of the dispute itself. Mr Meacher said in evidence that he took exception to the allegation that he 'drove' Mr Moonman out of the Labour Party. The *Observer* did not make that allegation; *The Times* made it. Yet he sued the *Observer*, not *The Times*.

Mr Meacher had tried to improve his case by imputing meanings that were not there. He had 'played down' his social origins – implied that they were 'lower' rather than middle class (Mr Hartley continued to talk about 'low' and 'lower' class) – not, as Mr Bishop said, to ingratiate himself with his constituents and with the Labour Party but to save himself from embarrassment. On the Moonman dispute, Mr Bishop said that my words meant that he had resigned from the Labour Party because of 'mean and despicable conduct' on Mr Meacher's part. But it was for the jury to decide what was meant by 'admittedly shabby episode'. They had to decide whether the words complained of tended to lower the plaintiff in the estimation of right-thinking members of society generally.

To answer that, they had to have in mind who the plaintiff was. He was an MP, 'a person very much in the public eye'. There were privileges to being an MP: membership of an exclusive club, freedom to say what one liked in Parliament under the rule of absolute privilege. But there were some disadvantages too: anything one did or said would inevitably attract 'the attention of the media'. Were these allegations sufficiently serious to lower Mr Meacher's reputation in the way counsel had just described? It was up to them to decide.

Over the Moonman dispute, most of the national press had used the emotive word 'spy'. I had not, and should be given credit for that. Mr Meacher had also claimed that if I had inserted 'he says' the 'he' referring to Mr Moonman, before the reference to the questionnaire, the words would not be defamatory. This was 'clearly absurd'.

Nor did the words 'because the life suited him better' carry the meaning which Mr Meacher had suggested for the very first time in the witness box. The jury knew why the words were used: they had heard my evidence. We should be given credit for using those words instead of referring to a nervous breakdown. The words covered the truth and should not be given any other meaning. The sentence about jumping off the Terrace into the Thames was important because it had initially been relied on as evidence of malice, yet Mr Meacher said in his evidence that he had no objection to it. This showed how thin the case of malice was.

As for the louse and the flea, it was a joke. The jury might think it was a good joke or a bad joke. (Mr Hartley evidently thought the latter.) It had also been referred to as vulgar abuse. It was 'plainly not something that should give rise to your being taken for two weeks from your employment'. As for the whole passage, it was something that should have been 'taken on the chin'. Alternatively, it was so serious that it should have caused Mr Meacher to rush off immediately for redress. The fact that he did not do so showed that it was not serious.

The second issue was whether the words were true. Mr Hartley began with the Moonman allegations (on which we were pleading justification as well as fair comment). Was sending out the questionnaire a shabby thing to do? Kenneth Clarke thought it was. Mr Meacher had tried to place the responsibility for some of the questions on his researchers. Was he there trying to pass the buck a little? Yet he did not seem to accept for one moment that the questionnaire might be thought of as spying.

What did the jury think? That was the important thing. Was there something nasty, underhand, about it? How would they like it if they were sitting on one of those health authorities and the person next to them was answering a questionnaire about them? 'Shabby' was exactly the right word: it captured the feeling the ordinary man would have on hearing of the sending-out of the questionnaire.

The second limb of the case concerned Mr Meacher's family background. Mr Hartley suggested that this could be boiled down to one question: had Mr Meacher ever claimed that his father was a farm worker? At the end of his evidence on the fourth day he was emphatic that he had never, ever said that his father was a farm worker. Yet in his statement to his solicitors (which the jury had before them) he asserted the opposite: 'I have always said ...' His position now was that he had never said he was 'the son of a farm worker, full stop'.

Mr Meacher had been 'well and truly hooked' and 'no amount of wriggling' would get him off the hook. Mr Hartley read various questions-and-answers from the transcript (which the jury did not have before them) in an attempt to illustrate the 'contradictions' between his evidence and his statement: 'Can you, faced with that, really believe one word he says?' The court had been able to 'nail a lie' because of the 'unique situation' of the jury's being able to see the statement, which was 'devastating'.

The plaintiff objected most strongly to my statement that his father was an accountant who retired to the family farm because the life suited him better. But suppose I had written that his father was an articled clerk in London who suffered a nervous breakdown and went back to the family farm. Would there have been no complaint then? What was the difference between them?

We know [Mr Hartley said] that everything Mr Meacher's father stood for is complete anathema to the Labour Party – inherited wealth, gentleman farmer, public school, a maid, living off unearned income, leafy suburbs and tennis clubs. One can understand it is not quite the picture one would want to have of your Labour MP.

Mr Hartley ended with a robust defence of fair comment, which he defined or described as 'unfair comment'. This was both clever and legally sound – the test being honesty rather than reasonableness – but it was possibly risky all the same. No harm seemed to have been done, however. Mr Hartley had certainly earned his money in his closing speech. Mr Howard wrote him a congratulatory note, and I expressed my appreciation. He had taken all day Tuesday and part of Wednesday 8 June.

Mr Bishop's speech

I had thought of missing Mr Bishop's closing speech, partly because I did not want to become upset and angry, but more because I showed my feelings easily; not only showed them, but exaggerated them, amusement, scorn, disbelief, usually of the mock variety. No doubt a lifetime spent talking to – or, more often, listening to – politicians had played a part in this disposition of mine. Earlier in the trial Mr Nathan had spoken to me about it: juries, he said, did not like it, so would I please sit still and keep quiet. I put my head down during Mr Bishop's speech and took a note, as I had done during Mr Hartley's speech also.

Mr Bishop began by repeating the two questions for the jury agreed by judge and counsel and posed earlier by Mr Hartley. Before answering them the jury had to decide the following issues: Were the words defamatory? Were the facts true? Was the allegation about the questionnaire ('admittedly shabby episode') fair comment? Was malice present? What damages were appropriate?

He suggested that the jury would have 'little difficulty' in concluding that the words were defamatory – were damaging to the plaintiff's reputation. To say of Mr Meacher that he claimed his father was an agricultural labourer when in fact he was an accountant was to accuse him of lying about his origins for political advantage. What was being said was that he was making his father's background out to be 'very low' when in fact it was 'quite high'. This was clearly damaging to Mr Meacher. Maybe it would be less damaging to 'some politicians' but it was 'very damaging to Mr Meacher, who is a man with a reputation for integrity, as Mr Watkins agreed'. Mr Meacher's reputation was 'enviable indeed'. One of the most priceless of assets was a reputation for honour and integrity. This was what I had damaged and what Mr Hartley in cross-examination – and more savagely in his closing speech – had attacked.

It was clear that what was being said was that Mr Moonman resigned from the Labour Party because of the questionnaire sent out by Mr Meacher. It was clearly said that Mr Moonman resigned because of the behaviour of Mr Meacher. There followed the allegation of shabbiness in relation to Mr Meacher's action. To say that Mr Meacher's conduct was shabby, and that that conduct had led to the resignation of another member of the Labour Party, was 'obviously damaging' to his reputation.

The implication was that the plaintiff pursued the politics of intolerance – behaviour such as caused other members to leave the party. Mr Meacher had said that he was tolerant of all views in the party. That was not challenged. It could be shown that Mr Moonman gave the questionnaire as his reason for leaving the Labour Party. But there was no evidence that this was the reason, because Mr Moonman had not been asked. The result was that we could say only that sending out the questionnaire itself was a shabby thing to do.

As to the background allegations, the highest we could put our case, on our evidence, was that Mr Meacher had said his father was a farm worker on 'a couple of occasions'. That was why Mr Hartley put it that the case boiled down to whether Mr Meacher said his father was a farm worker. As a test, this was 'nonsense'. But even if the jury rejected Mr Meacher's evidence, our case could be put no higher than that. Even if it could be so put, it did not justify what I wrote in the article.

What I wrote was not that Mr Meacher said his father was a farm worker but that he said his father was an 'agricultural labourer' when in fact he was a 'professional man'. I was setting something 'very low' against something 'very high'. It might be helpful for the jury to look at it as if it were a pair of scales. Mr Meacher said that something was 'low on the scales' whereas in fact it was 'actually up there'. (At this point Mr Bishop illustrated with his hands the operation of scales.) I was saying that there was a 'great gap' between the two, and that this represented 'the lie Mr Meacher was putting about to improve his image'.

What evidence was there that Mr Meacher ever claimed his father was an agricultural labourer? Mr Meacher accepted that the distinction between 'farm worker' and 'agricultural labourer' was a 'very fine one'. Nevertheless he denied using the latter phrase and no evidence had been called to show that he had ever done so.

It was 'ludicrous and obviously absurd' for me to describe Mr Meacher's father as an accountant when he had worked for only a few months as an articled clerk in an accountant's office. When pressed on the matter, I had been compelled to admit that he was not really an accountant. Mr Howard realised this too, when I showed him my column, typed. So the statement was untrue.

It was untrue also that Mr Meacher senior 'retired' to the family farm because the life 'suited him better'; even though I had 'attempted to get around this in cross-examination' by saying that he retired to the farm in the same way as one retired to bed. But the impression of the ordinary reader would be that he had worked for a long time as an accountant and then retired to the family farm. This was 'simply not true'.

Mr Bishop reminded the jury that he had asked Mr Howard, who had qualified as a barrister, why he did not call himself a barrister who retired to become a journalist. His reply was that he saw no reason to answer the question. Of course not: it was as 'absurd' as to describe Mr Meacher's father as an accountant who retired to the family farm because the life suited him better. It was clear that that sentence was 'wrong'. (I was surprised that Mr Bishop chose to bring up his question to Mr Howard, which had ended the cross-examination and had alienated certainly the judge, and possibly the jury.[1])

There was 'really no difference' between Mr Meacher's statement to his solicitors and what he had told the court in his evidence. A 'great deal' had been made of the maid, but she was taken into the house to be looked after in her old age, and was 'not in any sense a maid' at that stage. Mr Hartley was asking the jury to accept one sentence in a statement but to disregard the rest of that statement and the whole of Mr Meacher's evidence.

On the contrary, they ought to consider the whole. Mr Meacher had always said that his father had worked on a farm, but he had gone on to make clear that it was his father's farm. To suggest otherwise contradicted the evidence of Mr Howard and of Mr Chester, to both of whom Mr Meacher had provided 'clear details' of his background.

Moreover, this statement was not a formal document such as an affidavit. Taken as a whole, it fitted with what Mr Meacher had told the court. Mr Hartley was now trying to say that Mr Meacher was a liar. This was a serious allegation. Mr Bishop invited the jury to consider Mr Meacher as an honest man who, as I had said in my own evidence, had earned a reputation for integrity.

Articles by John Winder of *The Times* and Mick Costello of the *Morning Star* had also been cited. Mr Winder was not relied on in our Defence in the Pleadings, but Mr Costello was. Yet he had not been called to give evidence. Mr Bishop 'invited' the jury to 'infer' that these two journalists, had they been called, would not have supported our evidence, because 'clearly' they would have been 'heard from otherwise'. (I thought that this was rich, not to say fruity. However, in accordance with custom and practice, the judge did not interrupt Mr Bishop. Mr Costello, by the way, was not asked because, on balance, our solicitors considered Mr Chester's recollection to be better. After Mr Chester's evidence they regretted not calling Mr Costello instead.)

Mr Bishop asked the jury to prefer Mr Chester's evidence to Mr

[1] See Chapter 13.

Knight's or Mr Taylor's. Mr Taylor had made a mistake about Mr Meacher's period in Italy with the Danilo Dolci Trust. The point was that one could not expect the article to be absolutely accurate: the interview on which it was based had been compressed. Mr Bishop suggested to the jury that Mr Meacher had told him the details of the farm, but that he had compressed them. 'Journalists will try to protect the integrity of what has been written.' After five years, all that could remind Mr Taylor of what had been said was the article itself.

Similarly, Mr Knight recalled only 'one short, clipped sentence'. His article was an *'aide-mémoire'*. Was this the way Mr Meacher spoke? The jury might think it was not at all the way he spoke or answered questions. He 'went on at some length'. Mr Knight's version was 'simply not his style'. It was 'journalese', which Mr Bishop defined as the 'sort of statement a journalist would use'. As an example he would refer to the evidence of Mr Howard, not on this substantive point but to illustrate how journalists rather than politicians tended to speak.

> I came back and I said: 'Look, I think I have got the show on the road,' or words to that effect. You know: 'I think I have solved it. Nice lunch, Michael very friendly, a bit aggrieved, certainly still a bit aggrieved, but he has agreed that we should publish a correction of the one allegation' – absolutely clear that I had got Moonman completely out of the way – but he will want to see what we write.

'That,' Mr Bishop concluded, 'is the sort of language, short, staccato sentences, that journalists tend to use.'

It was clear that this opportunity had been used by me 'for whatever reason' deliberately to injure Mr Meacher. The jury had seen me in the box. I was, according to Mr Bishop, 'obviously a clever man', an 'expert in the precise use of words'. They might think that I 'chose each word very carefully'. They had to consider the state of mind I was in when I wrote the article. Was I 'just commenting'? Or was I 'intent on injuring the plaintiff'?

It had not been a wholly happy case for Mr Bishop – Miss Rouse's evidence cut off, Mr Meacher recalled, the judge showing greater irritation with him than with Mr Hartley. Nevertheless, he was a fighter in his way. He was certainly showing resilience. The day's proceedings ended with him demanding enormous damages.

More legal argument

There ensued a complicated legal discussion about the measure of damages, which was invited by the judge. Figures were not mentioned: Mr Bishop maintained that Mr Meacher was entitled to be compensated not only for the damage to his reputation but for pain and suffering, the absence of an apology, the defence of justification and 'the baselessness of the charge'. Mr Hartley demurred, cases were cited. The judge said that this was not an appropriate case for the award of punitive damages and that later he would direct the jury accordingly. The jury were present throughout. Mr Howard deplored this, as I did also. He feared the discussion would 'put ideas into their heads'.

Mr Bishop already had an idea in his head. This was that, in two days' time, the jury would award his client £7,500. Mr Meacher had, he told his friends in the Middle Temple, made an excellent impression in the box. Mr Howard and I went off to the Wig and Pen Club, opposite the Law Courts and adjoining the Middle Temple. He drank whisky, I brandy. He still thought we might 'go down on the one word "accountant" ', while I was confident only that the damages would be small. My real hope was for derisory damages. But there was nothing more anybody could do. It was now up to Mr Justice Hazan and the jury.

20

Summing-Up and Verdict

Mr Justice Cocklecarrot: The time has, I think, come for you, ladies and gentlemen of the jury, to consider this case on its merits.
Foreman of Jury: And what, sir, would you say were its merits?
Cocklecarrot: What would you?
Foreman: We have not so far understood one word of the proceedings.
Cocklecarrot: I must say there have been moments when I myself seemed to have lost touch with the real world. Nevertheless, certain facts stand out ... I intend to make a supreme and almost despairing attempt to sum up this most curious case.

J.B. Morton, *The Case of the Twelve Red-Bearded Dwarfs*

When the court case met on the morning of 9 June, I felt even more detached from the proceedings. Mr Justice Hazan had a quiet voice and a diffident manner. He more than ever resembled some furry little denizen of field or woodland – judicial accoutrements enhancing the aspect of a small mammal – that was being required to go through various motions. The jury were attentive.

In this case, he said, which they had been trying together for the past two-and-a-half weeks, they had different parts to play. His task was to direct them as to the law applicable. They had to accept that and apply it to the facts. Their task was to decide the case: they, and they alone, were the judges of fact. They did this by considering the evidence they had heard, having seen the witnesses under examination and cross-examination, and making up their minds about the witnesses they believed and those they did not believe. What the proper inferences were to draw from the evidence was entirely for them. They decided on the evidence, not on counsel's speeches.

If, in the course of his summing-up, he made any comments, or appeared to hold any views, these were not intended to influence their verdict but to draw their attention to matters which might assist them in the case. If they thought he held a view which happened to accord with theirs, that was 'fine', but if his view did not so accord they must disregard it.

No politics

The first matter he had to make 'perfectly clear' was that in deciding the case they must put aside political considerations altogether. Inevitably it was a case about politics – about political decisions or political disputes which arose in relation to them. But they must not decide in favour of the plaintiff because they were members or supporters of his party. Nor must they decide against him because they were members or supporters of another party. It did not end there, for 'another matter came in with the Meacher-Moonman dispute': that there were various factions within the Labour Party. So, again, their decision should not depend on which faction they supported. He mentioned that because they would remember that Mr Meacher had told them in evidence that until 1981 he had been a supporter of Mr Benn but had then withdrawn his support.

Next, they had to decide the case 'purely on its merits'. They must not say: 'Here is a national newspaper. The plaintiff is making a complaint against it. It can afford to pay.' At one stage the plaintiff was asking for only 'modest' damages but he was now, through counsel, asking for 'substantial' damages.

Equally, they must not be affected by the attempts to settle. They should not consider the case as if it had almost been settled – or should have been settled and never have come to court. The evidence about a settlement arose solely because one of the defences put forward was that an agreement was reached, which would bar damages altogether. But the evidence of Mr Howard was that they did not reach an agreement. The jury might think they got very near, and hoped for, an agreement. However, the only reason the jury heard the evidence was our defence of an agreement.

Finally, they must not say, whichever side they decided for: 'Who is going to pay the costs and how are the costs going to be paid?' That was 'totally irrelevant'. They must decide on the merits of the case.

A bulwark of democracy

The jury might think that I had 'laid about Mr Meacher with considerable vigour'. (This was certainly not my own view.) But, the judge went on, 'a free press is the bulwark of democracy'. Britain was a country with a tradition of 'trenchant' criticism of politicians and political decisions. It was no use merely 'paying lip service' to the concept of press freedom without putting it into practice. It was President Truman – was it not? – who said: 'If you can't stand the heat, keep out of the kitchen.'[1]

Did they not think it obvious, whatever the rights and wrongs of the matter, that sending out the questionnaire – and no one was questioning

[1] The more generally accepted version of this saying has 'get' instead of 'keep': see Nigel Rees, *A Dictionary of Twentieth Century Quotations* (1987), 434.

Mr Meacher's integrity in sending it out – was 'bound to arouse acute controversy'? This was not a political point against the Labour Party. 'What is sauce for the goose is sauce for the gander'. Suppose the Conservative Party in Opposition had done this. Did they not think the reaction would be the same?

Did it cause concern? Did they think it right that 'only one or two wrote to complain'? Or did it go further? Did it, for example, cause concern to Mr Kinnock? The basis of this suggestion by the judge, as he explained to the jury, was Mr Moonman's letter to the *Health and Social Services Journal*,[2] in which he wrote: 'When I first heard of his [Mr Meacher's] investigation last September, I got in touch with the Labour leader's office to find that they were unaware of the range of information being sought and assured me, after inquiries, that no further questionnaire would be sent out.' However, in his affidavit, which was not produced in evidence, Mr Kinnock said that he had possessed no knowledge of the affair and that Mr Meacher had been within his remit as a Shadow Minister in doing what he did.[3]

Mr Meacher had told the jury that he had heard nothing from Mr Kinnock's office about the matter. Neither did he communicate with him before the document was sent out. 'You may think that is strange but there it is.' It did not 'end there', however, because Kenneth Clarke, the then Health Minister, had said in evidence that in November 1984 or thereabouts he had been 'getting back' these questionnaires, which he had presumed were being returned by irate members of the health authorities. So if that was so they might think there was 'considerable concern'.

An un-English questionnaire

In fact, they might think that what was happening here was 'decidedly un-English' and 'bound to arouse acute controversy. I say that,' the judge continued, 'because in this country a man's politics and his religion are private matters unless he decides to disclose them.' (That effectively disposed of the Moonman allegations as a cause for libel. Whether the learned judge went too far is a matter of opinion.)

The judge proceeded to tell the jury that the first thing they had to decide was what the words meant. They were the sole judges of that. They would then go on to consider whether the words were defamatory. The test in law was: would the words tend to lower the plaintiff in the estimation of right-thinking members of society generally? They, the jury, represented society. 'Mere vulgar abuse is not of course defamatory.' (That disposed of the louse and the flea.)

One of the factors that might or might not assist them was what

[2] 28 March 1985.   [3] See Chapter 5.

happened after the publication of the article. Apparently there was 'a deafening silence'. Colleagues did not rush forward saying: have you seen the article? Nobody took it amiss. 'Mr Watkins told you he had to attend Parliament and no MP ever complained to him or said he had been a bit hard on Meacher.'

If, and only if, they came to the conclusion that the words were defamatory would they go on to consider the first defence, justification – that what was said was true. If that was established, it was a complete defence to the action. It was for the defendants to establish on the balance of probabilities that the defence was made out. The jury would appreciate that there were two matters here. The first was the allegation about Mr Meacher's father, the second the one about the Moonman dispute. Only if they rejected justification would they then go on to consider the next defence of fair comment, which related solely to the Moonman allegation.

First, fair comment must be on a matter of public interest. That was not in dispute here. Second, it must be based on facts which were true. Here it was based on the questionnaire and, partly, on Mr Moonman's resignation. It was said by counsel for the plaintiff that Mr Moonman had not been called. But the jury might think it clear from his article in *The Times* that the questionnaire 'was the last straw as far as he was concerned'. Then – and this was important – could any fair-minded man have said what I had written, on the proved facts? The test was: would any fair-minded man, however prejudiced he might be, or however exaggerated or obstinate his views, make that comment? The test was not whether the jury agreed with what was said.

The law of malice

The defence of fair comment could, however, be defeated by what was called malice. There the burden of proof reverted to the plaintiff because it was for the plaintiff to satisfy them on the balance of probabilities that the defendant was actuated by malice and to reject the defence of fair comment on that ground. What was meant by malice? Some improper motive: for example, a desire to injure the plaintiff, which was the sole or dominant motive. If the defendant did not believe that what he wrote was true, or was reckless about its truth, then maybe the jury would find no difficulty in considering that to be evidence of malice.

Such evidence could be extrinsic or intrinsic. It was agreed that there was no extrinsic evidence here: 'nobody suggests Mr Watkins was out to do Mr Meacher down.' What the jury had to consider was the allegation by Mr Bishop that for some reason – Mr Bishop did not know the reason – I had a desire to injure the plaintiff. 'If no reason can be pointed out to you,' the judge said, 'it may or may not assist you because none can be suggested.'

Mr Hartley had described this as 'the thinnest case of malice' and invited them to note how late it was raised, after three years, solely to destroy a valid defence of fair comment. The jury should be slow to draw the inference of malice unless I did not believe the words to be true, knew they were false or was totally indifferent as to whether they were true or false. It had been suggested that it was inconsistent to allege that I knew them to be false and yet should have checked with Mr Meacher. All these were matters for them.

The law of damages

Mr Justice Hazan then turned to the law about damages. The jury would appreciate that the question arose only if they found for the plaintiff. Damages were intended to compensate him. They were not allowed by the law to award punitive damages. They could not award damages to punish the defendants or to deter them, as a 'slap on the wrist' from publishing further libels, because that assumed that was what the defendants were going to do. The award should compensate for injury to feelings, for anxiety in the litigation and for the baselessness of the charge. They could consider 'the extent of publication' of the *Observer* and also the unsuccessful plea of justification. Similarly, if they found malice, defeating fair comment, that could be taken into account.

However, there might be cases when the defendant put forward a defence of justification but was unable to prove sufficient facts to bring it within section 5 of the Defamation Act 1952. (This provides that, when there are two or more distinct charges against the plaintiff, a defence of justification shall not fail only because the truth of every charge is not proved, 'if the words not proved to be true do not materially injure the plaintiff's reputation having regard to the truth of the remaining charges'. This provision had been referred to by counsel during legal argument, in the presence of the jury, and by Mr Hartley in his closing speech. It must have been taxing for the jury.) If, the judge went on, sufficient facts were not proved, the defendant was nevertheless entitled to rely on those facts which had been proved to reduce damages 'even to vanishing point'.

The evidence of the plaintiff

Having outlined the law, the judge gave the jury a deserved break of ten minutes. He then turned to the evidence. The jury might think that Mr Meacher had 'pursued a career of distinction'. It was 'very much to his own credit for which he needn't be shy but proud, though modesty would forbid him saying so.' He had gone to Oxford where he had obtained 'a first-class honours degree in arts' (an attempt to make 'Greats' more comprehensible to the jury).

He had said in evidence that he had never claimed to be the son of an agricultural labourer, though at one point the jury might think that he had been prepared to equate 'farm worker' with 'agricultural labourer'. The jury must compare his evidence with that of the journalists. Then there was his statement. 'Normally such documents would be privileged but the plaintiff waived privilege by referring to it and it became evidence by the questions counsel asked the plaintiff in re-examination.' The defendants' counsel said it was 'dynamite' because it 'blows the plaintiff's case sky-high'. The plaintiff's counsel said 'not at all'. There were 'no inconsistencies'. The judge was 'not making any comment on that. It is a matter for you to decide.'

Mr Meacher had not read the *Observer* article until 'some days after it came out'. When he did read it he was 'stunned and angry' because it suggested that he had 'hounded' Mr Moonman out of the Labour Party. He had sought the advice of solicitors. 'Then we have a whole series of discussions and negotiations between the parties about the apology.' He eventually decided he would have to proceed with the action because he felt 'aggrieved'.

In cross-examination, it had been pointed out to him that, if he had really thought the article defamatory, it was odd that something like two-and-a-third months elapsed before his solicitor wrote to the defendants. It had been said that there were several ironies in the case. Mr Hartley had asked how he could say that he had been libelled by the *Observer* when he himself was submitting articles to the paper. He had replied that he had thought at the time that the two matters were different. He had said the last thing he had wanted was to get into a legal fight with the *Observer*. It was the 'injustice' that had given him concern. He wanted 'modest' damages to 'punish' the paper. (The judge had pointed out earlier that Mr Bishop was calling for 'substantial' damages.)

He had said in cross-examination that in interviews with the press he had 'never claimed to be working class'. He had accepted that from 1926 his father had lived on inherited income from a capital of what would today be worth £150,000. He had maintained that he had never told anyone that his father was a farm worker. The jury would 'no doubt' want to compare that with 'other evidence'. He had denied that the action was 'a storm in a tea cup'.

The plaintiff's witnesses

Miss Burton had recalled that he had written to her in November 1984 and that she had seen him in January 1985. She had not been keen on his having the lunch with Mr Howard which later took place. She had then described the negotiations to settle. Mr Justice Hazan would not trouble the jury with that (because he had held earlier that, as a matter of law, there was no evidence of a concluded agreement to go before them). In her evidence, she had agreed that 'the usual thing to do' was to ask for an apology as soon as possible and that this had not been done here. She accepted responsibility. Though it would have taken only a 'short time' to write the letter, she did not write it till the end of January.

They had heard from Miss Rouse that there had been 'trouble and dispute' in Islington about health service issues: for example, cuts and privatisation in the NHS. There had been disputes about policy; some people wanted Mr Moonman to be removed as chairman of the health authority. She had put forward a motion to this effect in June 1984 which had been defeated. It was in November 1984 that he resigned.

Then they had heard Canon Wilkinson, 'a retired gentleman described as a surprise witness'. He came because he had read a report in a newspaper. He had described what he knew of the Meacher family. The jury might think that 'he thought very highly of the plaintiff'. He had described the Meacher family as having had 'a real struggle'. The furniture was shabby. Mr Meacher senior was withdrawn and would not talk. Mr Meacher's mother 'carried the family'. Nobody could have anything but the 'greatest sympathy' for Mr Meacher senior's situation and the 'greatest admiration' for Mr Meacher's mother. She had been not only 'extremely anxious for the best for her son' but had set out to achieve it.

When cross-examined, the Canon had said he did not know that the plaintiff had inherited money or that his father had inherited in 1926. Undoubtedly, the judge said, Mr Meacher senior had owned some capital. Whether or not it was enough or, as was often the case, he was reluctant to draw on it was a matter to be considered.

> Canon Wilkinson was obviously an honest witness. Nobody is suggesting that he came deliberately to lie. But the question is, on the further evidence that the plaintiff gave, whether inadvertently in his enthusiasm for the plaintiff he has exaggerated the situation. It is entirely a matter for you.

The case for the defendants

Mr Justice Hazan turned to the case for the defendants and began with my evidence. Mr Howard had told me in 1983 'with some excitement' the story of Mr Meacher's father. I had accordingly used the phrase 'because the life suited him better'. The jury might think this was 'useful' in indicating what my motives were here. I was not trying to injure the plaintiff when writing the article.

I had taken 'a low view' of the questionnaire, saying that Mr Moonman should have told Mr Meacher where to put it. 'The louse and the flea' was 'a literary joke'. It certainly contained 'an element of vulgar abuse'. I had recognised the plaintiff as 'among the decent though rather dull leadership of the Labour Party'. I had said I had been 'astonished' to receive the writ and that the person responsible 'obviously did not understand the meaning of fair comment'. I had said that Mr Meacher had 'only a small walk-on part'. I was not, I claimed, actuated by malice in what I wrote.

Cross-examined, I had said I did not recognise the plaintiff or Mr Moonman as a major politician. I had recognised the plaintiff as 'a middle-rank politician but a decent man of integrity'. I had been asked about the use of the words 'admittedly shabby'. I had said I thought it was 'improper' to ask members of authorities to give the information requested, though I accepted that the plaintiff thought he was doing the right thing in sending out the questionnaire. 'Is that a man motivated by malice or not?' I had said it was fair to describe the episode as 'admittedly shabby' because the Labour Party did not support the sending out of the questionnaire. This had apparently 'sparked off' Mr Moonman's resignation but I was not suggesting that Mr Meacher 'hounded' Mr Moonman out of the Labour Party.

Asked about the 'likes to claim ...' sentence, I had said that, in writing an article of this kind, the writer had 'to fill in a certain amount of interesting background'. I had described it (in 'a vivid phrase') as 'the currant in the suet pudding'. I had told the jury that I had never been sued for libel in my life and was 'shocked' by the allegations against me. It was Mr Meacher who was dragging his father through the Law Courts, not I. (I was pleased the judge managed to get that in.)

Then Mr Clarke had said that, though he did not know the political affiliations of all members of health authorities, he tried for a 'rough balance' but he had agreed that he did not always succeed. He had 'expected a certain amount of trouble' from the dispatch of the questionnaires. As to 'admittedly shabby', Mr Clarke did not decide, any more than any other witness, but the jury decided whether 'a fair-minded person would have made that comment'.

Mr Howard had said that the *Observer* was not the Conservatives' favourite newspaper. He himself had been a member of the Labour Party for 35 years. He had said he had believed that the plaintiff came from 'humble agricultural origins'. He recollected asking Mr Meacher about his background. Mr Meacher had replied that it was 'embarrassing' because it was 'complicated'. His father had gone to London from the family farm to try to become an accountant. But it did not work out because of his nervous disposition. So he came back to work on the farm.

Some three weeks later Mr Howard had spoken to Mr Hillmore, who had written the item in 'Pendennis'. The jury, the judge said, should remember that this was dated 2 October 1983. The judge then read it out. Mr Howard had said that he did not recall any complaint from Mr Meacher's supporters following this item. It 'never crossed his mind' that my 1984 column was defamatory. Indeed, no complaint had been received until January 1985.

Mr Howard had said that he 'could not believe his eyes' when he received the solicitor's letter after Mr Meacher's prospective article. He decided to sort out the matter on a personal level, so arranged lunch. He had started off by saying to Mr Meacher that it was 'a strange way to behave'. In cross-examination he had denied any suggestion of negotiating specific sums of money with the plaintiff. 'That leaves me to deal with the evidence of the journalists,' the judge said, concluding the morning's proceedings.

For the first time during the case, I thought we were going to win outright. The references to the 'deafening silence', to President Truman, the heat and the kitchen and to the 'un-English' quality of Mr Meacher's questionnaire had been like torpedoes. The robust defence of a free press had been useful as well. The judge had even suggested that Canon Wilkinson's evidence might have been 'exaggerated'. Mr Howard, Mr Millinship, Tim Walker and I went off to El Vino's for wine and sandwiches. For the first time during the case, I drank more than I should have done at lunch.

The judge resumed by reminding the jury that, in his now-disclosed statement to his solicitors (or proof of evidence), Mr Meacher had written that he had 'always' described his father as a 'farm worker' but had gone on to provide further details 'spontaneously'. What Mr Taylor had testified was that the plaintiff had said that his father had 'worked on a farm' but not mentioned the trainee accountancy or the nervous breakdown. 'Quite understandably', Mr Taylor had added. He had said that there had been 'no complaint' to him about the article. In cross-examination, he had said that Mr Meacher had not been honest about his background, but for understandable reasons. He had said that Mr Meacher had been hesitant, using phrases such as: 'Let's say ...' Overall, he had been left with the impression that Mr Meacher senior had been a farm worker or agricultural labourer.

Then there was Mr Chester. He had said that he 'was not sure' of the exact words which the plaintiff had used to describe his father. He had received the impression that he had worked on his own father's farm.

Mr Knight's article 'gave rise to some amusement', though he had insisted it was a 'serious article'. He had said that during the interview Mr Meacher had discussed the question of his background quickly. According to his recollection, Mr Meacher had *not* said that Mr Meacher senior had worked on his father's farm. When cross-examined, Mr Knight had said he had received the impression that the Meacher family had lived in a 'modest rural manner'.

The judge tidies up

That concluded Mr Justice Hazan's review of the evidence. He now did some tidying-up. Mr Meacher had said that his disclosed statement was a 'concoction' of his solicitors. What he had clearly meant was not that they had made it up but that they had compiled it. The judge also disposed of Mr Bishop's invitation to the jury to infer that, if Mr Winder and Mr Costello had been called, they would have supported Mr Chester rather than Mr Taylor and Mr Knight. They should not decide a case by speculating on what a witness might have said.

We had been back for only 20 minutes when the judge adjourned till the next day, Friday, at ten. He said he would clear up a few matters briefly and so provide them with a complete day for their deliberations. I thought he could have sent them out on the Thursday afternoon.

For the defendants

On the final day Mr Trelford turned up: his previous appearance had been on the Tuesday morning when I was finishing my evidence and Mr Howard starting his. The new Mrs Meacher turned up as well (she had been an assiduous attender in the closing days of the trial), and she was accompanied by her daughter, a young woman. The presence of the latter indicated the expectation of a verdict for the plaintiff, and perhaps – who could tell? – a vindication of Mr Bishop's estimate of £7,500 damages. The press benches were packed with, among others, Michael O'Flaherty of the *Daily Express* (who had attended more often and written more than anybody else), Frank Thompson of the *Daily Mail*, Alan Rusbridger of the *Guardian*, James Dalrymple and Mark Lawson of the *Independent*, Robin Young of *The Times* and Terence Shaw of the *Daily Telegraph*.

Mr Justice Hazan, in the course of summarising his summing-up of the previous day, reminded the jury that, in his evidence-in-chief, Mr Meacher had said that he would always explain, if possible, that his father had gone to London to train as an accountant. His proof of evidence, however – on which he had been further cross-examined – stated that he 'always said that his father was a farm worker'. Did they see a difference there? But then, as Mr Bishop had pointed out, the proof further stated that Mr Meacher would always go on to provide a further explanation. Did the jury think he did?

This was distinctly helpful to our cause. What the judge said next was of even greater assistance. The jury must consider whether the article was 'libellous at all' and whether the action was 'really a storm in a tea cup'. With the heat in the kitchen and the 'un-English' nature of Mr Meacher's questionnaire, this was a phrase that was remembered. If it was a storm in a tea cup, it

is evidenced by the fact that none of his colleagues mentioned it to Mr Meacher. Mr Watkins was in the House of Commons and nobody said anything to him. Nobody mentioned it at all. Does that help you in deciding whether the article lowered the plaintiff in the estimation of right-thinking members of society generally? ... By your verdict you will answer those questions ... When you get to the room will you elect a foreman? ...

The foreman turned out to be a sensible-looking, middle-aged man who had sat on the far right of the front row. After half-an-hour the jury sent out for tea and coffee. There was later a rumour, which proved to be unfounded, that they had sent out for sandwiches as well. This is traditionally considered a 'bad sign' because the jury are at odds or at any rate realise that they are in for a lengthy sequestration. After 91 minutes they trooped in. As Mr Howard was to express it in the *Observer* two days later:[4]

> In criminal trials it is always said you can foretell the outcome from the final demeanour of the jury. If, when they return to deliver their verdict, they avoid looking at the accused, then that is bad news for him; if they risk a full-frontal gaze, then he can breathe again.
>
> That was not much help to me – not that I, or anyone else, was criminally accused of anything – last Friday morning in Court No. 14 of the Royal Courts of Justice in the Strand. The *Observer* was merely involved as a defendant in a libel action, but the jury remained as impenetrable at the end as it had been at the beginning. Not until the foreman stood forward to announce, in reply to the question 'Do you find for the plaintiff or the defendants?', the magic words 'For the defendants', did I have the remotest idea of what had gone through their minds in the three separate weeks (with a Whitsun adjournment) we had spent together.

Later that day, when we had got over the excitement, Mr Howard and I agreed that, in the time they had spent, the jury would have been unlikely to consider the defences of justification for the background allegations and of both justification and fair comment for the Moonman allegations. They would probably have considered only whether the words were defamatory in the first place – and had concluded that the whole case really was, as the learned judge had suggested to them, a storm in a tea-cup.

---

[4] 13 June 1988.

Aftermath

London is the libel capital of the world. Society hostesses, faded ex-starlets, politicians with no sense of humour, and assorted nutcases with axes to grind into the shoulders of their sworn enemies sue each other for expressing facts and opinions which are of no conceivable interest to anyone else.

David Pannick, *Judges*

Mr Meacher blinked and looked at the press box. Mrs Meacher crumpled. Her daughter Helen looked both miserable and angry, and later pushed journalists aside as she was leaving the court, telling them to 'get out of my way'. Such behaviour was only to be expected in someone of her age, around 20, who had been brought along to witness a triumph which had failed to materialise.

Mr Hartley asked for costs and was awarded them. Mr Bishop asked for a proportion of the costs to be borne by us on the basis that our conduct of the defence in claiming accord and satisfaction had 'unnecessarily lengthened' the trial. Mr Justice Hazan refused this application.

The judge is cross

He was, however, concerned at the time the trial had taken. On this he exchanged pleasantries with the jury, whom he excused service for ten years. With learned counsel he was more severe. Mr Hartley looked cross, as if he thought a barrister of his seniority and distinction should not be addressed in this schoolmasterly fashion. The judge said the plaintiff's side had estimated that the case would run for two days. This would have been 'quite impossible'. The defendants' estimate had been five to eight days. But the trial had lasted 14 days. This had caused 'great inconvenience and difficulty' and 'considerable anxiety to everybody concerned'.

The trial had certainly gone on for a long time. But Mr Justice Hazan had played his part in this prolongation. Every afternoon he had adjourned at 3.50 instead of at the more usual time of 4.30. Indeed, to say that the learned judge 'adjourned' the court implies a greater deliberation and formality than he in fact displayed. There are some people who possess an ability to disappear from any gathering, though it is usually in a bar or at a party. At one minute they are there, talking away like

217

anything; at the next, they are gone. The journalist Richard West, for instance, has this gift, if gift it is. Mr Justice Hazan was like Mr West in this respect. At ten-to-four he would murmur a few words to counsel, rise, bow (rather, bob) and be off and away through the back door hardly before the usher had found time to order the court to get to its feet too.

Moreover, in the second week of the trial the court had sat effectively only until the Wednesday: Thursday morning had been given over to legal argument. Then the Whitsun holiday had begun. Again, the judge could have sent the jury out on the afternoon of the final Thursday, instead of bringing them back on the Friday. Judges like to send a jury out early in the day not only because they are fresher then but also because they are more likely to produce a verdict before the end of the afternoon, so allowing everyone to go home.

If Mr Hartley had kept Mr Meacher in the witness box for a long time, Mr Bishop had been similarly lengthy – and even more repetitious – with both Mr Howard and me. The other witnesses of both sides were disposed of in a reasonably short time. The truth is, however, that this was a difficult and complicated case. It would have taken us three to four days to present our side properly; Mr Meacher's counsel would have required similar time. Allowing for closing speeches, summing-up, retirement and verdict, the lowest estimate would have been eight days; a more realistic estimate would have been ten, which was what someone from our camp told me shortly before the trial began.

Assorted responses

Mr and Mrs Meacher left the court by – mistakenly, it appeared – the back entrance, the one I had favoured through most of the trial. Mr Meacher made a statement:

> This is not the end of the matter. There are many disturbing aspects to this case. I have discussed the matter with my solicitors and they have advised me that I have very strong grounds for appeal. Notice of appeal will therefore be served on the *Observer* on Monday.

Mr Trelford and Mr Howard had left the court on the retirement of the jury to return to the *Observer's* offices over Chelsea Bridge; they now made a dangerously fast journey back again in the office car, in time to catch the verdict. Mr Trelford said that any appeal would be 'vigorously resisted' and added:

> There is a tradition in this country of trenchant political comment and I think that would have been imperilled if we had lost this case. I understand there have been 39[1] successive libel cases in which the newspapers have lost. This one turns the tide. It was essential to the freedom of the press that

---

[1] Other estimates put the number in the low forties.

we should win ... We have been vindicated. I think it was quite clear from the judge's summing-up that this case should never have come to court. Politicians have got to learn to give and take with the rough-and-tumble of political life.

Mr Howard was more judicious and more subdued:

I naturally feel very sorry indeed for Mr Meacher. I have no ill-will towards him at all. He has been a friend of mine for some 15 years, and I hope our friendship will continue. Obviously he is under great strain today. I tried to settle this action on, I think, two separate occasions. I can only say he brought it on his own head.

He was asked whether his reputation and mine had been 'on the line' and replied:

Yes, we were both anxious. I would certainly be feeling very different today if Mr Meacher had won. I realise the great difficulties he is in because of the very high costs he has incurred, but if you are a public figure and you sue you must take these things into account. He is not really a private citizen. I have always had great sympathy for private citizens who are defamed, but public figures are in a different category.

Mr Howard was to expand on this distinction in his article of two days later in the *Observer*, part of which has already been quoted in Chapter 20. He suggested that a wider 'public interest' defence where politicians or other public figures had been defamed should be the *quid pro quo* for a 'right to privacy' where the lives of ordinary citizens had been invaded. However, he saw no realistic prospect of this bargain's being struck.

He also said, immediately after the verdict:

Alan Watkins is a very trenchant journalist, and I am sure there will be more of that type of journalism in the future. This case will not inhibit him or the *Observer*.

I am not sure that Mr Howard really meant these last few sentences. He knew me as a journalist as well as anyone. I had never regarded my work as specially trenchant. It possessed other qualities maybe. That was for others to judge. But I certainly did not look on myself as an opinionated or polemical writer. Indeed, Mr Howard in a sense acknowledged this in his Sunday article, where he correctly pointed out that the suggestion which had made Mr Meacher so cross had originally been put forward 'in more robust terms' by Mr Hillmore in his 'Pendennis' column.

Frank Johnson controverted Mr Trelford in the *Sunday Telegraph*:[2]

[2] 12 June 1988.

Mr Trelford, the *Observer's* editor, said after the Meacher libel action that Britain's 'tradition of trenchant political comment' would have been 'imperilled' had his paper lost. In fact, the case was much more serious than that. There is no shortage of, or threat to, trenchant political comment in Britain. Readers and viewers must find it hard to avoid the stuff. This was not like the legal actions involving newspapers in the Peter Wright case – a trivial affair to do with the right of journalists to strike poses about the national interest. The tradition 'imperilled' in the Meacher trial was the right of British newspaper readers to laugh at Labour MPs with middle-class antecedents who go on about their working-class background. Victory for Mr Meacher would have meant the banishment from the newspapers of one of the stock figures of British comedy – the prolier-than-thou socialist. Much of the life's work of ... Mr Watkins ... would have been in vain because of one irresponsible jury verdict.

I had taken the same line, expressing myself less amusingly, when interviewed by Independent Television News, shortly after the verdict. I said that, if Mr Meacher had won, it would have been open season for politicians to sue commentators – in particular, parliamentary sketch-writers (of whom Mr Johnson was himself once an ornament), who as a group specialised in more or less wounding personal references. This interview took place in the Clachan public house, a few yards from El Vino's. The television people had wished to set up the event in the latter establishment, but the management rightly demurred, saying that they could not allow cameras on the premises.

Mr Meacher appeals

The costs were estimated at £200,000 in the newspapers, though the costs the *Observer* had incurred in defending the action were nearer £130,000 than £100,000. How was Mr Meacher to pay? The *canard* that he had a 'rich wife' who was 'financing' his action has already been disposed of in these pages. One course open to him was to appeal, which he had already indicated he would take. There was some ignorance in Westminster and Fleet Street about the nature of an appeal in libel cases (though I have no reason to believe that Mr Meacher shared it, despite the innocence of legal matters which he had displayed throughout the trial). A few acquaintances were under the impression that the Court of Appeal could reverse the verdict of the jury in the defendants' favour, and even award a sum of damages to the plaintiff off their own bat.

Such was not the case. The most the court could do was to order a new trial. Mr Meacher might be unsuccessful in these second proceedings as well. In this event he would be liable to pay the costs both of the appeal and of the second hearing, in addition to the costs for which he was already liable. This was an alarming prospect. Alternatively, the court might dismiss the appeal, when he would be liable to costs also, though on a smaller scale. The third possibility, the only one satisfactory to Mr

Meacher – that both the Court of Appeal and another jury would find in his favour – was, to put the matter at its lowest, something of a gamble. Nevertheless, on 17 June 1988 Messrs Seifert Sedley Williams served a Notice of Appeal, signed by Mr Bishop. It contained ten grounds.

(i) We improperly put forward a defence of accord and satisfaction which we knew must fail. As a result, evidence of negotiations between Mr Meacher and us was put before the jury and prejudiced his case.

(ii) The judge erred in holding that evidence from Kenneth Clarke about his opinion of the questionnaire was admissible. The evidence was irrelevant to any issue in the case and was prejudicial to Mr Meacher.

(iii) The judge misdirected the jury by failing to tell them to ignore all evidence relating to the negotiations for a settlement.

(iv) The judge misdirected the jury by telling them that Mr Clarke's evidence was capable of supporting our case that a reasonable person could hold the view that Mr Meacher's conduct had been 'shabby'.

(v) The judge misdirected the jury by telling them that, in considering whether the words complained of were or were not defamatory, they were entitled to take into account what did or did not happen after my article had been published.

(vi) The judge misdirected the jury by failing to tell them that they had to decide whether my allegation that Mr Meacher's conduct had been 'shabby' was a statement of fact or a comment *before* deciding whether it was true or fair comment.

(vii) The judge misdirected the jury by inviting them to infer that the questionnaire had caused concern to Mr Kinnock from the fact that Mr Moonman had written a letter to the *Health and Social Services Journal* in which he had said that he had drawn it to Mr Kinnock's attention and had received an assurance that no further questionnaire would be sent out. Mr Moonman was not called as a witness. Nor was a Civil Evidence Act Notice served in respect of the latter. The judge thereby invited the jury to rely on inadmissible hearsay evidence.

(viii) The judge failed to put Mr Meacher's case to the jury 'properly, fairly or at all'.

(ix) The judge failed properly to remind the jury of the evidence given in the trial, even though his summing-up began 14 days after the last evidence had been given.

(x) The judge, in ordering Mr Meacher to pay all our costs, and refusing his application that we should pay that part of his costs which was incurred by our defence of accord and satisfaction, failed to exercise his discretion about costs 'properly or at all'.

Legal acquaintances thought that these grounds were 'pretty thin' and that I had little to worry about, principally because it was virtually unheard-of for the Court of Appeal to overturn a jury's verdict in favour of a defendant in a libel action. I noted that none of the grounds was concerned specifically with the father or background allegations. Nevertheless, the Notice of Appeal *was* worrying. I had no wish to spend another 14 days in the High Court, three of them (part-days, admittedly) in the witness-box.

My principal feeling was relief that, in Mr Howard's phrase, the wretched affair had been brought to what was from my point of view a successful conclusion. I felt exhausted rather than exhilarated, as I had done, briefly, during my period in the witness-box. Indeed, there was a sense of anti-climax, such as I had experienced in my youth after taking examinations. On this later occasion I also knew the result. I had passed. But I still felt no overpowering desire to celebrate the victory.

A few messages

Others were less restrained. Peter Cook sent me a congratulatory telegram. One *Observer* reader wrote me a letter starting 'You louse', and adding that he was making a 'literary joke'. Another reader stated that the action had been caused by 'the way you write' and that I had brought the trouble on my own head. I did not reply to these letters. The majority of them, however (which did receive replies), were friendly enough.

Auberon Waugh said to me that all the case showed was that juries disliked left-wing Labour MPs even more strongly than they did liberal newspapers. Paul Johnson wrote in the *Spectator*[3] that the verdict depended on the singular facts of the case and that journalists and proprietors would be imprudent to regard it as 'the turn of the tide' as far as libel juries were concerned. This was a prediction which, with the award of £300,000 to Koo Stark, the settlement of £1,000,000 by the *Sun* on Elton John and the award of £1,500,000 to Lord Aldington, turned out to be correct. An Irish legislator, Maurice Manning, welcomed the verdict in the Dublin magazine *Magill*[4] and wrote that 'only someone as priggish as Mr Meacher would have brought such a case in the first place ... and only someone as self-righteous as Mr Meacher would have persisted in the face of common sense and honest advice to drop the matter'. A lengthy account of the case also appeared in Gujarati, in a newspaper for speakers of that language in Britain.

Lord Goodman intervenes

To mark the case as one of major public import, Lord Goodman now intervened. He did so on behalf of Mr Meacher. Who put him up to it I do not know. Perhaps he acted on his own initiative. As a friend of Mr Trelford and a former director of the *Observer* (albeit one who had urged

---

[3] 18 June 1988.　　　　　[4] July 1988.

David Astor to sell the paper to Rupert Murdoch in 1976), he met the editor and asked him whether it would be possible for the *Observer* to waive Mr Meacher's costs. Lord Goodman's arguments were that Mr Meacher was not a rich man, he and the paper were fundamentally on the same side, and it would appear vindictive – would do the paper no good – for the *Observer* to pursue Mr Meacher for money. If the paper adopted this course, Mr Meacher would not, of course, continue with his appeal.

It is not unknown for successful defendants in libel cases (an increasingly rare breed) to waive their costs, or part of them. The BBC, for example, did so when they were unsuccessfully sued by Derek Jameson, the broadcaster and former journalist, in respect of a skit broadcast on a 'satirical' sound programme. The costs here were around £75,000. The costs in Mr Meacher's case were substantially higher than this. Mr Trelford replied that the decision was not for him but that he would pass Lord Goodman's request on to the appropriate authority, in this case the then managing director, Nicholas Morrell. Mr Morrell said that he was disinclined to assist Mr Meacher but that, if Lord Goodman wished to approach R.W. ('Tiny') Rowland of Lonrho, he was welcome to do so. As far as I know, this meeting did not take place.

A change of solicitors

In the meantime, Mr Meacher had changed his solicitors. He was not only dissatisfied with Seifert Sedley Williams for their conduct of the case but now wished to sue them for professional negligence. He turned to Bindman and Partners.

By coincidence, Geoffrey Bindman had written me a friendly letter immediately after the case. Its occasion was another reference of mine to Dr Johnson. Composing my column for 12 June 1988, I wrote that one of Roy Hattersley's amiable characteristics was that, like the would-be philosopher referred to by Dr Johnson, cheerfulness would keep breaking in. But it was not Johnson who said this of somebody but his old Pembroke College contemporary Edwards, who said it of himself. My error arose because Edwards's words were quoted in Boswell's *Life of Johnson*, 17 April 1788: 'I have tried too in my time to be a philosopher; but, I don't know how, cheerfulness was always breaking in.' Mr Bindman gently pointed out my mistake and suggested that Johnson was a dangerous author to quote. He now took charge of Mr Meacher's dealings with the *Observer* and of his complaint against Seifert Sedley Williams, with which I was not (and am not) concerned.

On 19 August 1988 Mr Justice Hazan died suddenly of a heart attack while on holiday in Cornwall. He was only 61, and had suffered heart trouble before. The obituaries were generous, lamenting the short time he had served on the High Court Bench. Some of them paid tribute to the judicious way in which he had handled the Meacher case. A woman friend

of mine suggested that Mrs Meacher had put a curse on the learned judge
and that I would be next on the list.

Voted off

At the beginning of October Mr Meacher suffered another setback. He
was voted off the constituency section of the Labour Party's National
Executive Committee, on which he had sat since 1983. He was in tears
and had to be consoled on the platform by Renée Short. He was replaced
by Robin Cook and was runner-up-but-one, with 248,000 votes as
compared to 320,000 in 1987. He attributed his defeat to Mr Cook's
acknowledged parliamentary successes, attacking the government's
policies on the health service. Mr Cook had supplanted Mr Meacher, who
had gone to Employment, in this opposition role. He had proved distinctly
sharper than Mr Meacher – though it is fair to say that in Mr Cook's
period the area became one of more acute political controversy.

The *Independent*, however, reported that 'the belief was widespread at
the conference that Mr Meacher had diminished himself by unsuccessfully taking a libel action against the *Observer* earlier this year'.[5] On
Wednesday 5 October 1988 I was sitting in my Blackpool hotel-room
watching the morning's proceedings on television, as I often do, rather
than sitting in the conference hall. Mr Meacher was being interviewed by
Vivian White of the BBC following that morning's debate on employment,
the subject with which the interview was principally concerned. Mr
White, however, threw in a legitimate question about whether Mr
Meacher thought his libel action had contributed to his removal two days
previously from the NEC. In my dressing-gown, pad on knee, I noted his
reply:

> I would have thought that there were many delegates who are actually
> sympathetic to politicians who simply are not going to take lies from the
> press and do stand up and fight it. The fact that I lost the court action as
> opposed to winning it I don't believe is a reason why delegates to the Labour
> Party would turn against me.

I was mildly cross rather than hopping with rage. But I wondered, not
for the first time, how such an intelligent and acute man could be so
foolish and imprudent. I should not have expected him to admit that he
had been beaten fair and square, by the unanimous verdict of a jury
delivered after a trial lasting 14 days. That would have been too much to
ask of an unsuccessful plaintiff, whose cry must ever be: 'We wuz robbed.'
But I should have expected someone of Mr Meacher's experience, occupy-
ing his position, to refrain from gratuitously landing himself in further

[5] *Independent*, 4 October 1988.

possible legal trouble. He should have known that 'lies' – along with 'fraud' and 'crook', to name only a few – was a legally perilous word in any event, quite apart the issue's already having been decided in the High Court. It was not so much that we might sue Mr Meacher and try the case all over again as that he, or Mr Bindman acting on his behalf, was already in the process of asking the *Observer* for leniency over the costs.

Negotiations on costs

For on 30 September 1988 Mr Bindman had conducted a conversation with Paul Fox of our solicitors, Turner Kenneth Brown, when he had offered, on Mr Meacher's behalf, to agree the *Observer*'s costs at £70,000. If that were to be agreed the sum, Mr Bindman had suggested, would be repaid by four equal instalments of £17,500, the first to be paid on 1 April 1989, and the remaining three at quarterly intervals, on 1 July 1989, 1 October 1989 and 1 January 1990.

On 12 October 1988 David O'Callaghan of Turner Kenneth Brown wrote to Mr Bindman insisting on £80,000 and rejecting the instalment plan: it was 'quite inconceivable that Mr Meacher should have pursued his libel action to trial without having made financial provision for the possibility that he would lose the action'. Mr O'Callaghan quoted Mr Meacher's televised remarks to Mr White, of which the authorised version had been obtained from the BBC by Julia Braybrook, the *Observer*'s new in-house solicitor. He continued:

> Mr Meacher should not be surprised that the *Observer* were extremely angry when they discovered that he had accused them of lies before a television audience of millions, especially at a time when his solicitor was entreating the *Observer* to make generous concessions to him. I have no doubt that Mr Meacher's statement on television was defamatory.

Later, however, Mr O'Callaghan and the *Observer's* management relented over the instalment plan. Nevertheless Mr Meacher paid the £80,000 in a lump sum. I had nothing to do with these decisions. Nor was there any reason why I should. My sole action was, on my return from Blackpool on 7 October 1988, to draw the attention of Miss Braybrook and Mr Morrell to Mr Meacher's accusation of 'lies'.

There was no financial appeal on behalf of Mr Meacher conducted either by the Labour Party or by any wider grouping. After Harold Laski's unsuccessful action against the *Newark Advertiser* and the *Daily Express*, the fund was over-subscribed. Supporters contributed generously to Barbara Castle's appeal after her unsuccessful action against Christopher Chataway and the BBC.[6] There was, as far as I know, no proposal or even suggestion for a Meacher fund. Westminster wags suggested that I

[6] See above, Chapter 1.

should contribute generously to one, were it to be set up, but it was never a serious possibility. Stanley Orme, the chairman of the Parliamentary Labour Party, told me shortly after the end of the case that no one had suggested such an appeal to him and that he doubted whether it would be successful were it to be made. The most that was now raised by the party, he said, tended to be £5-6,000, and the usual, virtually the sole, circumstances were the surcharging of councillors by the District Auditor.

Mr Meacher's case was far removed from these. In any event, he had been an isolated character in court, supported only by Mrs Meacher, Miss Burton and Mr Delaney or Priggen, with Mr Grant daily looking as if he wished he were somewhere else. It would be unfair to the Labour Party to say that it had let him down: several colleagues, including Mr Kinnock, had urged him to desist in his action, and were dismayed when he persisted.

But all was not disappointment for Mr Meacher. In November 1988 he was, against some expectations, re-elected to the Shadow Cabinet, even though in a lower position in the order, 10th out of 15. On 1 December 1988 I attended Mr Justice Hazan's memorial service in Lincoln's Inn chapel. It was not an unfamiliar building to me, for I was a member of the Inn myself, and still made use of its excellent library – had, indeed, composed several of my columns there while the case was proceeding, after the court had risen, between four and seven on the Thursday. This was what I was proudest of: not that we had won comprehensively, but that for four successive Sundays while the trial was going on, 22 May, 29 May, 5 June and 12 June, my column had appeared in the *Observer*, in its usual place.

The appeal is withdrawn

In December 1988 Mr O'Callaghan sent me the following document, stamped 13 December 1988 by the Court of Appeal:

WEDNESDAY the 30th day of NOVEMBER 1988
IN THE COURT OF APPEAL
QUEEN'S BENCH DIVISION
BEFORE MR REGISTRAR ADAMS
IN CHAMBERS
BETWEEN

        MICHAEL HUGH MEACHER

                                   Plaintiff

and
1) DONALD TRELFORD
2) The Observer Limited
3) Alan Watkins

                                   Defendants

UPON READING the notice of consent dated the 22nd November 1988 signed by the Solicitors for the Plaintiff and for the Defendant[7]

BY CONSENT

IT IS ORDERED that the Plaintiffs Appeal from the order of the Honourable Justice Hazan made on the 10th June 1988 be dismissed with no order as to costs

BY THE COURT

What this meant was that Mr Meacher had withdrawn his appeal. The reference to 'no order as to costs' was to the abandoned appeal, not to the action in the High Court. The bloody business or wretched affair was over.

[7] The document used the singular form here.

Mr Knight's Article

A dark horse dreams of being Kinnock's deputy
John Knight face to face with Michael Meacher

His eyes blink earnestly behind rimless spectacles, and Oscar, the family poodle, darts around our feet as we stand in the long garden of his house in London's prosperous Highgate.

I am not fooled by the tranquil scene.

For I am talking to Michael Meacher, the dark horse, who has suddenly appeared in Labour's leadership race.

And, for the moderates, turned what was to be the Dream Ticket into the Nightmare Ticket.

'Yes,' says Meacher, 'of course I am a close friend of Tony Benn. I am not going to kick him in the face or reject him now he isn't in Parliament.'

'He will come and support me in my campaign.'

That campaign is to make Michael Meacher, 43, the deputy leader in two months' time when Neil Kinnock, 41, is almost certain to be elected Labour's leader.

Then it's going to be a whole new ball game. Gone from the centre stage will be the shambling, evangelical figure of Michael Foot. No longer will we flee the fearsome sight of Denis Healey's puce countenance.

Yesterday's men, alas. But what of tomorrow's?

Distant tinkle

I must confess that six months ago the names of Kinnock and Roy Hattersley did not exactly ring mighty bells in my mind. Meacher was only a distant tinkle.

But in four or five years two of them (who, indeed, is to say?) may be running the country.

It was to be the Dream Ticket (a ghastly phrase invented by union boss Clive Jenkins) of Left-wing Kinnock and moderate Hattersley doing a balancing act running the turbulent Party.

Now this dream has been broken by Meacher, the outsider, appearing to streak ahead for the deputy's job.

So poor Hatters, already a bad bet to become leader, could be knocked right out of the running even as deputy.

Well, there's a long way to go before the finishing post at Labour's annual conference in Brighton when, on Sunday October 2, a computer sorts out the winners.

The nightmare to Labour's middle-of-the-road politicians is that the Kinnock-Meacher duo would present too solid a Left-wing front.

Still licking wounds from the election debacle, there are Labour MPs who regard Meacher as Benn's puppet-on-a-string.

Good chance

Now that he has lost his power base at Westminster, they argue that Benn sees Meacher as his spokesman there, and is using all his influence with the unions and constituency parties to promote his protégé to high office.

My impression of Meacher is that he is very much his own man.

There is a close association between the two of them which started when Meacher was Benn's junior minister during the period he ran the Department of Trade in the Wilson Government.

But the coolly intellectual Meacher is more than capable of getting his own act together.

'I think I am in with a very good chance', he says. 'None of it is tied up. It's all open. But from my contacts I believe I have a very good chance.'

He works it out this way: 'Let's be perfectly honest. My view is that I shall get around three-quarters of the constituency party votes because I am the candidate of the Left.

'Among the MPs, I have clear evidence I shall get one-third, and that's the bottom line.

'In the trade union section, I should get 16 or 17 points out of 40.'

(Under the electoral college system of voting for the Labour leadership, the unions have 40 per cent of the voting strength, and the Parliamentary Labour Party and the constituency parties 30 per cent each.)

Meacher was standing as Party Treasurer in the elections when 'people of the Left' called him, asking him to stand instead as deputy leader.

What does he think about reports that Kinnock would prefer Hattersley as deputy?

'I would like to know the source of that,' he says. 'There is so much black propaganda and fantasy.

'I can't honestly see why he would prefer Hattersley. I don't think in the last three weeks he has presented himself as being easily compatible with Neil Kinnock.

Sums right

'In terms of compatibility I am the obvious running mate. Ours is a Unity Ticket as opposed to a Conflict Ticket.'

Michael Meacher, a mild-mannered man, has got the jargon to communicate to the thickest union brother's mind.

Meacher has more than likely got his sums right. His reputation is that of a brilliant statistician.

As a young Labour back-bencher, he so bombarded the Tory Government with embarrassing statistics that Prime Minister Ted Heath issued orders to try to discredit him.

Meacher has an immaculate background which appeals to Socialist romantics. His father was a farm worker (outside lavatory and bath in kitchen), and his brainy son won a scholarship to a public school and went on to get a First at Oxford.

Lecturer in Social Administration at the London School of Economics, and then the Confederation of Health Service Employees (COHSE) launched him into politics by sponsoring him as MP for Oldham West.

Meacher isn't one of your loony Left. He is a leader of the thinking left and has a first-hand knowledge of world affairs having travelled as a minister to America, China, Russia, the Middle East and Africa.

He has four delightful children aged from 11 to 20, and his wife, Molly, is the Director of Information to the National Association of Citizens' Advice Bureaux.

With his family he has just left for a two-week holiday in Northern Italy.

I tell him that I hear Neil Kinnock is departing on holiday at the same time to the same area.

'It would be very nice to bump into him,' he says. 'But I assure you nothing has been arranged.'

I am convinced, however, the ambitious Michael Meacher will be on the constant look-out for a freckle-faced fellow with a Welsh accent.

Sunday Mirror, 7 August 1983

Biographical Details

Bishop, Gordon William. Cambridge. Called to Bar, Middle Temple, 1968. Practised from 10 South Square, Gray's Inn, a well-known libel, commercial and general chambers headed by Andrew Bateson, QC.

Clarke, Kenneth Harry. b 2 July 1940, ec Kenneth Clarke, jeweller, Nottingham. Nottingham HS; Gonville and Caius C, Cambridge. Chairman, Cambridge U Conservative Association, 1961; President, Cambridge Union, 1963. Called to Bar, Gray's Inn, 1963; QC, 1980. MP (Conservative), Rushcliffe, 1970. PPS, Solicitor-General, 1971-2. Assistant Government Whip, 1972-4. Parliamentary Secretary, Transport, 1979-81; Under-Secretary, 1981-2. Minister of State, Health, DHSS, 1982-5. PC, 1984. Paymaster General and Minister for Employment, 1985-7. Chancellor, Duchy of Lancaster and Minister for Trade and Industry, 1987-8. Minister of Health, 1988. *New Hope for the Regions* (1979).

Hartley, Richard Leslie Clifford. b 31 May 1932, s Arthur Clifford Hartley, CBE. Marlborough C; Sidney Sussex C, Cambridge. Called to Bar, Gray's Inn, 1956; Bencher, 1986; QC, 1976.

Hazan, John Boris Roderick. 3 October 1926–19 August 1988, s Selik Hazan. King's C, Taunton; King's C, London. Called to Bar, Lincoln's Inn, 1948; Bencher, 1977; QC, 1969. Prosecuting Counsel to Inland Revenue, SE Circuit, 1967-9. JP Surrey, 1969. Deputy Chairman, Surrey QS, 1969-71. Recorder, Crown Court, 1972-82. Circuit Judge, Central Criminal Court, 1982-8. Kt and Judge, QBD, 1988.

Howard, Anthony Michell. b 12 February 1934, os Canon Guy Howard. Westminster S; Christ Church, Oxford. Chairman, Oxford U Labour Club, 1954; President, Oxford Union, 1955. Called to Bar, Inner Temple, 1956. Political Correspondent, *Reynolds News*, 1958-9; *New Statesman*, 1961-4. Editorial Staff, *Manchester Guardian*, 1959-61 (Harkness Fellow, USA, 1960). Whitehall Correspondent, *Sunday Times*, 1965. Washington Correspondent, *Observer*, 1966-9; Political Columnist, 1971-2; Deputy Editor, 1981-8. Assistant Editor, *New Statesman*, 1970-2; Editor, 1972-8. Editor, *Listener*, 1979-81. Presenter, *Face the Press*, 1982-5. Columnist, *Independent*, 1989-90. (with R. West) *The Making of the Prime Minister* (1965), (ed.) *The Crossman Diaries: Selections* (1979), *Rab* (1987).

Meacher, Michael Hugh. b 4 November 1939, oc G.H. Meacher, gentleman, Berkhamsted, Herts. Berkhamsted S; New C, Oxford. Secretary, Danilo Dolci Trust, 1964. Research Fellow, Essex U, 1965-6. Lecturer in Social Administration, York U, 1967-9; LSE, 1970. MP (Labour), Oldham West, 1970. Under-Secretary, Industry, 1974-5; DHSS, 1975-6; Trade, 1976-9. Member, Shadow Cabinet, 1983; Labour NEC, 1983-8. *Taken for a Ride* (1972); pamphlets and essays: *The Care of the Old* (1969), *Wealth: Labour's Achilles Heel* (1972), *Socialism with a Human Face* (1981).

Meale, Joseph Alan. b 31 July 1949, s A.H. Meale. St Joseph's S; Ruskin C,

Oxford. Seaman, Merchant Navy, 1964-8. Engineering worker, 1968-75. National Employment Officer, NACRO, 1977-80. Assistant to General Secretary, ASLEF, 1980-3. Parliamentary and Political Adviser to M. Meacher, MP, 1983-7. MP (Labour), Mansfield, 1987.

Millinship, William. b 11 September 1929, s T.B. Millinship, shipwright, Newport, Gwent. St Julian's HS, Newport; Keble C, Oxford. French Radio, Paris. Assistant Paris Correspondent, *Observer*, 1957-8; Paris Correspondent, 1959-64; Chief Reporter, Magazine, 1964-6; News Editor, 1966-70; Washington Correspondent, 1970-3; Foreign News Editor, 1973-9; Managing Editor, 1979-88; Moscow Correspondent, 1988.

Moonman, Eric. b 29 April 1929, s Borach Moonman, dairyman. Rathbone S, Liverpool; Christ Church, Southport; Liverpool U and Manchester U. Human Relations Adviser, British Institute of Management, 1956-62. Senior Lecturer in Industrial Relations, SW Essex Technical C, 1962-4. Senior Research Fellow in Management Sciences, Manchester U, 1964-6. MP (Labour), Billericay, 1966-70; Basildon, 1974-9. Director, Centre for Contemporary Studies, 1979. Chairman, Islington Health Authority, 1981. *The Manager and the Organisation* (1961), *Employee Security* (1962), *European Science and Technology* (1968), *Communication in an Expanding Organisation* (1970), *Reluctant Partnership* (1970), *Alternative Government* (1984).

Trelford, Donald Gilchrist. b 9 November 1937, s Thomas Trelford, wholesale manager. Bablake S, Coventry; Selwyn C, Cambridge. Reporter and Sub-Editor, *Coventry Standard* and *Sheffield Telegraph*, 1960-3. Editor, *Times of Malawi*, and Correspondent, *Observer*, *The Times* and BBC, 1963-6. Deputy News Editor, *Observer*, 1966-8; Assistant Managing Editor, 1968-9; Deputy Editor, 1968-75; Editor, 1975. *Siege* (1980), *Snookered* (1986), (with G. Kasparov) *Child of Change* (1987).

Watkins, Alan Rhun. b 3 April 1933, oc D.J. Watkins, schoolmaster, Tycroes, Dyfed. Amman Valley GS, Ammanford; Queens' C, Cambridge. Chairman, Cambridge U Labour Club, 1954. Called to Bar, Lincoln's Inn, 1957. Research Assistant, LSE, 1958-9. Editorial Staff, *Sunday Express*, 1959-64 (New York Correspondent, 1961; Crossbencher Columnist, 1963-4). Political Correspondent, *Spectator*, 1964-7; *New Statesman*, 1967-76. Political Columnist, *Sunday Mirror*, 1968-9; *Observer*, 1976. Columnist, *Evening Standard*, 1974-5. Rugby Columnist, *Field*, 1984-6; *Independent*, 1986. *The Liberal Dilemma* (1966), (with A. Alexander) *The Making of the Prime Minister 1970* (1970), *Brief Lives* (1982), *Sportswriter's Eye* (1989).

Wilkinson, Wilfred Badger. b 1921. King's C, London. Curate, Luton, 1950-3; Berkhamsted, 1953-7. Curate-in-Charge, Wythenshawe, 1957-65. Rector, Clifton, Nottingham, 1965. Honorary Canon of Southwell.

Select Bibliography

Iain Adamson: *The Old Fox* (1963)
Muriel Box: *Rebel Advocate* (1983)
P.F. Carter-Ruck and R. Walker (eds): *Carter-Ruck on Libel and Slander* (3rd edn 1985)
Randolph S. Churchill: *What I Said about the Press* (1957)
Robert Connor: *Cassandra* (1969)
Hugh Cudlipp: *Walking on the Water* (1976)
Daily Express: *Laski Libel Trial* (1946)
Joseph Dean: *Hatred, Ridicule or Contempt* (1953, Pan edn 1955)
Neville Faulks: *No Mitigating Circumstances* (1977)
    A Law Unto Myself (1978)
Michael Foot: *Aneurin Bevan*, II (1973)
John G. Foster: 'Randolph and the Law' in Kay Halle (ed.): *Randolph Churchill* (1971)
Patrick Hastings: *Cases in Court* (1949)
David Hooper: *Public Scandal, Odium and Contempt* (1984)
H. Montgomery Hyde: *Their Good Name* (1970)
Richard Ingrams: *Goldenballs* (1979)
P.S.C. Lewis (ed.) *Gatley on Libel and Slander* (8th edn 1981)
Patrick Marnham: *The Private Eye Story* (1982)
Kingsley Martin: *Harold Laski* (1953, new edn 1969)
Janet Morgan (ed.): *The Backbench Diaries of Richard Crossman* (1981)
B. Neill and R. Rampton (eds): *Duncan and Neill on Defamation* (2nd edn 1983)
Adam Raphael: *My Learned Friends* (1989)
Report of the Committee on Defamation, Cmnd 5909 (1975)
Michael Rubinstein (ed.): *Wicked, Wicked Libels* (1972)

Index